The San Francisco Irish, 1848–1880

The
San Francisco Irish
1848–1880

R. A. Burchell

University of California Press

University of California Press
Berkeley and Los Angeles, California

Copyright © 1980 by R. A. Burchell

ISBN 0-520-04003-1

Library of Congress Cataloging in Publication Data

Burchell, R A
   The San Francisco Irish, 1848-1880.
   Includes bibliographical references and index.
   1. Irish Americans — California — San Francisco — Social conditions. 2. Irish Americans — California — San Francisco — History. 3. San Francisco — Social Conditions. 4. San Francisco — History. I. Title.
F869.S391653   979.4'61'0049162   79-65764
ISBN 0-520-04003-1

Contents

	Tables	*page* vii
	Preface and acknowledgements	ix
Chapter I	Introduction	1
II	The expanding city, 1848–80	15
III	Arrival and settlement	34
IV	The material world	52
V	Family and community	73
VI	Irish associationalism	96
VII	The politics of adjustment	116
VIII	The limits of satisfaction	155
IX	Cosmopolitanism *v.* sectarianism	179
Appendix	The Irish United States Senators from California in the middle nineteenth century	186
	A note on sources	188
	Notes	191
	Index	223

Tables

1	Length of residence of employed males in 1880, by nativity and ethnicity	page 11
2	Irish-born residential patterns, by ward, 1870	47
3	Irish residential patterns, by ward, 1880	48
4	Age structure, Irish-born, 1852–80	50
5	Occupational structure, Irish-born, 1852–80	54
6	Occupational structure, second-generation Irish, 1880	56
7	Comparison of occupational profile, first- and second-generation Irish, 1880	57
8	Comparison of occupational structure of native-born of native parents with that of Irish community: males, 1880	59
9	Occupational structure of all forty-year-old native-, Irish- and German-born males compared, 1870	60
10	Property-owning, real and personal, all forty-year-old Irish-, native- and German-born males, 1870	61
11	Comparison of residential concentration and mean property-holding by ward, Irish-born, 1870	63
12	Occupational structure, Irish community, by ward, and by sex, 1880	65
13	Comparison of wage rates, San Francisco and New York City, 1870 and 1880	67
14	Percentage boarders and lodgers in each occupational status, Seventh ward, 1880, for first- and second-generation employed Irish males	75
15	Percentage distribution of total first- and second-generation employed male Irish boarders and lodgers, by occupational status, Seventh ward, 1880	75

16	First-generation Irish marital patterns, 1852, 1870, 1880	79
17	Marital patterns, American-born of two Irish-born parents, 1880	80
18	Marital patterns, Irish-born with non-British foreign-born, 1880	82
19	Marital patterns, second-generation Irish with non-British foreign-born, 1880	83
20	Parental birthplaces of Irish couples, 1880	84
21	Numbers and percentages of Irish-born appearing in various *Municipal Reports*, 1859–80	157
22	Numbers and percentages of Irish children attending school, by ward, 1880	167

Preface and acknowledgements

No one in Britain working on the history of California and relying heavily on primary sources could do so without frequent visits to the west coast of the United States and without the co-operation of library staffs there. The University of Manchester, the Social Science Research Council and the Sir Ernest Cassel Educational Trust most generously helped provide the first; the staffs of the State Library at Sacramento, the San Francisco Public Library, the Society of California Pioneers and, most importantly and most impressively, the Bancroft Library, gave the second. The US Government Printing Office gave permission to reproduce the biographical details in the appendix. Thanks are also due to individuals, to Dr Philip Taylor, for his very helpful and acute criticisms of an earlier draft; to Dr Barry Brunt for his map of San Francisco, and to Margaret Lear for all the time and energy she invested in typing the manuscript. It is an odd feeling to have finished a work that has been in progress for five years, particularly as the author is aware of some dark areas in his attempted panorama of Irish life in San Francisco between 1848 and 1880, suggesting that even now that past needs further illumination. Whether readers will judge the sins of commission more severely than the sins of omission remains to be seen; hopefully the view that permeates the work that not all immigrants in industrialising America suffered dislocation, alienation or despair will not irritate too many.

R.A.B.

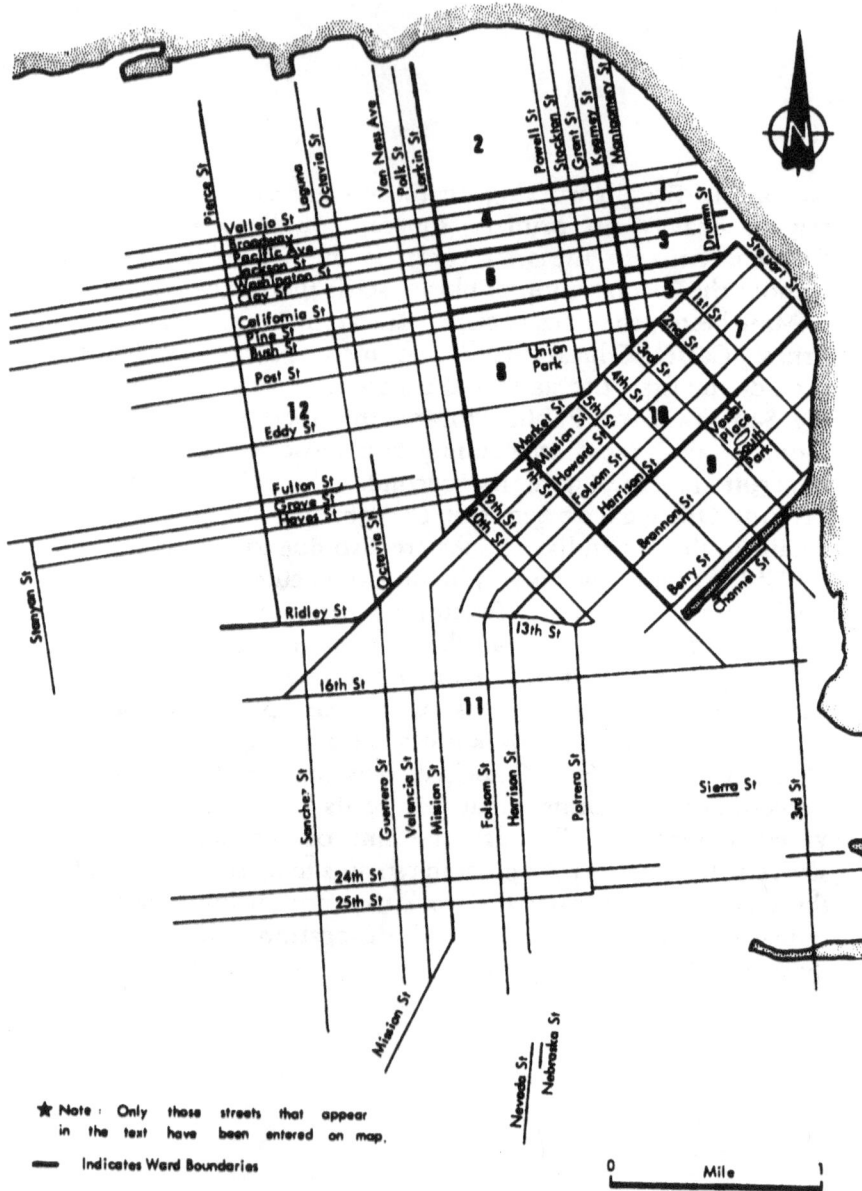

Chapter I
Introduction

The year 1851 saw 221,253 Irish arrivals in the United States, the largest number ever to arrive in a twelve-month period. Numbers had been rising since the mid-'thirties, when they exceeded 20,000 a year for the first time, although as late as 1843 there were only 19,670. In 1845, however, the potato crop failed in Ireland, as it did in successive years up to 1849. Whereas it was possible to regard the first failure as an accident, to be redeemed by the success of the crop of 1846, its failure, too, created a mood of despair that was reflected in a sharp, responsive rise in the numbers leaving Ireland. In 1847 the United States received over 100,000 immigrants from Ireland. It was not until 1855 that the panic subsided and numbers returned to pre-Famine levels. Altogether, whereas only 278,000 Irish arrived in the United States in the comparatively easy years of 1840–46, over 1,180,000 arrived between 1847 and 1854. Fewer than that number, a little over 1,140,000, were to arrive in the next quarter of a century. The United States, therefore, took in, in forty years, over 2,600,000 refugees from Irish economic, social and political conditions.[1]

The Irish arrived on the east coast of the United States and there the majority of them stayed, settling particularly as a result of their low level of skills and capital in the ill prepared urban areas. Even in 1870, when sufficient time had passed for Irish immigrants to have joined the westward movement, over half the Irish-born population of the country lived in the three states of New York, Pennsylvania and Massachusetts, producing a very important Irish presence in the towns and cities of New York, Brooklyn, Albany, Buffalo, Troy, Philadelphia, Pittsburgh, Scranton, Boston, Fall River, Lawrence and Lowell.[2] Studies of the Irish reception in these far from open-minded communities have emphasised the distress, confusion and dislocation experienced by the newcomers, forced by poverty and ignorance to take the poorest-paid jobs, to live in the worst housing, to suffer high rates of unemployment, disease and death, all the time being made to feel unwanted by the host community.[3] The Irish were disliked not merely for their strangeness but also for their Catholicism. Anti-Catholicism was as old as the republic and never completely dormant. It gave respectability to the activities of nativists who felt anxious and imperilled by the increasing numbers of foreign-born arrivals, with their strange ways of acting and their tendency to seek security among their own kind. Cultural antipathies reflecting class, religious and economic divisions led to anti-Irish feeling being forcibly expressed long before the Famine years. In 1829 Irish Catholic homes in Boston were stoned over three days. Violence reached new levels with the burning of the Ursuline convent in Charlestown in 1834.[4] Ten years later ethnic conflict generated the Philadelphia riots, which killed at least twenty persons and injured over a hundred others.[5] Instinctive dislike of the challenge to basically Protestant British ways from Irish and Germans helped produce the negative response of the Know Nothing movement. The New York City draft riots of 1863 showed up a society that had, seemingly, little knowledge of or ability to deal with the increasingly destructive cracks appearing in the urban fabric.[6] If, after the Civil War, nativists grew more self-confident and therefore less aggressive, there were always undercurrents of distrust and displeasure at the immigrant presence, particularly when the immigrant adjusted to his new society with the passage of time, and began to appear in areas of society, the economy and politics of which had been the preserve of the native stock.[7]

This, though, was the story in the eastern United States, where immigrants found themselves in communities that could have, by 1850, two hundred years of history, where much of the power and status had been handed down from generation to generation within a group of often intermarried families.[8] The immigrant faced an enemy who stood behind prepared and massive fortifications. It was as if the newcomer was advancing up a valley with the surrounding heights most surely in the hands of the foe. In such conditions his fate was very likely to be that of General Braddock. Yet there was, contemporaneously in the United States, an area where the eastern pattern of interaction between native stock and immigrant was missing, where local conditions produced idiosyncratic factors that distinguished the region even from the Middle West, which also lacked historic white communities.[9] That region was California, where the gold discoveries of 1848–49 produced cataclysmic changes in the structure of society, destroying old forms as completely as they can ever be destroyed, and replacing them with strange new ones. It was not merely that in California Anglo-America suppressed Hispanic America; it was not only that Anglo-America incorporated California into its cultural domain; the most important point was the speed with which the conquest was made and the amount of activity that was squeezed into very few years.[10] Nowhere in California were change and growth more marked in the period 1848–80 than in San Francisco. Nowhere, therefore, in the United States presents a better case study of what happened to the immigrant in mid-nineteenth-century America, when the traditional mould was broken and relations between native stock and immigrant were set free from the shackles of history, to take a new course.

In January 1848 San Francisco had under 200 buildings and fewer than 1,000 inhabitants.[11] By 1870 it had, astoundingly, become the tenth largest city in the country, with a population of 150,000, and by 1880 it had, including its suburbs, about a quarter of a million inhabitants.[12] From the first it had a large foreign-born population. In 1870 the native-born outnumbered the foreign-born by only 75,754 to 73,719, so there is no doubt that, taking second-generation immigrants into account, the native stock were in the minority in the city, perhaps outnumbered by as much as three to one.[13] Among the foreign-born the Irish were most numerous. By 1852 there were over 4,200 first-generation in the city; by 1880 over 30,000. In 1852 there were also over 1,400 Irish children in the city, not born in Ireland, and by 1870 there were 20,015 of this second generation. In 1880 the city officially contained 30,721 first-generation Irish, 13·1 per cent of the population, but a study of the manuscript schedules of the census of that year shows at least another 43,000 second-generation, 4,700 third-generation, and even—if for the moment Irishness can be taken to survive the passage of so many generations—some eighteen fourth-generation Irish.[14] Thus in 1880 one-third of the city's inhabitants belonged to the Irish community, or about 37 per cent of the city's white population. This made the group the largest of any in San Francisco; its history becomes a major part of the history of the city in the period. These Irish appear to have been largely Catholic, for in 1880 there were only two small branches of the Loyal Orange Institution of the United States in the city, and when the Scotch-Irish Society of America was founded support was warm but limited.[15] Thus the history of the Irish in San Francisco is also part of the history of ethnic rivalries in which religion played a major part.

Considering the Irish experience in the east, ethnic rivalries in San Francisco should have produced a hostile, destructive and unfortunate environment dominated by a nativist desire to limit the success and progress of the immigrant. There is no reason to suppose that nativists left their prejudices at the Sierra Nevada or on the Isthmus of Panama. Yet the odd thing is that, on the surface at least, contemporary Irish opinion on, for instance, the most important matter of the state and status of the Catholic religion in San Francisco, was far from pessimistic—on the contrary, it was excited and triumphant. The editor of the longest-surviving Irish and Catholic newspaper in the city, the *Monitor,* articulated this feeling when he said in April 1869 that if Irish readers were thinking of migration, not merely to San Francisco, but to California in general,

> Our Countrymen need not fear ... that they will have to encounter the prejudices against their race or religion, that are such drawbacks to their settlement in many parts of the Eastern States. Irishmen have made themselves a position here fully equal to that of any other nationality in our cosmopolitan population, and newcomers of the same race need fear to find no prejudice to bar their advancement, unless what any fault of their own may raise against individuals. Catholicity, too, has struck as firm a root in California as in any part of the United States, not excepting Maryland or Louisiana; and, as probably over a third, if not a full half, of the population of our State belong to her fold, Catholics need not fear the loss of their faith for want of Churches and Catholic associations, even in the more thickly settled districts.[16]

The same confident and encouraging message had been given

wide publicity in the previous year in a work influenced by the unfaltering editorial stance of the *Monitor,* namely John F. Maguire's *The Irish in America.* It too generally praised California, but also particularly pointed out the satisfactory position of Catholicism in San Francisco.[17] The fact that the Catholic hierarchy shared such views suggests that Maguire and the *Monitor* were not engaged in any conspiracy to defraud either contemporary Irish immigrants or later historians. As early as 1862 Archbishop Joseph Alemany had written to his flock that

when we look over this wide portion of the Kingdom of Christ under our own care, see the strong foundations on which the Church therein rests, the vast dimensions it already displays, and the hope of continued growth it gives, we cannot but rejoice.[18]

Four years later the sense of pleasure had been offered to a wider audience, through an article published in the *Dublin Review* of January 1866, by Father Hubert Vaughan, future Cardinal Archbishop of Westminster. This was later reprinted in the *Catholic Herald,* published in New York. According to Father Vaughan, the Catholic Church in California was 'the only representative of religious unity, order, and revelation'. As the foremost religious body it led the way in 'popular instruction, orphanages and hospitals', which, he added, were all works particularly attributable to the zeal of the Irish. Father Vaughan's clear message to the world was that, in California, 'In a word, Catholicity is in the ascendant, the sects are in the decline'.[19]

Six years later the first major summary of the Catholic position in the state, by the Reverend William Gleeson, was no less forthright and satisfied. It concluded that 'of the entire American Church, there is not probably any other portion of it, except the diocese of Chicago, where our holy religion has attained such a position within the last generation'.[20] The census of 1870 certainly seemed to support his and similar views. Roman Catholicism was not only the largest denomination in California but it was stronger there than in any other state. In the city the number of seats in Roman Catholic churches had grown from 6,050 in 1860 to 21,000 in 1870, giving solid assistance to the immigrant who wished to keep the faith.[21] No wonder, then, that in July 1875, on the occasion of Archbishop Alemany's silver jubilee, the address of his clergy displayed a marked sense of pleasure. 'Under your Grace's administration,' it read, 'the Church has fairly distanced all her competitors in this new field of religious rivalry. With scarcely equal advantages, and without any earthly favour, the State in general, and this metropolis in particular, have become more and more Catholic with the advance of years.'[22]

There is thus evidence to suggest that a significant and important section of the Catholic community believed that relations between the various religious groups were not only peaceful but aided the advance of Catholicism. In 1878 one who would have been very quick to sense any threat to his Church, the prickly Father Hugh Quigley, suggested that tolerance and mutual forbearance among the clergy were a major factor behind the religious peace. He pointed out

that a very remarkable harmony exists among the clergy of all denominations. We seldom hear of any lectures or invectives against the religion of their neighbours by over-zealous preachers, as is too frequently the case in the Eastern States, or was in past times. People here, even in religion, have come to the conlcusion to 'live and let live', and their common sense teaches them that to attack your neighbour's religion or his character is a pitiable way to defend your own.[23]

It could be questioned whether, say, Protestant abstention from invective was due to being outnumbered by Catholics, or whether San Francisco Protestants had a genuine and positive commitment to toleration which they had acquired on their way west, but, for the moment, it is undeniable that Catholic–Protestant relations were not in California then as they were in the east.

In January 1849, within a year of the American acquisition of San Francisco, and while the United States was being flooded by immigrants, causing alarm and hostility in the east, the San Francisco newspaper the *Alta California* commented that 'If there be a people whose condition is worthy of a world-wide commiseration and sympathy, it is that of tyrannised and famished Ireland'.[24] It is very possible that such a detached and humanitarian attitude could be taken because there was little chance that the refugees from the Famine would be cast up on the shores of California, but it is also possible that San

Francisco was ready to value the Irish immigrant differently from eastern cities. Certainly, within three years, in June 1851, the British consul in San Francisco was reporting to London that Terence Bellew McManus, having escaped from 'Her Majesty's penal colonies', had arrived in the city and had been given 'a Public Dinner' attended by 'the Mayor and other authorities'. Two years later Patrick O'Donohue followed in June, while in October the Governor of California, the Mayor of San Francisco and leading citizens gave a banquet for a third arrival, John Mitchell.[25] It is possible that such generosity was intended to catch votes, but, if that is true, as it well might be, such politicking suggests that from the first the Irish vote was valuable and needed courting, by, it should be noticed, Whigs and Democrats alike. There was no instinctive official attitude to regard McManus or Mitchell as representatives of a dangerous and culturally subversive group, to be shunned if not attacked. The official view was to identify with the cause of Irish freedom.

It is generally known that Boston elected an Irish mayor in 1884; that New York did so in 1880.[26] What is less well known is that San Francisco elected its first Irish mayor, Frank McCoppin, in 1867. Less well known, too, than it ought to be is that on 4 March 1863 John Conness, born not in the United States but in Abbey, County Galway, began his term in the United States Senate, and, moreover, that on 4 March 1869 he was followed by Eugene Casserly, born in Mullingar, County Westmeath. Casserly's political base, unlike that of Conness, lay firmly in San Francisco, so that his election particularly shows how Irish political muscle was already being exercised in the city within a decade of the ending of the Famine emigration.[27] Even his triumph, however, was preceded by that of David C. Broderick, who though born in Washington, D.C., was of Irish parentage, and very Irish in his political style and associations. He became United States Senator from California on 4 March 1857, again depending to a great extent on the backing of San Francisco at the state capital.[28] These political triumphs, dating from well before the era usually ascribed to the arrival of the Irish in national politics, suggest, again, San Francisco's deviation from the norm of Irish experiences in the United States.

On 11 July 1868 Eugene Casserly acted as a pallbearer at the funeral of Mrs Mary Ann Donahue in St Mary's Cathedral.²⁹ She was the widow of the prominent James Donahue, president of the San Francisco Gas Company, and sister-in-law to the eminent banker and industrialist Peter Donahue. Peter, another pallbearer, James and their brother Michael, Glaswegians of Irish parentage, had built the first ironworks, done the first iron casting, produced the first printing press, steam engine, mining machinery, quartz mill, gasworks and street railway in the city.³⁰ A third pallbearer was the Irish-born John Sullivan, who had come to San Francisco in 1845 and had made a fortune out of real estate. He had been one of the founders of the premier banking institution in the city, the Hibernia Savings and Loan Society, and had played an important part, as will be seen, in establishing the Catholic Church in the city.³¹ An Irish-born fellow director of his, Miles D. Sweeny, was another pallbearer, known to the city partly as the supervisor of the Second ward between 1861 and 1863 on, it should be noted, the People's or non-Democratic ticket.³² Close by stood D. J. Oliver, born in Galway in 1823, who would have been known to the congregation not merely for his wealth in real estate but also as the man, knighted by Pius IX in 1849, who had had the enviable distinction of seeing two of his children receive their first communion from the Pope himself; and Daniel J. Murphy, who developed the largest dry goods house west of Chicago.³³ Outside the cathedral was a vast crowd, while the number of carriages in the funeral procession exceeded one hundred. 'The procession,' it was reported, 'was upward of a mile in length, and many of the principal buildings in the city displayed flags at half-mast while the cortège was passing through the streets.'³⁴ This pattern of events does not suggest a concourse of shanty Irish.

The same edition of the San Francisco *Irish News* which reported the funeral procession carried news of the death of Colonel Thomas Hayes while acting as a delegate to the National Democratic Convention in New York. Hayes, from County Cork, had landed in San Francisco in 1849, had been deputy sheriff of the county of San Francisco in 1850 and 1851, had given his name to Hayes Valley, had acted as assistant alderman, forerunner of the later Supervisor, from the Eighth ward for 1852–53, but probably owed most of his fame to his skill in pre-empting 160 acres in the heart of San Francisco. He acted as county clerk from 1853 to 1856 and was president of the Market Street Railroad, the creation of Peter Donahue. By 1860 he claimed real estate to the value of $100,000.[35] When his will was proved it included an annuity of $500 to his father and an equal one to a sister; a bequest of $250 to an aunt; $5,000 to another sister, $5,000 to his sister-in-law, Maria Hayes, $1,000 to a brother, $2,000 to James Van Ness, Mayor of San Francisco 1855–56 and into whose family Frank McCoppin married to continue the mayoral tradition; $2,500 to Nellie Yale, 'daughter of Gregory Yale', with the residue to his nieces and nephews.[36] Here, too, was evidence of a wealthy Irish community in the city.

Earlier in the same year, to give more evidence of the position of the Irish in community affairs, the Archbishop of San Francisco, Joseph S. Alemany, had appealed to his flock for donations to liquidate the debt hanging over the cathedral. A committee of 'fifteen gentlemen' was appointed, including D. J. Oliver, John Sullivan, Myles D. Sweeny and Peter Donahue. This, however, was only the tip of the Irish iceberg.[37] Others who served with them included Cornelius D. O'Sullivan, reportedly known as 'the Irish lord', controller of a successful mining and commercial business, and another original founder of the Hibernia Bank; Joseph A. Donohue, an Irish-American of New York, and another very prominent banker, associated with the early beginnings of William C. Ralston in the city; Richard Tobin, from Tipperary, again connected with the Hibernia Bank; John T. Doyle, another New York Irish-American, described by Bancroft as 'a very conspicuous and reputable jurist; recognised not only as among the ablest lawyers on the coast, but as one who [could] be depended upon to maintain the honor and dignity of the bar; and withal, a scholar of rare culture and refinement'; as well as D. C. McGlynn and John Kelley Jr.[38] At a subsequent meeting the committee heard that it had collected $1,000 from Donohue Kelly & Co., $1,000 from D. J. Murphy, $500 from D. J. Oliver, $500 from Peter Donahue, $500 from Conroy and O'Connor, $500 from Sullivan and Cashman, Irish firms, $500 from Thomas Tobin, from County Tipperary, who had opened a clothing business in the city in 1851, and $500 from John Sullivan.[39] The cathedral was one of the most important buildings in the city, both architecturally and functionally. The Irish were its financiers. Their role in this suggests a far from unimportant one in civic life in general, and an unparalleled status within the Catholic community at least.

In July 1851 Archbishop, then Bishop, Alemany, was given a lot of land in Market Street, for a Roman Catholic orphan asylum, by John Sullivan, Timothy Murphy and Jasper O'Farrell. Murphy and O'Farrell symbolised the early connection of the Irish with the city, the former having arrived in California in 1828, the latter in 1843. Murphy acted as land commissioner from 1847 to 1848, after the American takeover, and had time to lay the foundations of a fortune based on real estate; O'Farrell made the first important survey of San Francisco in the same years and also collected real estate on the way.[40] The first president of the asylum was John A. McGlynn, a prominent Democratic politician, and among others who served as trustees in its early years were James A. Donohue, John Sullivan, Peter Donahue, and Philip A. Roach, who became president in June 1856. Roach, from Cork, had been American consul in Lisbon before coming to California, and acted as United States Appraiser at San Francisco from 1853 to 1861. He was part-owner of the *Examiner,* and became state senator from the city in 1873.[41] The composition of the board of trustees suggests, once again, the importance of the Irish in the founding of social institutions. What is also important, because it reflects the weight these men had in the civic community as a whole, is the reaction of the general public and the politicians to bodies like the asylum. Here in San Francisco there was no sustained, well orchestrated nativist attack on such civic enterprise in the hands of Romanists: rather, when, in 1868, a state legislative committee investigated charitable institutions, it did little but praise those in which there was an Irish influence. The Catholic orphan asylum was 'doing great good by dispensing a needed charity to many destitute children', it said, also praising similar work in the Magdalen asylum, another Irish-dominated institution.[42] This tolerant attitude was not new. The state had given the Roman Catholic orphan asylum $5,000 as early as 1855, while from 1870 it granted $50 per year for each orphan and $25 per year for children with only one parent, in recognised institutions, without sectarian distinction.[43] In 1862 the state legislature gave the Magdalen asylum, under the direction of the Sisters of Mercy, $5,000 for a new building and the responsibility for looking after the girls formerly sent to the Industrial School. Between 1863 and 1878 the legislature gave the asylum $30,000 and, though the new constitution of 1879 forbade general charitable grants, continued to pass money to the asylum on a *per capita* basis.[44] Clearly the balance of social and political power was not, as in the east, heavily weighted against the Irish community and all its works. The city was ready to accept its welfare institutions, even to pay for some of them.

The evidence produced so far for agreeing with contemporary accounts of Irish satisfaction with San Francisco has an élitist cast. Yet a modern authority has produced figures which suggest that the comparative gratification in the Irish community may have been widespread, for, as time went on, and the Irish presence became more defined, and more central, in the city, the Irish settled there permanently in greater proportions, for longer periods, as Table 1 shows.[45] Although the sample is small it does show that at some stage after 1860 the Irish ceased to flow in and out of the city at the

Table 1

Length of residence in San Francisco of employed males in 1880, by nativity and ethnicity

	Age (years)				
	1–9	10–19	20–29	30+	N
Native-born	78	14	5	3	297
Foreign-born	67	24	6	3	422
English-Scottish	63	18	12	8	51
Irish	56	31	9	4	146
German	73	22	4	1	109
French	84	11		5	19
Italian	94	6			16
Other	72	28			81
All	72	20	6	3	719

general rate of the population, appearing to decide that they had now found a favourable environment for a permanent home. It is not impossible that the exalted social, economic and political position reached by some of their countrymen persuaded others, more lowly, to stay. It is also likely that they considered there were very good reasons for doing so, for there was nothing, otherwise, to prevent them from leaving. This evidence of voting with the feet is very important in the final analysis.

None of this, however, should lead to exaggerated claims for the Irish position in San Francisco. The figures in Table 1 do not show the ideal of one hundred per cent persistence. The Irish community developed its character and identity in relation to the community at large, and that community was troubled about the relationship between host and immigrant cultures in the city as elsewhere. At the same time the Irish immigrant culture itself underwent the strain of redefinition in a new environment and was disturbed by the problems of relocation and adjustment. The San Francisco Irish had a number of substantial reasons for dissatisfaction, not all of them the product of nativism, which limited their sense of progress. American society was inegalitarian: therefore some men and women were poorer than others. It believed in the inheritance of property and thus allowed some to begin their lives better equipped materially. The standard of living in Ireland, the amount of property heritable there, were lower than in the United States, so that Irish immigrants, irrespective of their cultural unfamiliarity with their new home, were likely to be worse off than their American native counterparts.

On top of this, the San Francisco Irish lived in a society which had received the legacy of the Reformation from the past. Historically the Reformation had produced two equally exclusive views of Christian orthodoxy, both adamant that each possessed the secret of eternal salvation. Protestants happened to be in the majority in the formative years of American society; Catholic immigrants therefore necessarily had to wage an uphill fight for acceptance. The Catholic position was, however, vulnerable in one important respect. Catholic allegiance to the Pope lacked universally accepted definition, partly because, historically, the Popes had found it difficult to separate religion and geopolitics, as the excommunication of monarchs clearly showed. By the nineteenth century the Pope's secular power was minimal, but the problem of his relationship to Catholics remained a vital one in the United States, where there was continuing disagreement over what allegiances were transferred by migration to the New World.[46] When the British government, before 1871, refused to accept that its subjects could transfer their nationality and when immigrants by and large found it impossible to forget the values of their childhood, it was hardly surprising that men could doubt the loyalty of newcomers and ask what it was they identified with in the United States. The Reformation was still a live issue to the mid-nineteenth-century mind, which regarded the event with either disgust or adulation. Disagreements stemming from it were bound to exist and divide communities, as was the fact that immigrants had not, by definition, been born in the United States. The very first editorial of the San Francisco *Catholic Guardian,* without meaning to do so, set out the pressures which must work on the Irish community in San Francisco. 'As American citizens,' it said,

we owe allegiance to our Government, are bound to uphold its laws and to consult, so far as is in our power and within our sphere of duty, the public good. Of course, we cannot forget the land that gave us birth—the home of our childhood. Ireland is the mother country of the immense majority of American Catholics, and, as such, is dear to us all.[47]

San Francisco Irish were Irish, largely Catholic, and also largely, citizens of the United States. They were not American-born Protestant citizens of the republic. This was the crucial difference, the one that had a great effect on the Irish experience in San Francisco. But simultaneously, healing the breach, was the mutual identification by both groups with the future of the United States. In the end, because San Francisco had no past, because it looked only to the future, its development gave opportunity to native-born and immigrant alike in their commitment to that future. The opportunity may not have been equal in every respect, but it was not wildly dissimilar.

As a result, in viewing the Irish experience in San Francisco in terms of two formative sets of circumstances, namely locally derived ones that brought material opportunity and an ever-developing sense of importance in the city, and nationally derived ones that never ceased to remind the Irish that they were immigrants in a strange country, both need to be given weight. The unusual features of the San Francisco story for the Irish in this period were, however, that the two sets did not weigh equally on the immigrant, and certainly that the effect and force of nativism were much blunted in the spread of Anglo-American culture to the Pacific coast. The music of the time therefore had two themes; a major and minor one, the major being the local circumstances that produced the feelings of satisfaction and complacency already outlined, the minor stemming from the host culture's at best ambivalence, at worst hostility, to the immigrant presence. The purpose of the work that follows is to analyse the components of the melody in terms of the two themes. The place to begin is the extraordinary development of the urban centre of San Francisco.

Chapter II
The expanding city, 1848-1880

It is one of the axioms of modern thought that economic growth and development, though with some costs, are substantially necessary to produce a contented population. This being so, it is important, as far as the Irish of San Francisco are concerned, that they lived, in the period under discussion, in a city in which both took place. There were minor down-swings from time to time, but by 1880 the economic life of the city was complex and highly developed. In that year 104,650 persons were employed in the city, which now ranked ninth largest in the nation.[1] The economic history of its expansion can be divided into three periods: the first, running from the days of the Gold Rush to 1858 or 1859, was marked by an early boom, lasting until the end of 1849 or the beginning of 1850; a two-year depression; another boom of approximately eighteen months; and then a depression that dragged on from the late months of 1853. The second period was one of steady growth, helped by the increasing self-sufficiency of California, particularly in foodstuffs, which lasted until the mid-1870s. The Civil War and the transcontinental railroad caused minor upheavals, particularly in distribution networks, but also acted as accelerators, creating new markets. The development of the Nevada mines was controlled from the city, and their expansion helped fuel this boom. The decreasing profitability of these mines, however, added to the reverberations from the national slump of 1873, helped to bring the second period to a close. By 1877 there was a fully-fledged financial panic to destroy confidence and partly create the conditions that produced the political, economic and social challenge of the Workingmen's Party. The depression, however, was short-lived, and over by 1880, so there was no sense, at the end of the period, that the city had reached the limits of its growth.[2] Even during the last more troubled decade the numbers in employment had risen by 53 per cent. The Irish immigrants benefited from this growth, for it provided them with jobs. By 1880 17,012 first-generation and 10,810 second-generation were employed in San Francisco, comprising 27 per cent of the workforce.[3]

Throughout the period 1848–80 the city's economy was closely influenced by the development of San Francisco's role as the chief *entrepôt* of the Pacific coast. The commercial growth, stimulated by the need to provide for the new mining areas of the state, was instantaneous and enormous. By 1851 the port, which had hardly existed in 1848, was dealing with a volume of foreign commerce that ranked it fourth in the nation. Exports were slower to develop than imports, being limited in the early years almost exclusively to gold, but by 1855 they had begun to include flour, barley, oats and, most important, wheat. Later canned goods, wine, refined sugar, explosives and lumber were added to the list of exports.[4] Distribution of goods between the city and its economic hinterland was as important to the economy as the long-distance trade, so that the coasting trade quickly developed a role equal to that of trade with the east.[5]

Local demand coupled with distance from eastern suppliers brought the development of a manufacturing sector too, which grew so that by 1880 San Francisco had become the ninth largest manufacturing centre in the country, measured both by industrial output, in terms of 'value added' and by the percentage of the city's population employed.[6] It was believed that for some time manufacturing was held back by a number of factors, including high wages, 'the larger profits of elementary industries, the lack of water-power in eligible quarters, the cost of transportation, the high value of good sites, and doubtful land titles, scanty population, unsettled conditions, the limited quantity of iron and hard wood, and the high price of coal', not to mention frontier rates of interest. Indeed, in the 'fifties, if the value of refined metals is not counted, the manufacturing output of San Francisco actually declined by over 50 per cent. Its expansion did not take place until the 'sixties, when labour, particularly, became more plentiful. Employment opportunities then rose in that decade with the growth of manufacturing and did not disappear even during the 'seventies, when manufacturing came to rest on larger and more efficient units, although owners of smaller units of production might have suffered in the general industrial rationalisation. The more intricate and diversified manufacturing sector needed less unskilled labour but, conversely, increased the demand for skilled labour, allowing greater opportunity for upward mobility where the individual was able to take advantage of the demand for skill. Between 1852 and 1880, according to one analysis, the mean occupational prestige score of the general employed population rose by 5·2 points, that of the blue-collar workers by 6·0. At the same time the percentage of blue-collar workers in the total workforce was falling from 64 to 56, while that of white-collar workers was rising from 36 to 44. Both commerce and manufacturing were producing conditions permitting upward mobility for the Irish, if they could seize them.[7]

In detail, the 'fifties saw the establishment of a number of ironworks, brass foundries, shipyards, food processing plants, sawmills, flour mills, wagon-making establishments, factories producing mining implements, bag factories, type factories, potteries and glassworks.[8] In 1860 the city possessed 229 manufacturing establishments capitalised at over $2 million, employing 1,525 males and thirty-nine females, and producing over $19 million worth of goods. There was, however, little sign of the development of a large heavy industrial sector, for food processing had as much importance as the production of machinery, steam engines, tin, copper or sheet-iron ware. Nevertheless the manufacture of machinery and steam engines did employ the largest numbers, some 222, followed, in order, by 151 in the printing industry, 120 in sugar refining, eighty in brick-making, seventy-eight in producing malt liquors, sixty-one in bread-making and fifty-nine in the production of tin, copper and sheet-iron ware.[9]

The 'sixties witnessed expansion and diversification in response to population growth, the wheat trade, the Civil War, which interrupted eastern imports but permitted favourable currency manipulations, and receipts from the new Nevada mines.[10] The number of manufacturing establishments rose to 1,223 and the number of hands employed to 12,377. This growth still failed to bring about significant heavy industrialisation, and, for instance, the numbers engaged in producing machinery, engines and boilers only rose to 626. These employees were outnumbered by the 1,794 occupied in making cigars, or the 854 engaged in boot and shoe making.[11] Consequently there was a sense of hyperbole in the remarks of a visitor in 1871 that though he 'had supposed San Francisco to be a second Liverpool' he 'was not prepared to find that it was also a second Birmingham'. It was perhaps true in quality but certainly not in quantity that in San Francisco 'There are saw manufactories which rival those of Sheffield; locomotive and steam-engine works which compare favourably with those of Philadelphia and Newcastle; rolling mills, which are admitted to be most complete in their arrangements'. It was not heavy industry alone that left 'The greater part of the lower town enveloped in a dense cloud of smoke', from furnaces burning Mount Diablo coal, for it was used in all branches of manufacture.[12] More dispassionate observation admitted that there had been some industrial development, but particularly noted the lack of heavy manufacturing, despite the 'Cars, locomotives, steam-engines, [and] all machinery for mining purposes'.[13] In 1880, after further growth to the point where there were 2,971 manufacturing establishments in the city, capitalised at over $35 million and employing 28,442 persons, there were only fifty-eight foundry and machine shops, and they were capitalised at little over $2 million. Meat-packing and slaughtering claimed the greatest dollar value for its products, just over $6 million, while only three branches of industry paid out over a million dollars annually in wages. Only nine of a named 115 were capitalised at over $1 million. If foundries and machine shops employed 1,888 of the 23,662 males of sixteen years of age and over, the manufacturers of tobacco employed 3,110 and boot and shoe makers 2,464. The city's economy continued to be characterised by increasing diversity in its manufacturing sector, but contained only one establishment in 1880 manufacturing iron and steel, to a value of $780,000.[14]

Surprisingly, perhaps, the city's economy had an agricultural sector during the period. Even in 1860 there were twenty-four farms in the city and county of San Francisco over 100 acres in size, producing mainly peas, beans, potatoes, other market garden products, and milk.[15] In 1870 the value of farm products was over $840,000; the county had 406 farms, including seven over 500 acres; and its 3,169 milch cows produced nearly two million gallons of milk yearly.[16] By 1880 the number of farms had fallen to 164, but thirteen of these were now over 1,000 acres. The principal products were eggs, milk and potatoes, with the 4,213 cows now giving nearly five and a half million gallons of milk in 1879.[17] These farms lay mainly to the south, towards the San Mateo boundary, and permitted some Irish San Franciscans to retain traditional links with agriculture.

Throughout most of the period the city was governed under the terms of the charter of 1856, often referred to as the Consolidation Act, as it had consolidated city and county government into one.[18] If the Irish immigrants were fiscal conservatives they would have been satisfied by that most important municipal burden, the level of taxation. Before 1856 a series of three short-lived charters had been far less unobjectionable in this respect, mainly because the city fathers had had almost unlimited freedom to tax and spend under the so-called omnibus clause, permitting them 'to make by-laws and ordinances not repugnant to the Constitution and laws of the United States or of this state'.[19] In the earliest days of the American period, too, the sense of permanent commitment to the city was weak, so that it was not difficult to run up massive debts, leaving the problem of paying them to an unknown posterity. In the last year before the 1856 charter, spending peaked at $2¼ million, by no means all of it on what the solid citizen would consider legitimate projects. By May 1851 the city debt had already reached the alarming figure of $1¼ million.[20]

The Consolidation Act coincided with the beginning of a ten-year period of rule by the People's Party. Though, as will be seen, there were strong reasons why the Irish should dislike the party, the taxpayers among them had little to complain of. In 1857 the city administration in the hands of the new party spent only $353,000.[21] The level of expenditure remained low until the party's demise in 1866–67, when it began to rise again, reaching $2¼ million in 1869 and $4¼ million in 1876. By this time the taxpayers were alarmed, and the state legislature stepped in with the curious One-twelfth Act, whereby all revenues were divided into twelve parts, and monthly expenditures were not to exceed one-twelfth of the annual appropriation.[22] Tax rates were kept comparatively low under the Consolidation Act: whereas in 1852–53 the total city, county and state taxes amounted to $4.41½ per centum, the new government of 1856 set them at a total of $1.60, though the level of services that this rate permitted was so low that in 1859–60 it was raised to $2.56 9/10 per centum. Rising real estate values led to a reduction to $1.20 in 1863–64, but 1871–72 saw a rise to $2.10¼. A change in valuation, from a forced-sale to a cash one, led to an increase in the assessed property values and consequently to a new low tax rate of $1 in 1872–73. Poor times led to a lower assessment in 1879–80, so that the rate had to be lifted to $1.69, though in 1880–81 it was to be lowered slightly to $1.57. The propertied reacted to the rise of the early 'seventies by beginning an agitation for a new city charter, arguing, in part, that the loss of control of some powers to Sacramento in 1856 had been responsible for the jobbery and corruption producing higher taxes. The people in general, however, turned down proposals for a new charter in 1874 and were to do so again in 1883 and 1887.[23]

Civic satisfaction did not begin and end with the tax rate. Equally important were the services provided by spending what the taxes raised. So much was done in San Francisco in a very short time that, despite the understandable calls for even further improvements, public and private agencies could feel reasonably proud of their achievements. There was no sense that San Francisco had degenerated into some form of civic barbarism because of its remote position on the Pacific frontier. Irish San Franciscans, as others, benefited from the twin urges that all western replicas of eastern societies in the United States shared, the drives to equal and excel. When Anthony Trollope visited the Mid-west he noted of civic leaders there, what was equally true of San Francisco's, that they 'have had the experience of the world before them. They have known of sanitary laws as they began. That sewerage, and water, and gas, and good air would be needed for a thriving community has been to them as much a matter of fact as are the well understood combination between timber and nails, and bricks and mortar.'[24] The San Franciscan demanded a level of urban services at least equal to that which he or she had experienced in the east, and, by and large, received at least an acceptable approximation. Although the physical, spatial growth and transformation of the city was one index of its progress, and a sense of progress was vital to the well-being of the citizen, equally important, because far more immediate, was the feeling that the quality of life was improving, measured by the number of paved streets, the purity of the water supply, the efficiency of the sewerage system, the increase in educational facilities or the development of welfare institutions. The historical record shows that San Franciscans had no reason to feel that they lived in a limited or regressive society. Irish San Franciscans' view of their situation would have been buoyed up by the growth and development of services which they saw all around them. It should be recalled that they were San Franciscans as well as Irish when evaluating their experience.

The major item of the municipal budget was the provision of roads. Between 1856 and 1870 the city spent $9,750,000 on them, reaching $1,246,000 in 1869–70. By 1880 the city had over five hundred miles of streets, of which twenty-five miles were paved with cobblestones, twenty miles with stone blocks, five miles with asphalt or similar material, fifty-seven miles with broken stone, and thirty-one miles with wood. Twenty-seven miles of the wood was laid in planks; four miles in blocks. Repairs were effected by day labour, once the roadway had been accepted by the city, but were not wholly satisfactory, according to much contemporary comment. Despite the attempt to cut costs, they rose continually, reaching $1,862,194 in 1876–77, when the drive for economy was renewed. Even then, the city would normally spend over half a million dollars annually on its streets.[25] Before 1871 it looked after the sidewalks, but in that year it restricted itself to the roadway alone. Not surprisingly, there was much adverse comment about the resulting decline in quality, but much had been done.[26]

The first street lighting was privately provided, but in 1851 the city council hired contractors to illuminate the area between Battery, Kearny, Jackson and California. In 1852 it ratified an agreement with James Donahue to provide coal-gas street lighting but had to wait until February 1854 for results.[27] The company was given a fifteen-year monopoly and reacted by charging what were thought to be high prices. Hardly surprisingly the result was very sparse street lighting in the city, but in 1871 it was calculated that San Francisco possessed 3,600 gas lamps and ran them at a cost of about $200,000 per annum.[28] For some time the city saved money by lighting streets only on moonless nights, a somewhat unsatisfactory procedure. There was criticism of the quality of the gas furnished, which produced too much 'smoke and damage to household comfort' as well as 'pulmonary derangements' and, unhappily, little light, but there was at least a system in operation.[29]

The city cleaned its streets, too. By 1880 it had graded them into four classes, according to the amount of use, and they were cleaned, respectively, by contract, once a week, once a fortnight, once a month and once every two months, at a cost of $47 per mile per year. Private refuse had to be privately disposed of, usually once a week at a cost of about fifty cents per month, paid to specialist removers. Liquid household wastes and the refuse from water closets either ran into the sewers or into cesspools or privy vaults. When vaults were emptied the 'night soil' from them was taken out to sea by boat and dumped.[30] The system might not always work, but, again, it had been developed.

The expansion of the police force mirrored the growth of the city. In early 1849 it consisted of some six men. After the election of 1 August 1849 it was expanded to thirty to enable it to face the new era. Demand for the policemen's services continued to outrun supply, so that the force was increased again to fifty by February 1850 and to seventy-five by 1851. In January 1852 an economy drive left the force's strength at thirty men, but by the end of the year numbers had to be increased to fifty. In 1853 a further increase took place, to fifty-six; in 1854 a further twenty-four were recruited. Economy then became the order of the day once more, and at the onset of the Committee of Vigilance of 1856 the force was reduced to thirty-four men. Their effectiveness was limited by the fact that, even when the city had fifty-six policemen, only fifteen were on the beat at any one time, patrolling a very small area. One result was that San Francisco began to experiment with 'specials' to supplement the regulars and, discovering advantages in not having to pay fixed salaries, continued the arrangement beyond the end of the period.[51]

The Consolidation Act reorganised matters to some degree, abolishing annual contracts and providing for an elective police chief, who, together with the mayor and police judge, would comprise a police commission. In the next eighteen years only three men, two certainly Irish, filled the office: James Curtiss, Martin Burke and Patrick Crowley.[52] In 1856, too, the number of men was raised to 150; in 1857 they were put into uniform.[53] Economy, however, kept real numbers down; there were only fifty-four policemen between 1862 and 1864; sixty-six between 1864 and 1865; eighty-four between 1865 and 1868; and 104—100 men and four captains—in 1870, when the ratio of policemen to the total inhabitants of the city and county was 1 to 1,437.[54] The growth of unemployment in the early 1870s seemed to offer a chance to remedy the ills of such small numbers, and in 1873 Mayor Alvord proposed reducing salaries by 20 per cent, to allow numbers to increase by 25 per cent. 'The present pay of Officers would seem to be small enough,' he said,

> considering the risks pertaining to their duties; but when so many persons are willing to assume the same risks, why should not the City favour the employment of more men, and render greater protection to the lives and property of her inhabitants?[35]

Numbers were not increased, however, and the city continued to be patrolled by between thirty-seven and forty men at any one time, making them of limited effect.[36] Numbers employed did rise to 121 in 1873–74, to just over 150 in 1875–77, and to 172 in 1877–78.[37] Eventually, in 1878, the legislature permitted an increase in the force to 400 men, and tried to remove it further from politics by putting it under a commission of three 'representative' citizens chosen by judges of the Fourth, Twelfth, and Fifteenth judicial districts. Among the first appointees was Irish-born Robert Tobin of the Hibernia Bank, who with his fellows set out to oversee a force that rose from 329 in 1878–79 and 340 in 1879–80 to 400 in 1880–81.[38] In 1880 San Francisco had one police officer for every 685 of its population as a result, which did not give it quite as good a proportion as New York, where in 1876 the ratio was one to 435, nor as Boston, where in 1880 the ratio was one to 527, but brought the city close to Philadelphia's ratio of one to 672 and much exceeded Chicago's of one to 1,071.[39]

The growth of the police force did not uncover a markedly criminal society, despite the views of those who mourned the passing of the spirit that had produced the Committee of Vigilance of 1856 and its political child, the People's Party.[40] Although the number of arrests quadrupled between 1862–63 and 1879–80, the number of arrests per policeman dropped from 100 to sixty-two.[41] Although there were 21,063 arrests in the latter year, they were the result not of an unnaturally violent population but rather of one unable to control its baser instincts. Only about 10 per cent of arrests were for assault and battery, while 9,127 were for drunkenness, 470 for gambling, 547 for soliciting for a house of ill fame, 1,037 for obscene language, seventy-eight for furious riding or driving, and twenty-five for riding or driving on the sidewalk.[42] San Franciscans should have felt reasonably safe on their streets and that the forces of law and order were keeping pace with the growth of the problems that went with greater population density.

The history of the fire service during the period was also one of increasing commitment on the part of the city to the safety of the citizens and their property. The first volunteer company was founded on 25 December 1849, and by 1854 there were three hook-and-ladder companies, with thirteen engines and 950 certified members, partly rewarded by the city by being exempted from jury service.[43] The volunteer companies were exclusive bodies to which entry was difficult, if their admission procedures can be believed. A system was used that kept men out who received as few as two black balls.[44] San Francisco began regularising this volunteer labour in June 1850, when the city passed an ordinance to set up a fire department, but it was a year before serious work was done. The city did establish cisterns, some sixty by 1855, and did proscribe wooden buildings within certain very narrow limits of the downtown area. Under George H. Hossefross it set up a system of governing the volunteer companies and agreed on a method of dividing expenses with them. There the matter rested until 1865. Meanwhile the Consolidation Act, pursuing economy, established an annual budget of $8,000 in 1856.[45] In 1863–64 the legislature passed an Act empowering the city to establish a telegraph system for fire alarms, but San Francisco found costs prohibitive. Instead, for a time, it relied on bells which tolled out an elaborate code. The city was divided into districts and then subdivided again. News of fires was carried to the town hall: 'The big bell tolls five times quickly, and then after a pause six times. The firemen all know where to go, and people in the streets turn to their pocket-books to see where the fire has broken out.'[46]

In 1865–66 the legislature permitted the city to have a paid department. Some felt that San Francisco had lost part of its colour with the disappearance of the mad rush of rival companies to be first at a fire, and also to outshine others at the Fourth of July processions, but fire was too serious a matter to be left to private enterprise.[47] In 1874 the city reorganised its fire limits—that is, the area within which buildings had to be of other material than wood—to comprise the block between Stockton and Dupont, four blocks in length, from Bush to Clay.[48] Private enterprise was still forced to relieve the city to some extent. In May 1875 the Board of Fire Underwriters set up a Fire Patrol that guaranteed fourteen men on duty, day and night.[49] Perhaps both city and private effort was necessary because of the widespread use of wood in building. It was reported in 1874 that the rate of insurance was 'nearly ten times higher than in Europe'.[50] The Fire Department was generally believed to be extremely efficient by the 1870s, to the safety and satisfaction of San Franciscans.[51] By 1880 the total force numbered 303 men, who used seventeen steam fire-engines, eighteen two-wheel tenders, six four-wheel hose carriages and five hook-and-ladder trucks. They also had seventy-two horses and 24,150 ft of hose. The city possessed 1,352 fire hydrants, forty-three of which were private, and fifty-five cisterns, with a total capacity of over two million gallons. The telegraph system developed during the late 'seventies, and by 1880 had 120 miles of wire with 150 signal-boxes. Altogether the Fire Department cost over $266,000 per annum, and the telegraph over $18,000 per annum.[52]

The problem of fire prevention was intricately bound up with that of a water supply. To begin with, the city relied on an unsystematised supply. Local springs and wells provided some water; more was brought from Suasalito. By 1855 the city had 175 artesian wells, some with windmills, but, before that, had taken steps to put the water supply on a more regular footing. Azro D. Merrifield was given permission to pipe water into the city for twenty years in June 1851, with exclusive privileges during the first five. The city was to have free water, but was not to inherit the works at the expiry of the contract. Merrifield sold his franchise to others who demanded a monopoly, which they received. They began to construct their works but had not completed them by an extended deadline of 1 January 1857. Their grant then passed to the San Francisco City Water Works, which eventually began supplying the city in September 1858.[53]

Before that date, however, on 23 April 1858, the state legislature passed 'An Act to authorise George H. Ensign and others, Owners of the Spring Valley Water Works, to lay down Water Pipes in the Public Streets of the City and County of San Francisco'.[54] This company gradually achieved a stranglehold over the city's water supply, particularly after 1862, taking over the City Water Works in February 1865, and by 1867 it had won a monopoly position.[55] Consumption of water rose from 2.36 million gallons in 1865 to 17,050 million in 1880, but though the company met demand it also suffered increasing criticism as the 1870s wore on.[56] Complaints centred on the cost. In 1879 Henry George maintained that

Water in San Francisco costs more than bread, more than light; it is a very serious item in the living expenses of every family, and one of the large expenses of every manufacturing establishment. There is no large city in the civilized world where water costs so much. And even then the supply is neither as good nor as plentiful as it should be.[57]

In fact it was not until 1928 that San Francisco voters approved a bond issue to purchase the properties of the Spring Valley Water Company, now valued at $41 million.[58] Despite arguments over the cost and the possibility of municipal control, however, the company's achievements should not be underestimated in bringing and expanding a water supply to an area with few local sources.

James Donahue provided the city with its first gas supply. The first mains were laid in 1854; by 1855 there were ten miles of them, serving 563 consumers who paid $15 per 1,000 cu. ft. By 1860 6,172 consumers paid $8 per 1,000 cu. ft. and used 60 million.[59] The legislature attempted to provide competition after 1860. At least two franchises were granted to supply gas in 1861 and 1862, and Von Schmidt *et al.* were authorised to lay gas pipes in 1863. The benefits of rival producers were not to be reaped, however, until the 1870s. One of the results then was a jump in the number of consumers from 9,400 in 1870 to 14,300 in 1880, when 489 million cu. ft were used. Prices in the 1870s ranged from $1.50 to $4.50 per 1,000 cu. ft.[60] The city paid 14½ cents for each street lamp in 1880.[61] The fall in prices from those of earlier days helped make inhabitants more willing to tolerate private control, but did not entirely satisfy them. The legislature of 1877–78 produced a law to regulate prices, which should not exceed $3 per 1,000 cu. ft, and tried to stimulate competition once again with the Free Gas and Water Act.[62] The period ended with the gas supply still a monopoly, but one that had been responsible for the massive development of yet another service. Further evidence that San Francisco was, despite its late start, among the most forward-looking and progressive cities is to be seen in the opening of the American Speaking Telephone Company in February 1878, even if it had but eighteen subscribers to begin with.[63] Electricity had appeared privately on 4 July 1876, but had not reached the public by 1880.[64] The city would be quite ready to adopt it when the time came.

The sewerage system was perhaps San Francisco's most disastrous service. In 1892 I. H. Stallard gave what he called 'A Polyclinic Lecture' on the problem. It was his unequivocal view that there was not 'one single yard of sewer in this city which fulfils its duty with safety to the public health'.[65] Difficulties with the sewerage system began to emerge in the 1860s when citizens came to realise that what had been provided so far was proving increasingly ineffective in dealing with the growing amount of city waste. The *ad hoc* arrangements hitherto adopted had worked as well as they had because sewerage could, at first, be allowed to run out into the Bay, down the generally sloping site of the city. When the foreshore was developed, however, its level rose; simultaneously the growth of population produced more waste, while the rainfall to expel it remained the same. Waste deposits began to gather under city streets; their smells signalled danger and the citizens began to link them with disease. In the late 'seventies matters at last began to improve, under the direction of William P. Humphreys, the City and County Surveyor. In 1880 Mayor Andrew J. Bryant felt there had been a decided improvement in the last four years. 'The sewer on Channel Street and the work done at Washerwoman's Bay,' he said, 'have materially contributed to a better condition of the public health.'[66] By the end of the period the city had thus begun to retrieve its position even here, and to provide the inhabitants with the service they needed. In 1870 an advance had been made on an associated front with the Act to Establish a Quarantine and Sanitary Laws for the City and County of San Francisco, which set up a Board of Health and led to a number of important 'Orders and Regulations' governing the depositing of rubbish, action during smallpox epidemics, the use of slaughterhouses, the clearing of vaults, drainage, the working of night carts and other potential health hazards.[67] Though much remained to be done, and since much will always remain to be done in the provision of urban services, it is better to look at the distance travelled, not that remaining, in judging the city's exertions. As far as the material services went, San Francisco certainly provided enough to convince its inhabitants that they lived in a dynamic, developing and successful urban centre. It had, after all, begun with nothing.

The same may be said of the city's educational and welfare institutions. The major social service to develop was education. The first, short-lived school was begun by Thomas Douglas, early in 1848; the city adopted its first Ordinance of Regulation of Public Schools on 8 April 1850; and the first Public School Report of 4 May 1850 showed that 152 pupils were enrolled.[68] By 1880, as a result of thirty years of construction, San Francisco had two High Schools, fifteen Grammar Schools, thirty-seven public schools and one ungraded school.[69] It spent 13·8 per cent of its revenues on education in the year 1879–80, on nearly forty thousand pupils.[70] In 1856 the Union Grammar School, the first High School in California, had been opened in the same year as Chicago's first, and only eight years after the first similar establishment in New York.[71] In 1864 the city had set up a separate Girls' High School, and in 1865 had even attempted a Latin School, which unfortunately only lasted three years.[72] Such developments were of use to all citizens and showed a broad definition of civic commitment. Particularly useful to Irish immigrants was the night school, which began by charging $2 a month, lowered it to $1, and then, in 1868, accepted John Swett's decision not to collect a fee.[73] According to Swett, the foremost Californian educator of his day, the school owed much to Joseph O'Connor, 'who had just come over from Ireland', begun a class in book-keeping and then developed the school to one 'excelled by no other city in the United States'.[74] There were other educational developments of importance. In 1876 San Francisco established a class for graduates of the High School who wished to be trained to teach in the elementary schools.[75] In 1879 the city opened its first public kindergarten, run by Emma Marwedel, adding it to a number of private ones, including one set up in 1878 by the Sisters of the Holy Family, to give shelter and care to the small children of widows and working women.[76] There was also a small home for the education of deaf and dumb and blind children from 1860 to 1865, when the school moved to Berkeley.[77]

The city had also established a number of other social services by 1880. There was an Industrial School on the San Jose road, about six miles south-west of City Hall, for 250 'ungovernable' boys. This institution dated back to 1859; its neighbour on the same lot, the House of Correction, to an Act of the legislature of 1871–72.[78] There was a City and County Hospital on a ten-acre lot between Potrero, Nevada, Sierra and Nebraska; the Twenty-sixth Street Hospital for contagious diseases; and a City and County Alms House near Lake Honda.[79] San Francisco had also been given state funds for an institution to care for the mentally ill and deficient, by an Act of 1851, but lost it in 1855 when the state decided to concentrate its efforts on a single hospital in Stockton. The provision of a state institution did mean, however, that the City and County Hospital in San Francisco, unlike many in the United States, was free from the need to care for the insane of the city. After 1855 the Board of Supervisors had to distribute outdoor relief to the indigent sick. The unemployed were left to private organisations, aided by small grants of public money, and were mainly dealt with by the San Francisco Benevolent Association, which in 1878, for instance, helped 7,000 persons.[80] The city's criminals were housed either in the city jail, between Kearny and Dupont, or in the city prison, to be found in the basement of the old City Hall at the corner of Kearny and Washington.[81]

San Franciscans could be pleased not only that so much had been done but also that many believed that a fair standard had been reached. For instance, no less an authority than Charles Loring Brace remarked that, by the late sixties, 'If the time and obstacles be considered, no city in the Union has accomplished more for popular education than San Francisco'.[82] John Erastus Lester found in 1873 that the schools were 'much better than could have been expected'.[83] In 1884 Emily Faithfull, an experienced social observer, was to agree that 'San Francisco, altogether, takes a very high place for the educational advantages she affords'.[84] There may have been reasons for some dismay, feelings that the Industrial School was ineffective and badly run, that there was corruption in the appointment of teachers, that not enough was done to force children to attend school, but all these anxieties could only come about after a partly successful system of social institutions had begun to function.[85] Even dissatisfactions were evidence of the social construction that had gone on in the city.

The growth of public institutions was not the only index of satisfaction. Life was not only utilitarian and practical; there was also enjoyment and pleasure. By 1880 the city, through a combination of public and private effort, had provided the means to both. The major institution was the Golden Gate Park, which owed its beginnings in large measure to Frank McCoppin.[86] It was he who suggested that San Francisco should seek the advice of Frederick Law Olmstead, and though the city refused to adopt the proposals of Olmstead and his collaborator Calvert Vaux, it did begin to plan a park in 1870, signalling another level of commitment to providing the citizens with an acceptable environment.[87] By 1879-80 no fewer than 983,164 visitors came to enjoy its amenities, which, though in their infancy, were a great improvement on the sand dunes that had gone before.[88]

In its 1877–78 session the legislature passed an Act empowering the city to establish a free library. During the following two years slow progress was made, but it was reported in April 1879 that the library was about to open, and in its first year it attracted 10,500 cardholders who read 354,000 volumes.[89] Previously, private bodies had filled the need for books. Three major private collections had grown up in the Mercantile Library, the Mechanics' Institute and the Odd Fellows' Hall, comprising 47,000, 30,000 and 25,000 volumes, respectively, in 1880.[90] Altogether, in that year, there were ten libraries, including one for French and one for German readers, where there had been none in 1848. Some observers thought that private enterprise served the city well, but private subscription charges—$12 annually for the Mercantile, for instance—kept the poor from books.[91] The Mercantile flourished at first, but was eventually forced to amalgamate with the Mechanics' Institute, suggesting restricted public demand, perhaps because of the fee.[92] Other institutions of higher culture, like picture galleries and museums, were still lacking in 1880. The city may have been too young for these, but there were other bodies to fill the gap.[93]

Private enterprise quickly gave the city amusements of every sort: 'gardens, theatres, circuses, saloons, skating-rinks ...restaurants'.[94] Privately run gardens were the city's substitute park for a long while. Russ's Gardens dated back to May 1854 and remained popular until the early 1870s.[95] One visitor swore he heard the following snatch of conversation on California Street at the beginning of the 'seventies:

I and my husband are very happy the whole of the week, for if I wash clothes, and he mends old boots and shoes, from Monday morning until Saturday night, *we always go to Russ's gardens on Sundays.*[96]

Other early resorts were the Willows and the Mission Dolores.[97] From the mid-1860s to the end of the 1880s the major private resort was Woodward's Gardens.[98] There the San Franciscan watched acrobats and ballooning, visited the zoological section, looked at pictures, 'copies gorgeously framed, of many celebrated pictures from the Roman galleries', conservatories, sea-lions, aviaries, and fish. There was a funfair and a pond on which they could remain 'with the pleasant illusion of being at sea, until an attack of vertigo' drove them ashore.[99] A popular alternative was Cliff House and Ocean Beach, with their seals, one that appears to have particularly attracted the contemporary road-hog.[100]

The quality of life was also soon enhanced by the development of other pleasurable institutions. The number and standards of city restaurants were satisfying even discriminating New Yorkers by the 1860s, while the 'free lunch' and 'free supper' saloons developed early and were widely praised.[101] The hotels included not only the architectural pacemakers of the city but also a wide range of lesser quality such as the temperance 'What Cheer House', where meals and lodging cost fifty cents each.[102] San Franciscans early became avid theatre-goers. By 1880 they could choose among twelve.[103] Visitors usually felt that the best one or two had productions of some merit.[104] Below the theatres, in size and standards, were some twenty small concert and beer halls, with an average seating capacity of about five hundred.[105]

The analysis of the great variety of city institutions thus reveals that by 1880 San Francisco could properly consider itself a well functioning centre, with no major reason for complaint from the citizens, according to contemporary standards. There was no great obvious and glaring defect to life in the city and there were many advantages stemming from rapid growth and development. There may have been minor discomforts. Some visitors were appalled aesthetically by the appearance of the city, the lack of significant buildings, the poverty of architectural styles, the jumble of buildings and the unprepossessing town plan.[106] Frederick Law Olmstead objected to the last, saying that it had 'been contrived with scarcely any effort to adapt it to the peculiar topography of the situation ... in such a hilly position as that of San Francisco, it is very inappropriate'.[107] Another visitor was repelled by the climate, 'simply detestable—cold, raw mornings and evenings, occasional fogs, burning hot noons, and a running accompaniment of dust and sand at all times'.[108] These were the criticisms of visitors and strangers, aesthetes rather than practical men who had come to the city to make their fortune. Shrewd local inhabitants might have judged differently, relating to the tremendous and exciting expansion of their city. Irish immigrants would have been impressed to read that in 1880, according to the San Francisco Health Officer, the death rate per 1,000 during the calendar year was 18·5, compared with 20·49 in Brooklyn, 20·37 in Boston, 17·23 in Chicago, 25·82 in New York City, 23·65 in New Orleans, 17·17 in Philadelphia, 31·00 in Belfast, 29·00 in Cork, 36·00 in Dublin, 23·05 in Glasgow, 23·3 in London, 26·9 in Liverpool and 27·9 in Manchester. The Health Officer estimated the death rate for the city between 1866 and 1880 as having run from a high of 27·66 in the smallpox year of 1868–69 to a low of 14·75 in 1878–79. In eleven of the fourteen years the rate was below 20 per 1,000.[109] Equally significant to the local inhabitant would have been the eastern insurance companies' decision, around 1860, to cease making an extra charge of $10 per $1,000 for policy holders living in San Francisco.[110] The city had ceased to be a recognisably dangerous place in which to live.

All San Franciscans shared in their city's growth, but the development of the services and characteristics of large city life was no less important to the Irish than to others. They had known far less in the east and in Ireland. The provision and enjoyment of services would vary by class and by the linked factor of residence. The standards and the ability to enjoy life would depend on income. As the following two chapters suggest, there was no overwhelming reason why the Irish should have failed to benefit from the expansion of the city in all its aspects. They were among the prime beneficiaries, if for no other reason than that so many of them walked the streets and used the institutions provided by a city that in 1848 could have offered them nothing.

Chapter III
Arrival and settlement

One of the most important factors governing the Irish experience in San Francisco was that the Irish did not come direct from rural Irish communities. The main places of origin were the urban areas of the eastern United States, where, importantly, the Irish would have met the problems of urban society before and have spent a period of acculturation to American ways. The 1852 state census reveals that the first Irish in the city arrived equally from Australasia and from the eastern United States: 44·5 per cent from the west; 44·6 per cent from the east. Nearly 86 per cent of those from the east had come from the states of New York, Pennsylvania, Massachusetts and Louisiana. Within those states, the migrants came most frequently from New York City, Philadelphia, Boston and New Orleans. The Australasian element dried up after the discovery of gold in Victoria, and consequently the eastern United States became by far the most important point of origin of San Francisco's Irish population, and within the east, particularly, the states of New York, Massachusetts and Pennsylvania.[1] In 1880, of 12,902 children in Irish families in the city not born in California, 7,790, or 60·4 per cent, had been born in these three states.[2] There is little evidence of direct migration from Ireland. In 1852 only 5·1 per cent of the Irish-born in the city reported that they had come direct from Ireland, while there is nothing in the subsequent reports of the Commissioners of Emigration of the State of New York, the main highway for Irish into the United States, to suggest significantly greater direct migration from Ireland to San Francisco in later years.[3]

Before 1869 and the opening of the transcontinental railroad, immigrants mainly went to California through Central America, or trekked overland, with a very small minority braving Cape Horn. Precise figures are difficult to come by, but common sense suggests that, as San Francisco was a seaport, immigrants would choose to arrive by sea, should the city be their destination. In the early days of the Gold Rush most arrivals were headed for the mines of the interior, so that the overland route had attractions it later lost. By 1852, however, arrivals by sea in California outnumbered those by land by 67,000 to 30,000, and San Francisco had increasingly become a magnet in its own right. Consequently it is not surprising that, between 1855 and 1869, less than one quarter of arrivals in San Francisco had come overland.[4] Further, the Panama route was always the quickest in the early days. Before 1855 and the completion of the Panama Railroad, the trip from New York via Panama took from thirty-three to thirty-five days, dropping to twenty-three to twenty-six days thereafter and to around twenty-one days after 1865. Steerage prices from New York depended very much upon the amount of competition among steamship lines. In the pioneer years it was cheaper to buy two tickets, one from New York to Chagres, the other from Panama to San Francisco, rather than a through ticket. By 1851 steerage rates had settled at $100 for the through trip, and though fares fluctuated between $45 and $150 in the 'fifties, in the early 'sixties agreement among competing capitalists set the figure at $100.[5] This figure later fell. By April 1868 it was reported that steerage costs from New York to San Francisco were a mere $35.50.[6]

The opening of the transcontinental railroad did not have an immediate effect on immigrant traffic. The railway did not introduce emigrant trains or fares for some time. In August 1870 it was said that, including board, it cost almost twice as much to travel by rail as by steamer.[7] It was not until late in 1870 that 'emigrants could travel in freight trains from New York to San Francisco for seventy-five dollars, and from Omaha for sixty dollars, currency, but by 1871 through emigrant fares from New York to San Francisco had fallen to sixty dollars'.[8] Such fares were still for travel on freight trains which took seven days from Omaha.[9] Presumably those who travelled on them were ready to put up with their 'whiff of pure menagerie' and their discomfort for their cheapness.[10] The advent of emigrant trains appears to have changed some travelling habits. In 1870 44 per cent of arrivals in California came by rail, 56 per cent by sea. In 1871 only 23 per cent came by sea, 77 per cent by rail. As the 'seventies passed the proportion using the railroad rose until, excluding arrivals from China, it comprised seven-eighths of all arrivals.[11] Nevertheless some Irish were reported even then as travelling steerage class on the steamers, sleeping on bunks that consisted of 'three tiers of filthy canvas stretchers, supported by upright frames' and having to stand at table to eat.[12] The growth of the Irish population in the city proved that, whatever the fares and the conditions, they were not enough to prevent a large number making the long and tiring journey west.

One who left an account of his voyage was John Henry McCloskey. Part of his career was typical of that of many Irish: the details of his voyage were almost too ludicrous ever to have been repeated. McCloskey was born in Dublin in 1837 and, orphaned, went to New Orleans in 1845 or 1846. He became a carpenter and was reasonably successful, coming to own two city lots worth $700 which he sold in order to make the journey to California, departing on 1 May 1852 on a ship that he described as, unfortunately, 'little better than a flat boat'. The owner sold tickets at between $150 and $300, but, understandably in the light of what was to follow, fled the city on the day the ship sailed. He had sold so many tickets that it was immediately clear that the ship was inadequately provisioned, and the captain put into Savannah for more. At this point some of the passengers complained to the authorities that the ship was overloaded, and 'The same passengers who had entered these complaints then instituted civil suits for the recovery of their passage money, and attached the provisions of the ship'. It took two months to unravel this tangle, so that when the ship got under way not surprisingly there was great 'rejoicing'. Consequently 'Almost everyone on the vessel was drunk, and when about four miles down the river, the pilot being drunk, ran her into the bank'. The luckless passengers then learned they could not proceed until the next day, and some returned to Savannah for the night, where 'many of them were arrested on suspicion that they had returned to burn the city, and were lodged in jail until the following morning when, upon an explanation of the situation, they were released'.

The following day the ship set sail for Rio de Janeiro, 'but after passing the equator in the Atlantic, her coal gave out, and being almost keelless, she drifted by prevailing winds on to the coast of Africa. She put into Monrovia, where she was bonded, to get wood, water and provisions for the voyage to Rio de Janeiro.' This was not the end of the disasters, for 'When she was out about two days from Monrovia she caught fire, and but for the fortunate occurrence that the crew were at the time washing the decks, she would certainly have been destroyed with her passengers and crew'. The vessel was sold in Rio to satisfy the bond, and McCloskey transferred to an American ship, the *Dacota*, buying a ticket for fifty dollars and a gold watch. He eventually arrived at San Francisco on 1 April 1853 after a voyage of 335 days.[13]

Like Boston and New York, San Francisco was a port, and like them it had to face the problems posed by the arrival of immigrants like McCloskey who landed without immediate means. The response was legislation which could have presented a threat to the Irish immigrant in particular had he been identified with the problems being attacked, but in any case all the legislation of the 1850s against ex-convicts, 'lunatic, idiot, deaf, dumb, blind, crippled or infirm' arrivals and non-citizens ended in failure. They were supposed to post a two-year bond with the mayor for $500 or commute it for not less than $5 nor more than $10, but very few bothered.[14] As the clerk to the Superintendent of Immigration pointed out, he had 'no means of ascertaining the number of foreign passengers arriving from Panama, except for the statements of the masters of the steamers made under oath'. They ignored the law, and consequently 'The number usually reported by each steamer is from three to nine'.[15] A general lack of system, added to the difficulty of tracing an immigrant's origins, made it the easiest thing in the world to escape the tax. By 1860 an entire year's revenue amounted to only $2,344, almost all of it being received from vessels coming directly from foreign parts.[16] Most of these were coming from China, for the issue of Chinese immigration had begun to arise.[17] As it did so the city forgot its qualms about other immigrants, to the direct advantage of the Irish immigrant.

If the flow of Irish immigration was free from official restrictions, it also remained untouched by any artificial attempts to stimulate it. In the 1850s capitalists thought of founding an association to promote general immigration, but did not succeed. The state of California flirted with the idea of aiding immigration on the eve of the Civil War, but gave up, partly because of the expense. In the late 1860s a group of capitalists tried to obtain public money to underwrite their attempts to bring labour to the state, but failed, partly because of the opposition of groups of working men, including many Irish, who saw the move as a direct assault on wage rates.[18] Their attempts were a failure by 1872 and were not followed by others until the early 1880s.[19] During all the period from 1848 to 1880, therefore, the migration of Irish to the Pacific coast was very much a movement of self-supported individuals and families. It is a matter of speculation whether a particular psychological type was drawn from the Irish community in the United States, to make what was a very definite decision to migrate almost as far again as he or she had already moved from Ireland, but, as this study will argue, the results of remigration do not suggest general psychological deterioration in the move.[20] Two factors immediately distinguished the Irish migration to the west coast from that to the east: first, the period of previous residence in the United States; second, the failure of attempts to make the Irish feel unwelcome on arrival through harsh immigration laws. The landing at San Francisco was therefore an altogether different experience from that of the arrival at New York or Boston, and the later history of the immigrant in the city was not clouded by memories of shock and hostility.

Irish settlement patterns were partly determined by the city's spatial growth. San Francisco began down by the Bay, in the area marked out by the later California and Montgomery streets and Pacific and Dupont avenues.[21] In the following years, the city spread north, south and west, even east into the Bay. Some expansion to the north-west was held up by hills that stayed largely unconquered until the first cable car overcame them in 1873. The commercial development of the downtown area did not lead to a wholesale depopulation of the district. Immigrants and others continued to live at the old heart of the city. In February 1871 a visitor found that on Bush Street 'in the business part of town ... dwellings [were] interspersed among the business houses'.[22] Generally many in the downtown area 'lived in the upper stories of buildings whose ground floors were occupied by stores', beginning a practice that was continued until the eve of the great fire of 1906, helping to give the centre of the city its animation after nightfall.[23] There were no apartment houses as such, for these did not appear in the city until about 1884, but single-room dwellings were very common in this area.[24] These were largely lived in by the poorer classes, who needed to live closest to their work. These included many Irish.[25]

Slowly residential segregation by class, in terms of occupation and income, developed. By the late 'fifties the working classes were concentrated north of Jackson and east of Dupont in what, after 1864, was the First ward; south of California and north of Hayward in the Third, Fifth and Ninth wards, with heavy settlement, proportionately, in the area bounded by Market, Mission, Steuart and Second streets. Later the working class went west along Mission, Howard, Folsom and Harrison streets towards the Mission Dolores, settling the Ninth, Tenth, and Eleventh wards. The fashionable chose first of all to go south to Rincon Hill, and to South Park, developed in 1852, but withdrew in the 1870s when the area became increasingly industrialised, and the cable car made Nob Hill accessible.[26] Chinatown grew up between Kearny and Stockton, California and Broadway, giving very sharp distinctiveness to that part of the city, the east end of the Sixth ward. In 1880 the areas being developed for the first time, marking the edge of the city, were in the Western Addition, between Clay, Post and, roughly, Laguna and Pierce streets; and in the Mission district, along Valencia, Mission and Howard, between Sixteenth and Twenty-fourth streets. Further, 'An almost new town' had lately appeared at 'the southwestern outskirts of the Mission, between Twenty-fifth, Thirtieth, Guerrero and Sanchez streets', where it was noted, 'the buyers and builders were all people of small means'.[27]

The spatial expansion of the city was helped by the early development of a complex system of transport. The first horse-drawn omnibus service began in 1850, along Mission, a second along Powell in 1852, and a north–south line opened in 1854, between North Beach and South Park.[28] In 1860 the San

Francisco and Market Street steam line was established, and two years later the Howard Street and Folsom Street lines.[29] The first horse-drawn railway, the Omnibus line, founded by the Irish capitalist Peter Donahue, opened in 1861, and by 1880 there were twelve street railroad companies carrying the population to and fro, at the rate of about 35 million journeys annually. The centrifugal potential was, however, a little limited because of duplication of some of the routes.[30]

The first omnibus line charged a fare of fifty cents on weekdays and one dollar on Sundays, but these were Gold Rush prices, and by the early 1870s fares ran from three to seven cents, though, because of the dearth of coins of small value, change was given in tickets.[31] Transfer facilities developed during the 1860s.[32] Later, fares rose, until in the mid-1870s they reached ten cents, but in 1877–78 the state legislature lowered all to a uniform five cents.[33] Visitors were much impressed by the complexity of the city's transport system, especially after the development of the cable car lines.[34]

Some expansion took place across the Bay. Ferries left for Oakland as early as 1852, but it was not until the 1870s that the service settled into a regular groove.[35] By 1880 boats ran every half-hour and carried perhaps 10,000 passengers daily. In 1879 alone two thousand buildings were erected in Oakland, some as a result of the drift from San Francisco to its more pleasant suburbs away from fog, sand and wind.[36] Oakland remained, however, outside San Francisco municipal control.

One important factor affecting growth was confusion over land titles, which dated back to Congress's decision in 1851 not to recognise, without scrutiny, all titles claimed from the days of Mexican control. In 1853 Jose Limantour claimed four square leagues of land, extending into the heart of the city, under Mexican title, came close to success when the Land Commission approved his claim in 1856, and was only defeated by the decision of the United States District Court that there was a forged document at the bottom of the case. The Philadelphia Association, which had bought the possibly authentic claim to a three-league grant to Jose Santillan by Mexico, also came close to confirmation, but had its hopes dashed again on appeal by the District Court. In 1852 the city of San Francisco itself claimed four leagues as a one-time pueblo, but had not received the full claim in 1866, when Congress tried to quieten matters by confirming the city's title. Even then, it was not until 20 June 1884 that the United States government issued the patent for 17,754.36 acres to the city, ending this episode. Meanwhile, as a result, particularly after 1853, there were troubles with squatters, leading to loss of life.[37] Eventually in 1887 the California Title Insurance and Trust Company began to sell title insurance policies to San Franciscans, a sign that even then there was no ultimate security of tenure.[38]

The problem of land titles was a peculiarly Californian one. More common to all frontier communities were the high interest rates that helped depress the builders and developers. As late as 1859 mortgage loans on real estate were as high as 2 per cent per month, and sometimes 3 per cent. The middle classes apparently suffered more than the richer, for those who borrowed $40,000 were recorded as paying 1¾ per cent per month; those who took $1,000 to $4,000 paid as high as 3 per cent.[39] The Irish community was as eager as any group of San Franciscans to deal with the problem of raising mortgages and when, in 1857, the first Savings and Loan Society was founded, attracting deposits totalling $20,000 in the first six months, the Irish were not slow to follow suit.[40] On 12 April 1859 a group of Irish capitalists founded what proved to be the most successful of all such ventures, the Hibernia Savings and Loan Society. Ten years later its deposits amounted to $10,683,212 and its depositors numbered 14,544. Its nearest rival, the Savings and Loan Society, had 4,844 depositors, and deposits of $5,053,543.[41] The Hibernia was very successful in aiding prospective Irish home-owners, as it was in bringing down interest rates. *Langley's San Francisco Directory* for 1880 reported that, during the past year,

the leading savings bank (the Hibernia) has been loaning at 8 per cent. per year, it agreeing to pay the mortgage tax, which will consume 1¾ or 2 per cent. of the 8. This is practically loaning money at 6 per cent., which for California is certainly a low rate; but indeed, it is high enough, all things considered.[42]

No other institution was as successful as the Hibernia, but there were other unsuccessful Irish imitations that bore witness to the desire among the Irish to own their homes. On 31 October 1867 the balance sheet of the arch-promoter Thomas

Mooney's California Building and Loan Society read:

Assets

Loans on mortgages	$ 937,804 27
Loans on sundries	10,534 46
Bank premises	60,000 00
Insurance stocks	27,536 00
Furniture	685 00
Cash in coin	40,796 80
Cash in City S.F. bonds	60,020 00
	1,127,376 53
To depositors	1,008,614 55
Surplus to secure depositors	118,761 98

Unfortunately this seemingly solid structure collapsed in September 1870, momentarily deranging the real estate market, but demands for loans were strong enough to revive the system after a few months.[43] Home ownership was well within the grasp of those Irish who could convince their banker they were a good risk. The fact that the premier institution for lending money of the day was in Irish hands was a great advantage.

Irish home-buyers also benefited from another local development. In May 1861, and again in April 1864, the state legislature authorised corporations to provide members with suitable homesteads, which might be either urban or rural. By 1869 *Langley's Directory* was adamant that:

Owing to the number and general success that has attended the formation of these institutions, they may be considered one of the features of San Francisco, having been developed here on a grand scale and served as powerful auxiliaries in hastening forward the city's expansion. These associations... have been rapidly multiplied during the past two or three years, the list of those having their headquarters in San Francisco numbering about one hundred and fifteen, the lands of the greater portion of these being also situate near the city, though in a few instances they are at points more north.

The *Directory* ascribed the success of the associations to the high wages and high rents in the city, the first permitting men to join such bodies, the second compelling them to.[44] A society like the Abbey Homestead Association charged $250 for a share on joining, in return for a lot 100 ft square, and then asked for a monthly instalment of $10 for twenty-five months.

This association already had its eye on land three miles southeast of Mission Dolores, but, ostensibly at least, did not yet own it.[45] Another society, the Sunny Vale Homestead Association, seemingly had no specific tract of land in mind, but also charged $250 a share. Its prospectus bore a laudatory excerpt from the San Francisco *Herald,* which maintained not only the high social value of homestead associations but also, characteristically of its city, their speculative value too. 'In no other way,' said the newspaper,

> can a man of small means so cheaply obtain a homestead; and the time is rapidly slipping by in which eligible lots, of sufficient size for a convenient dwelling, can be had in the city limits at less than prices ranging above two thousand dollars each. Today you can, through one of these associations, for $300, payable in instalments of not over ten dollars per month, obtain a lot twenty-five by one hundred feet, in a district that before ten years have passed will be in the midst of the city, and worth fully ten times its present valuation.[46]

Such rates of repayment were not excessive, perhaps, but did demand a regular occupation and a level of creditworthiness which the labourer, who earned less than two dollars a day when working, would not have. It was, however, the view of the experienced social observer Charles Loring Brace that the city had developed extremely effective means of promoting home ownership by the late 1860s, far superior, for instance, to those of New York. He saw San Francisco and its suburbs as 'full of what to an economist's eye ought to be the happiest sight—poor men's homes'.[47] In 1880 another visitor reported that the scheme for providing homes was so far advanced that 'the Real Estate Association... build or sell, on an average, a house a day, and have done so these three years past'.[48] According to a third, the money for mortgages came from the 'steady labouring men [who] are not fond of mining speculations, but generally invest their wages in land, or deposit them in the savings bank'.[49] All in all, there is little doubt that San Franciscans had developed as advanced a method of promoting property ownership and speculation as any community in the country, promoting thereby both the public and private interest. The existence of the Hibernia Homestead Association in the city shows the Irish taking part in the movement to develop the suburbs.[50] But such developments were, of course, open only to those who were able to manage their repayments.

The expansion of the city proceeded with little municipal control. When in 1861 Mary Sweeny moved her shanty, ten by twelve feet, to a lot on Berry Street, and 'sought to have the removal concurred in by the City Fathers, the Fire Ordinance and the protests of several citizens to the contrary notwithstanding', her case was considered by the Board of Supervisors, who found against her. This was a rare example of the Board exercising its control over development, perhaps because of the fear of fire that the early history of American San Francisco had engendered in all its inhabitants.[51] Section 47 of the Orders and Regulations adopted by the San Francisco Board of Health in 1870 did try to deal with overcrowded tenements, as well as apartments that were 'used for lodgings that are damp, or not properly provided with water, or privies, or vaults', but prosecutions cost money and were rare.[52] The city's supervision remained nominal under these conditions. Consequently, as time went on, and the original housing stock decayed, particularly in the area by the waterfront, on the land reclaimed from the Bay, slum conditions began to emerge, despite the city's youth. In 1872 an eye witness of this, the oldest part of the city, said:

Even at the present day the lower part of the town is built entirely on piles; and the space beneath the houses, formerly occupied by water, but now generally left dry, owing to the work of filling up constantly extending itself in front, forms the home of myriads of rats, dogs, and escaped pigs; who, owing to the plentiful supply of refuse, seem to live together in a state of undisturbed enjoyment and continuous repletion. On the whole, a visit to this quarter makes one reflect with some gratulation on the fact that cholera is unknown on the Pacific coast.[53]

Eight years earlier a municipal reformer, speaking of the area along Dupont (Grant), Kearny, Broadway, Pacific and Jackson streets, had described the resulting living conditions: 'Whole families can... be found living in the back rooms of mere shanties, without pure air or any proper convenience for cleanliness.' The city had its 'crowded tenements', he reported, 'jammed together without regard to moral or sanitary results'.[54]

Some of the worst decay took place in the area that consolidated into Chinatown. In 1880 an admittedly hostile investigation found appalling conditions there. In Spofford Alley, for instance, it was said that

> Every house there is a direct violation of all sanitary and police regulations and fire ordinances. Filth, stench and smoke, overcrowded habitation, houses of prostitution of the vilest sort, court-yards covered with slime, etc., abound there in contradistinction to all civilization.

In eight houses on Washington Street, between Stockton and Dupont, the investigators found 'Filth; stink; remnants of dead animals; piles of dirt; fearful water closets and stench'.[55] Because of overcrowding of inadequate buildings in this area, it was to be compared with the contemporary Five Points of New York, or London's Seven Dials.[56] The waterfront buildings and those behind them in this older part of the city might look in fair order at a distance, but, close at hand, streets were plainly 'made up of decaying, smoke-grimmed [sic], wooden houses' of an 'old-fashioned appearance'.[57]

Much new housing was of a comparatively low quality and scarcely built to last. This was particularly true of the development south of Market Street which occurred after the Civil War. There streets rapidly filled with houses that began

> To assume the objectionable characteristics of the tenement system. There were no such large buildings as those in New York in which enough human beings to fill a small town were crowded, but there was an unmistakeable tendency in that direction.[58]

Reflecting this tendency, the area attracted the young, the immigrant, the transient and the poor, particularly towards its eastern end.[59] There were other more pleasant developments. Those who settled on the western edge of the city surrounded themselves with homes of some distinction and style. A general description of their dwellings read:

> Marble steps outside lead up to a porch, laid with encaustic tile, forming the entrance to a lofty house, always white, covered with carved-work framing in each door and window. Plate-glass is in every window, but all the house of wood. The rooms are large, light, commodious, well-furnished. Each house is surrounded with a little garden full of bright flowering shrubs and flowers.[60]

Consequently not all the city seemed in premature decay, and permanent settled San Franciscans could aspire to some comfort.

Such villas, however, would be for the minority, even of the middle class, not merely because of the financial burden in establishing them but also from a local preference for hotel life. San Francisco was renowned for the number of its inhabitants who lived in hotels. A wave of building began in 1862 with the Russ House, and by 1880 hotel living was so prevalent that even the census officials remarked on it.[61] The reason for this may once have lain in the high proportion of males and the absence of families in the transient sections of the population, and the tendency may have been strengthened by a continuing transience among later arrivals, but some of it had to do with the inevitable pressure on housing caused by the ever-rising population pressing on a housing stock that had scarcely existed in 1848. One result was relatively high rents. In the middle 1860s, after over a decade of building, 'a moderate-sized eight-roomed frame house' rented for between $40 and $45 per month; a brick house 'of similar size' for $50 to $60.[62] Some observers said that the shortage of servants in the city also hampered domestic life, further driving men and women into the hotels, but whatever the reason, the tendency towards hotel living was weaker among the Irish than among other groups. Certainly, unattached Irish labourers used boarding houses, especially in the waterfront wards, but the Irish in general chose family life if they could. This, as will be seen, affected their choice of residence.

By 1870 the Irish had the institutions for home ownership at their disposal. The economy was growing steadily providing jobs. The result was to work against any development of an Irish 'ghetto' in the city. There may have been some concentration of Irish-born, to begin with, on the slopes of Telegraph Hill, or around St Patrick's on Market Street, but this was neither heavy enough, nor long-lasting enough, for permanent importance.[63] The Irish residential pattern for 1870 is laid out in Table 2. There were, clearly, differences by ward, but the Irish-born were not sufficiently tightly packed into any one area to give it a ghetto quality. There was a north-eastern community in the First ward, separated by the downtown area

Arrival and settlement

from another concentration that ran from the Bay, south of Market Street, through the Seventh, Ninth and Tenth wards, into the Eleventh and up to the county line. If there was a centre in this area it lay in the Seventh ward, where the Irish-born population of the city was at its densest. The eastern end of this band of Irish population lay in the working-class areas described earlier, but the western end lay in the newly developing wealthier reaches of the vast Eleventh ward, circling north into the Twelfth ward as well.

Table 2

Irish-born residential patterns in San Francisco, by ward, 1870

Ward	Irish-born % of ward population	No. of Irish-born in ward	Index of Irish-born concentration
1	22.9	2,467	133
2	11.3	1,335	66
3	10.0	297	58
4	7.2	1,191	42
5	14.3	402	83
6	6.9	648	40
7	27.8	2,891	162
8	14.4	2,381	84
9	21.4	2,245	124
10	22.4	5,011	130
11	20.2	4,594	117
12	18.0	2,272	105
Total	17.2	25,735	100

Table 2 dealt with the Irish-born alone. Table 3 sets out the residential pattern, by ward, for the entire Irish community in 1880. Considering that ten years had intervened and that the community now being described included second and later generations, the patterns in 1880 were remarkably similar to those of 1870. The Seventh ward was still the most favoured by the Irish; the Sixth ward, least. At the extremes, the Irish community was apparently settling more heavily in the Ninth and Eleventh wards, on the southern side of the city, and was leaving the First, Third and Fifth, the waterfront heart of San Francisco. Since the figures for 1880 include other generations than the first, it is worth while looking more closely at the pattern of settlement of the second generation, and since residence and occupation were closely connected, particularly among the second-generation males in occupations. A comparison of these with first-generation males in occupations reveals a trend hidden in the general figures of Tables 2 and 3.

Table 3

Irish residential patterns in San Francisco by ward, 1880

Ward	Irish % of ward population	Total Irish community	Index of concentration
1	34·0	3,306	102
2	23·6	3,391	71
3	10·6	422	32
4	13·9	2,667	42
5	19·4	291	58
6	9·7	1,326	29
7	53·1	4,714	159
8	20·2	4,249	60
9	40·5	8,297	147
10	31·2	11,966	121
11	45·2	25,035	135
12	49·1	12,387	93
Total	33·4	78,051	100

In the Seventh ward the index of concentration in 1880 for the first generation was 214, and for the second, 157. The second generation, by contrast with the Irish community as a whole, was not moving into the Ninth ward: its index was 137, that of the first generation 153. The second generation was also settling less heavily in the Third ward than the first generation, with indexes of 54 as against 82. The wards experiencing heavier settlement by the second generation were the First, up from 121 to 139, the Second, up from 61 to 83, the Fourth, up from 38 to 57, and the Fifth, up from 111 to 139. There was no significant change in other wards. Those in which the change was occurring shared one characteristic: those losing Irish wage-earners were south of Market; those gaining them were to the north. The wards that lay farthest from the downtown area experienced least change, suggesting a complicated picture. Residential changes were occurring more frequently at the eastern end of the city than at the western end, for the Irish. The residential areas that were losing Irish were those of lowest status, while the drift of the second generation was most definitely into the highest-status wards, the Second, the Fourth and the Eighth. If the total Irish community were upwardly mobile, then the middle-status wards would lose Irish to the higher and gain them from the lower-status wards, and thus, if there was a uniform progress at work, keep a middle position in the hierarchy of residential choice. This appears to have been the case, for there is little evidence of abrupt and extreme mobility among the Irish from lower- to upper-class status in a single generation.

The greatest determinant of residential mobility was occupational mobility, the subject of the following chapter. Before moving to that, it is rewarding to look at two other sets of changes that were occurring in the Irish community in the period, namely its age and sex structure. Briefly, an increasingly middle-aged Irish-born community, living with a sex ratio that increasingly permitted the establishment of family groups, had different demands from one that was youthfully footloose and fancy free. The drive for home ownership, with all that it meant for residential patterns, could have been very different. In fact, to begin with, the Irish, like San Franciscans in general, were largely male and mainly young. The census of 1852 shows that 69·7 per cent of the Irish-born in the city were male and that only 14·4 per cent, of them were over forty years of age. The second generation was then very small, so that the character of the first generation heavily influenced that of the total community. Then in succeeding years two trends emerged. The first generation established families and simultaneously aged; the second generation grew in numbers and added its youth and more usual sex ratio to help create a demographically more normal community. By 1860 the inflow of Irish-born females was marked: the Irish-born of the city were only 53·4 per cent male. By 1870 the males had become a minority: they now comprised only 48·7 per cent of the Irish-born group. They did not recover their position in the following decade: in 1880 the Irish-born were only 48·2 per cent male.

Table 4

Age structure, Irish-born in San Francisco, 1852–80 (%)

Age	1852 M	1852 F	1860 M	1860 F	1870 M	1870 F	1880 M	1880 F
0–19	9·5	21·8	3·9	6·4	2·3	3·6	2·1	2·9
20–29	36·7	35·4	37·2	48·3	23·9	30·9	12·1	16·3
30–39	38·9	28·8	41·1	32·0	42·9	41·4	31·4	32·7
40–59	14·4	12·9	16·1	11·2	28·5	20·8	46·4	41·4
Over 60	0·4	0·8	1·7	2·1	2·4	3·3	8·0	6·7
Unknown	0·1	0·3						

As Table 4 shows, the Irish-born in the city aged somewhat more slowly than might have been expected before 1860, and rather more quickly after that year. The city appears to have become more attractive to the Irish-born, over the age of forty in particular, some time in the 1860s. It is possible that this ageing community was becoming less transient, but at the same time San Francisco was clearly failing to attract new inflows of younger Irish-born from other parts of the United States. Greater permanence would suggest greater satisfaction with conditions in the city, though it would be wrong to ascribe the ageing of the first generation entirely to this. It was also true that, since the headlong rush from Ireland of the Famine years was at an end, the Irish-born population of the United States was not being reinforced at the rate of the period 1845–54. The total Irish-born community of the country was ageing, affecting the age structure of the pool of Irish-born available, in other parts of the United States, to be drawn to San Francisco. The poor national economic conditions of the 'seventies and the unattractive image of California projected in the east, one of racial and economic turmoil, do not seem to have affected immigration to the state and to San Francisco. Its rate increased in the mid-'seventies.[64] Perhaps the increasing number of forty-year-olds and over among the Irish in the city was the result of the immigration of disproportionate numbers of middle-aged making, at least, a second attempt to secure their fortunes. It is highly probable that this was true to some extent, but it is unlikely that this immigration alone explains the rapid ageing of the Irish-born already in the city. As important, in this demographic change, was Irish persistence. This persistence was expressed in the growing number of Irish families and in changing residential demands. As a corollary, lower rates of persistence among other groups weakened their challenge to control the resources of the city, particularly in the case of the native stock, whose transience in the earliest, Gold Rush, days was one important reason why it did not fix an exclusive control over city affairs, to give opportunity for competition from the Irish.[65]

The Irish of San Francisco in the period would have welcomed the demographic changes that gave them the chance to set up families and homes. They would have benefited from the development of institutions making home ownership easier. Even such a possibly tangential development as that of the transport system made it even less likely that they would be cooped up in the decaying, older parts of the city. Residential mobility was possible, home life was possible, both very satisfactory. Both aims, however, depended on steady, well paid, easily accessible employment. The sense of progress would be very much connected to a feeling of upward occupational mobility, the extent of which is the subject of the next chapter.

Chapter IV
The material world

It may appear, though it is not its purpose to do so, that this study argues in some rightly suspicious and peculiar way that all members of the Irish community were well satisfied with their lives in San Francisco. This was hardly the case, though it would be going too far in the opposite direction to say that, since all Irish failed to achieve, for instance, white-collar status in the city, the record of the group must be called a failure. In looking now at the pattern of occupations taken up by the Irish in San Francisco, and the amount of economic mobility, this, as well as a number of other matters, must be borne in mind. These include, first, the performance of the San Francisco economy, which, as has been seen, most importantly ended a twenty-year period of prosperity in the third quarter of the 'seventies. Consequently, it could be expected that the Irish, like San Franciscans in general, would experience first a period of advance, and then one of slippage, that should not, for instance, be put down to nativism. Second, it can be doubted whether, given even very favourable economic conditions, what may be termed class values and the class structure would allow frictionless economic mobility. There is evidence to suggest that a simple exchange of status, as material and economic conditions improve or decline for the individual, is not likely to occur equally at all points on the occupational scale. Particularly, white-collar slippers are not likely to move to skilled blue-collar occupations: they would lack the skills to do so. Semi-skilled and skilled blue-collar workers are not always attracted by white-collar status. They may prefer to remain in an improved blue-collar one. Slippage from high white-collar occupations is less likely than from low white-collar ones; while, at the other end of the scale, the unskilled, unable to fall, are able only to rise. Past educational achievement acts as a brake on occupational performance, too, largely and differentially determined by the class position of the individual at the outset of his occupational career.

A third factor to be borne in mind has a connection with the educational background of the individual, in as much as his career may well be determined by the cultural values of the group to which he belongs, including the value placed on formal education.[1] In a broad sense the Irish were hindered by their rural, non-industrial background, though helped by their familiarity with the English language. This was, however, not an unlimited advantage, as the first generation, even though it had lived in the United States for some time, remained, as largely as not, illiterate. In the absence of a belief in protracted schooling, a group might, however, place a high value on the acquisition of real estate, which in the United States could, independently of occupation, bring its own status.[2] The relation between cultural values and status is thus complex rather than simple, affecting interpretation.

Nativism, the protracted, often institutionalised hostility of the native stock to the immigrant, could also act as a barrier to free flow between statuses, in two main ways. First, the native stock, from a superior economic and social position, could attempt, positively, to proscribe the immigrant and to prevent him from rising. This was difficult to do in San Francisco, where there were no inherited positions in a new community. Second, and more important in San Francisco, the native stock could use their superior cultural position, their familiarity with the values, modes of behaviour and institutions of society, to take a disproportionate share of its rewards. In one sense, this aspect of the inequality between native stock and immigrant group was the result of historical accident rather than of malevolent hostility, but in the long run its effects were the same as the more positive form of nativism, leading to differential amounts of opportunity. In San Francisco one consequence of this second feature of nativism was that, even if the Irish experienced some economic and social mobility, they did not manage thereby to exclude the native stock from a preponderant share in the city's development. In as much as San Francisco was part of the nation, the native stock held to its hereditary advantages, but in so far as the city was also a local community developing from nothing, the Irish broadened theirs.

The overall occupational progress of the Irish-born in San Francisco can be seen in Table 5.[3] The pattern of female occupations did not change significantly, since the city did not see a widening of opportunities for female workers, of any

Table 5

Occupational structure, Irish-born in San Francisco, total employed, 1852–80

	1852		1860		1870		1880	
	N	%	N	%	N	%	N	%
Males								
White-collar	395	15.4	706	15.8	1,949	17.3	2,748	19.9
Skilled blue-collar	501	19.6	913	20.5	2,404	21.4	2,568	18.6
Semi-skilled blue-collar	442	17.3	1,194	26.7	3,326	29.5	4,160	30.0
Unskilled	1,222	47.7	1,651	37.0	3,579	31.8	4,354	31.5
N	2,560		4,464		11,258		13,830	
Females								
White-collar	8	7.9	57	4.1	213	6.0	291	8.2
Skilled blue-collar			15	1.1	24	0.7	45	1.3
Semi-skilled blue-collar	67	66.3	1,231	88.2	3,063	85.9	2,992	84.0
Unskilled	26	25.8	93	6.6	263	7.4	233	6.5
N	101		1,396		3,563		3,561	

group, during the period. The occupational status of Irish-born males, however, improved slowly but surely until after 1870, when, presumably, the subsequent depression halted advances. Numerically, the most common occupations remained labouring for men and domestic service for women throughout the period. There were changes here, however, that highlight the progress being made by the Irish-born. In 1852 1,155 of the 2,560 Irish males employed in the city were labourers, 45.1 per cent of the total males employed. In 1860 there were 1,452 labourers out of 4,464 employed, a percentage of 32.5; in 1870 the figures were 3,472 of 11,258 and the percentage was 30·8; in 1880 3,532 of 13,821, or 25·5 per cent. The decline in the percentage of Irish employed as labourers was the major cause of the steady fall in the total percentage of Irish-born employed in unskilled occupations, brought on mainly by the developing demands of an increasingly complex economy for wider ranges of skills. This process did not, however, favour female labour. Once family life and households had been established in the city, the demand for domestic service remained constant throughout the period, and, in the absence of changes in the total demand for female labour, all-important in structuring the pattern of female employment. In 1852 fifty-eight of the 101 females employed in San Francisco were domestic servants (unspecified), a percentage of 57·4; in 1860 the figures were 968 out of 1,396, or a percentage of 69·3. In 1870 2,541 of 3,563, or a percentage of 71·3, were in unspecified domestic service; in 1880 the figures were 2,186 of 3,561, or 61·4 per cent.

It should not be thought that some improvement for female labour lies hidden in these figures. There was, for instance, little movement into regular factory employment, with perhaps only thirty Irish females in it, throughout the city, in 1880. The main alternative to domestic service for Irish-born females was the clothing trades, employing about 12 per cent of the total, while nursing, cooking and waiting further employed nearly 10 per cent of the Irish-born female workforce. The lack of demand for skilled female labour limited the possibilities open to women for upward social and economic mobility. It may well be that widowhood was one of the most significant factors behind the doubling of the percentage of Irish-born females, classifiable as white-collar, between 1860 and 1880. In 1880 there were only ten Irish-born female clerks in the city, but eighty-two boarding and lodging-house keepers, as well as thirty-seven owning a store of some kind, or a saloon. There were eighty Irish in religious houses, who in many cases provided educational services, together with forty-one lay schoolmistresses. There were no more than three or four in any other white-collar category of employment, or property owning, giving little evidence of a healthy multiplication of female economic roles in city life.

The figures in Table 5 suggest dependence on structural changes in the economy for a sense of upward mobility, though it should be added that some satisfaction was possible from the fact that the results of economic diversification were not monopolised by the native-born to the total exclusion of the first-generation Irish. Thorough consideration of the performance of the Irish community as a whole, however, requires two further steps. First, it is necessary to examine the progress of the second-generation Irish; second, to compare the progress of both Irish generations with that of other groups.

Table 6

Occupational structure, second-generation Irish in San Francisco, 1880

	White-collar		Skilled blue-collar		Semi-skilled blue-collar		Unskilled		Total
	N	%	N	%	N	%	N	%	N
Second-generation Irish b. U.S.A.									
Males	1,894	27·7	2,140	31·3	2,135	31·2	671	9·8	6,840
Females	601	20·6	151	5·2	2,126	72·8	42	1·4	2,920
Second-generation Irish b. elsewhere									
Males	220	27·1	280	34·5	215	26·5	96	11·8	811
Females	45	18.8	19	8.0	169	70·7	6	2·5	239

By 1880 the city was old enough to have a large second-generation Irish community, whose occupational distribution appears as Table 6. This and the subsequent two tables split the second-generation into two groups: those born in the United States, and those born elsewhere, almost exclusively in Great Britain, British North America and Australasia. The division was made in order to discover what advantage, if any, came to a second-generation Irish worker from birth in the United States. The evidence provided is not as clear-cut as it might be, since there is no reason to suppose that the second-generation born outside the United States spent their entire formative period there, and did not emigrate to the United States almost immediately after birth. As the figures stand, they suggest one point immediately: Irish-born outside the United States were certainly not disadvantaged later on in their American careers, by comparison with Irish-born in the United States. A comparison of both groups with the first-generation is laid out in Table 7.

Table 7

Comparison of occupational profile, first- and second-generation Irish in San Francisco, 1880 (%)

	Born in Ireland	Born in U.S.A.	Born elsewhere
Males			
White-collar	19·9	27·7 (+7·8)	27·1 (+7·2)
Skilled blue-collar	18·6	31·3 (+12.7)	34·5 (+15·9)
Semi-skilled blue-collar	30·0	31·2 (+1·2)	26·5 (−3·5)
Unskilled	31·5	9·7 (−21·7)	11·8 (−19·7)
N	13,830	6,840	811
Females			
White-collar	8·2	20·6 (+12·4)	18·8 (+10·6)
Skilled blue-collar	1·3	5·2 (+3·9)	8·0 (+6·7)
Semi-skilled blue-collar	84·0	72·8 (−11·2)	70·7 (−12·3)
Unskilled	6·5	1·4 (−5·1)	2·5 (−5·0)
N	3,561	2,920	239

Table 7 shows the considerable intergenerational advance made by the Irish community, even more marked than appears on the surface, since the second generation was towards the beginnings of its careers, while the first generation was towards the end. Particularly noticeable is the sharp decline in the percentages in unskilled occupations among males and the rise in the percentages of those employed in white-collar and skilled blue-collar occupations. Reflecting general social attitudes to women and the consequent more limited economic opportunities, the intergenerational progress of females was more limited, leaving over 70 per cent still in semi-skilled occupations. Since, however, it may be assumed that a good proportion of women in this category looked to marriage rather than to occupational progress for their future, such concentration in the semi-skilled occupations is less disturbing. At the same time, it is remarkable that one in four second-generation females had achieved high blue-collar or white-collar status.

Table 7 also shows that there was little difference in performance between the second generation born in the United States and that born elsewhere. If the percentage in white-collar occupations was higher among those born in the United States, the percentage in skilled blue-collar occupations was higher among those born elsewhere. If those born elsewhere produced a larger percentage of unskilled, it was small by comparison with the percentage of unskilled in the first generation. Overall, birth in the United States does not appear to have been of overwhelming advantage to the second generation. Thus, taking the first and second generations together, the Irish community was experiencing considerable mobility. If parents were disappointed in their own progress, they could take satisfaction from that of their children. The rapid ageing of the first generation may have had some connection with increasing immobility, while the youth of the second could have been related to its mobility. By 1880, at any rate, over one quarter of the second-generation Irish males of San Francisco were in white-collar occupations. Only one in ten, approximately, remained in the unskilled.

Comparison of the occupational state of the Irish community in 1880 with that of the total population presents problems, as the printed census does not distinguish occupations by level of skill or prestige. It is also difficult to believe that a straight comparison between those born in the United States and other groups produces a result of much validity, since a good proportion—for instance, over 20 per cent in the case of the Irish community—of the ostensibly native-born community belongs as much to the foreign-born community as it does to the host. It is also difficult to work in a situation where occupational statistics, by nativity, are not distinguished by sex.

It is possible, however, to look at the proportions of unskilled labourers in the total community and in first- and second-generation Irish communities. If an index figure of 100 is given to the incidence of labourers among all employed in San Francisco in 1880, then the index for the first-generation

Irish community could be 271; for the second, 85. The index for those born in the United States would be 42, while for those born in the United States minus second-generation Irish it would be 31. Using these figures as a benchmark, it is possible to say that, whereas the first-generation Irish were somewhat behind, the second was marginally in front of the total community in occupational status. Another way of looking at the same problem is to compare the occupational structure of that far from common group in the city, the native-born of native parents. A random sample of 1,000 males of this group in 1880 shows that 46·7 per cent of them had white-collar jobs; 21·3 per cent skilled blue-collar jobs; 26·0 per cent semi-skilled blue-collar jobs and only 6·0 per cent unskilled occupations.

Table 8

Comparison of occupational structure of native-born of native parents with that of the Irish community; San Francisco males, 1880

	Born U.S.	Born Ireland	Born U.S. of Irish parentage	Born outside U.S. and Ireland of Irish parentage
White-collar	100	42	59	60
Skilled blue-collar	100	87	147	161
Semi-skilled blue-collar	100	116	120	101
Unskilled	100	525	165	195

Table 8 compares this native-born occupational structure with the three groups of Irish in the city by means of index numbers. The native-born categories are each given the figure of 100; the Irish are to be seen in relation. The table shows that the occupations of first-generation Irish differed markedly from those of the native-born at the extremes of the occupational scale and that the two second-generation groups narrowed the gap, without, however, finally closing it. Since the sample of the native-born included some ten blacks, all in semi-skilled or unskilled occupations, the figures derived from it do not represent precisely the occupational performance of the white native-born. That was even more markedly concentrated in the white-collar sector.

Table 9

Occupational structure of all forty-year-old native-, Irish-, and German-born males compared, San Francisco, 1870 (%)

	Native-born		Irish-born		German-born	
	All	In employment	All	In employment	All	In employment
White-collar	45.4	48.7	15.2	15.7	47.4	49.0
Skilled blue-collar	24.2	26.0	21.6	22.2	18.4	19.0
Semi-skilled blue-collar	17.9	19.2	23.3	24.0	24.2	25.0
Unskilled	5.7	6.1	37.0	38.1	6.8	7.0
None	6.8	–	2.9	–	3.2	–
N	987	919	1,109	1,076	533	515

Ten years before, the situation had been very much the same. Table 9 surveys all native-born and Irish-born males in the city aged forty, adding, for comparison, all German-born males of the same age. All should have been performing at near their peak rate at this time in their lives. By now, immigrants would have had time to acculturate; all should have been well on their way to success in their chosen occupations. Table 9 is not precisely comparable with Table 8, for the native-born of Table 9 may have included some with foreign-born parents. The census schedules do not help on this matter. Nevertheless there is little difference in what the two tables show. The native-born are conspicuous by their absence in unskilled occupations, outnumbering the Irish-born by three to one in the white-collar occupations. The performance of the German-born, by comparison, is remarkable for its similarity to that of the native-born, and its superiority to that of the Irish-born. Particularly noticeable is the way in which the German-born had entered the white-collar occupations largely connected with commerce, reflecting, in part, the presence of a Jewish community.[4]

Table 10 carries the survey of these forty-year-old San Franciscans further, investigating the amount of real and personal property that they admitted to in 1870. The table shows that many San Franciscans at this age said they had no property, and that even one in three native-born forty-year-olds claimed this. As far as numbers reporting property went, the Irish-born compared relatively well with the native- and German-born, running behind them on personal property but exceeding them both when it came to claiming real estate. Almost one in three Irish-born San Fransciscans aged forty claimed some real estate. Comparison of both mean and median figures, however, suggests that if real estate was spread relatively widely through the Irish-born it was also spread somewhat thinly, for if a native-born San Franciscan did have real estate its value was likely to be, roughly, two and a half

Table 10

Property owning, real and personal, all forty-year-old Irish-, native- and German-born males, San Francisco, 1870 ($000)

	Irish-born		Native-born		German-born	
	Real estate	Personal	Real estate	Personal	Real estate	Personal
Ward I						
Total reported	210·4	190·65	114·0	127·6	58	56·6
N	112	112	45	45	32	32
N¹	44	77	14	30	11	20
Ward II						
Total reported	193·2	47·75	687·5	221·15	309	150·15
N	53	53	53	53	49	49
N¹	21	42	26	43	14	41
Ward III						
Total reported	8	1·65	125	15·1	0	5·5
N	17	17	25	25	8	8
N¹	1	4	3	8	0	2
Ward IV						
Total reported	60·7	23·9	181	169·9	94·5	62·6
N	54	54	73	73	60	60
N¹	19	42	20	61	11	44
Ward V						
Total reported	0	0·85	15	271·55	0	26·6
N	9	9	101	101	17	17
N¹	0	3	2	48	0	7

[continued overleaf

Table 10 continued

	Irish-born		Native-born		German-born	
	Real estate	Personal	Real estate	Personal	Real estate	Personal
Ward VI						
Total reported	50	22.9	416	496.65	230	109.75
N	24	24	98	98	29	29
N[1]	7	17	24	82	8	24
Ward VII						
Total reported	69.5	31.4	206.6	244.75	44.5	23.6
N	161	161	82	82	26	26
N[1]	12	47	8	24	5	12
Ward VIII						
Total reported	357.8	55.0	1876.0	826.5	388.85	593.85
N,	94	94	133	133	97	97
N[1]	29	39	54	69	27	60
Ward IX						
Total reported	167.2	45.185	370.6	314.65	67	64.4
N	79	79	67	67	29	29
N[1]	27	39	20	43	8	19
Ward X						
Total reported	529.08	96.15	428.13	343.92	99.8	100.33
N	202	202	160	160	99	99
N[1]	56	111	44	109	20	63
Ward XI						
Total reported	506.44	174.36	468.9	186.8	281.5	148.09
N	212	212	92	92	56	56
N[1]	106	151	42	73	28	46
Ward XII						
Total reported	273.1	100.115	277.7	136.495	197.8	107.1
N	92	92	58	58	31	31
N[1]	38	62	26	41	16	27
City						
Total reported	2,425.42	789.91	5,166.43	3,355.065	1,770.95	1,448.57
N	1,109	1109	987	987	533	533
N[1]	360	634	283	631	148	365
% reporting estate	32.5	57.2	28.7	63.9	27.8	68.5
Mean — all	2.187	0.712	5.234	3.399	3.322	2.718
Mean — propertied only	6.737	1.246	18.255	5.317	11.966	3.969
Median — all	0	0.1	0	0.4	0	0.25
Median— propertied only	4	0.5	8	1	5	1

N = Total number of forty-year-old males.
N[1] = Number of forty-year-old males reporting positive amounts of property.

times that of his Irish-born neighbour. Similarly the German-born would have owned a slightly greater value than the Irish-born. As far as personal property went, the median Irish-born would have had exactly half the value of the native- and German-born. Even if these figures suggest that the Irish-born had been out-performed by the other two groups, they also indicate that, if the Irish-born male had managed to amass any real or personal estate at all, in the median case, he would, in 1870, have owned $4,000 worth of real estate and $500 worth of personal estate. This was no small achievement.

The figures in Table 10 are presented by ward. They show that, on average, the wealthier Irish-born lived in the Second, Eighth and Twelfth wards, which ran in an arc through the northern and north-western parts of the city. Importantly, as far as the Irish-born community as a whole was concerned, poverty and density did not inevitably go hand-in-hand. The connection between the two factors was a complex one. It was not the general case that, as mean property-holding increased by ward, correlatively fewer Irish-born lived there. Table 11 shows that if the twelve wards are divided into three groups of

Table 11

Comparison of residential concentration and mean property-holding by ward, Irish-born, San Francisco, 1870

	Residential concentration		Mean total property-holding		
	Ward	Index	Ward	$000	
High	7	162	5	0.1	Low
	1	133	3	0.6	
	10	130	7	0.6	
	9	124	4	1.6	
Medium	11	117	9	2.7	Medium
	12	105	6	3.0	
	8	84	10	3.1	
	5	83	11	3.2	
Low	2	66	1	3.6	High
	3	58	12	4.1	
	4	42	8	4.4	
	6	40	2	4.5	

four wards each, and the groups ranked, first in terms of Irish concentration, as high, medium and low, and then, second, in terms of mean property-holding, only one ward, the Second, appears as having a relatively high degree of property-owning and a low index of concentration; only the Eleventh has a medium degree of both; and only one ward, the Seventh, has a high index of concentration and low mean property-owning. What this suggests is a complicated, differentiated Irish community, some of whose members were wealthy and lived among non-Irish neighbours, while others did not. Nor did the poor Irish cluster exclusively with their own kind except, noticeably, in the case of the Seventh ward. Altogether, the correlation coefficient between concentration and property-holding was 0·02: not significant.

Each ward, however, had its own character or occupational profile, and Irish occupational status varied by ward, as can be seen from Table 12. The extreme cases were the Seventh and Eighth wards, the first bounded by the waterfront, Harrison, Second and Market streets, the second by Market, Kearny, Pine and Larkin. In the Seventh ward only 12·7 per cent of the Irish males were in white-collar occupations; in the Eighth 44·6 per cent were. Conversely, in the Seventh, 33·5 per cent were in unskilled occupations, compared with 17·6 per cent in the Eighth.

Table 12 distinguishes the pattern of total Irish settlement by ward, sex and occupation. It is more useful for correlating male residence and occupation than female, for women were heavily employed in domestic service and largely lived-in with the families that employed them. Further, the census is not reliable on the occupations of widows or married women, so that its information must be used with caution. Males, however, were more able to live at a chosen distance from their occupation. Their residence patterns reveal that the heavy Irish concentration in the Seventh and Ninth wards was due, in the first case, to a clustering of unskilled workers, and, in the second, to a larger-than-average clustering of semi-skilled. The Irish of the Tenth and Eleventh wards, which contained a lesser yet still marked over-proportion of Irish in their population, were not, however, particularly concentrated at any occupational level. On the contrary, if anything, these

Table 12

Occupational structure, Irish community, by ward, and by sex, San Francisco, 1880 (%)

Ward	Male/ Female	White-collar	Skilled blue-collar	Semi-skilled blue-collar	Unskilled	N
1	M	13.7	10.5	51.2	24.6	1,320
	F	12.9	8.1	74.7	4.3	186
2	M	23.2	22.3	27.4	27.1	906
	F	27.2	1.8	69.6	1.4	283
3	M	17.9	13.3	47.6	21.2	330
	F	13.3	40.0	46.7	0.0	15
4	M	24.6	31.0	30.4	14.0	780
	F	14.7	3.4	77.4	4.5	265
5	M	44.3	12.7	24.2	18.8	149
	F	11.4	0.0	82.9	5.7	70
6	M	37.2	23.8	20.2	18.8	366
	F	9.7	2.2	82.8	5.3	227
7	M	12.7	25.2	28.6	33.5	1,752
	F	6.7	6.1	78.1	9.1	297
8	M	44.6	20.3	17.5	17.6	1,166
	F	12.4	0.9	82.6	4.1	807
9	M	16.1	22.4	35.6	25.9	2,399
	F	19.9	5.0	70.0	5.1	587
10	M	23.7	25.1	28.4	22.8	3,626
	F	13.5	5.1	78.0	3.4	990
11	M	21.5	25.2	29.4	23.9	5,887
	F	18.2	3.6	73.1	5.1	1,384
12	M	27.4	22.9	27.2	22.5	2,810
	F	8.9	1.3	87.0	2.8	1,609
City-wide	M	22.6	23.2	30.3	23.9	21,481
	F	13.9	3.2	78.7	4.2	6,720

wards were marked by an almost uniform distribution of Irish at all four occupational levels. One consequence of the occupational distribution in these wards, and in the Twelfth, was the general lack of Irish residential segregation already noticed, for these wards contained over 57 per cent of Irish males in occupations in the city.

Overall, the residential patterns of the Irish community do show some variations. There was heavy concentration in the lower-class areas of the city outside Chinatown, but there was also a significant Irish presence in all wards. The Irish settled more heavily south of Market Street than north of it, but the disproportion could have been far greater. South of Market the housing stock was inferior to that to the north, but none of it was a decayed remnant of the past. The Irish were definitely not held to the inner city, but spread with San Francisco's growth freely into the farther and newer suburbs. It is possible that there was a significant difference in degree between the Irish of the eastern end of the city and those farther west. Those to the east were possibly more transient, less wealthy and more unskilled. But neither group should stand as representative of the whole. The Irish community in San Francisco had no single character.[5]

One factor influencing residence was rent. At first, in the days of the Gold Rush, this was extremely expensive, with one of a dozen or fifty bunks in a lodging room costing from $6 to $20 a week.[6] Rapid building, successive economic crises and a falling off in immigration helped to stabilise prices at a lower level. By the early 'sixties an entire moderate-sized eight-roomed frame house could be rented for between $40 and $45 a month.[7] These prices were high, however, compared with those prevailing in other parts of the Union and could only be sustained by generally higher wages. These went through the same cycle as prices. In 1849–50 a labourer could expect $1 an hour; in 1854 $3 a day; by 1875, it has been said, $2 a day if he were fortunate.[8] In 1862 and 1863 the British consul in San Francisco more conservatively estimated that labourers might earn as little as eighty cents a day if unlucky, $1.20 if fortunate. Other wages were in proportion: for instance, the consul also reported for 1862 and 1863 that blacksmiths could earn between $2.40 and $3.20 a day, while in 1875 they might have received from $50 to $70 a month, all found.[9]

Since immigrant satisfaction might very well be a relative matter, comparative eastern rates of wages are important. One modern authority has attempted to establish the percentage ratio of average annual earnings in the Pacific region to those in the Middle Atlantic region for the following industries: malt liquors, leather, carriage and wagon making, foundries and machine shops, sawed lumber, cigars and cigarettes, distilled liquors, paper, agricultural implements, woollen goods, flour and grist mills, and brick and tile making. The comparison of the entire Pacific region with the Middle Atlantic poses its problems, but since San Francisco was the predominant manufacturing centre of the Pacific the resulting figures are very useful. According to them the median percentage ratio for these industries fell from 262 in 1860 to 125 in 1870 but rose to 139 in 1880. Taking a simple mean, the figures would be 255, 138 and 136 respectively.[10]

What these figures suggest is a massive fall in the wage differential in the 1860s but at least its maintenance in the 1870s. This is not precisely the picture to be drawn from a more detailed nineteenth-century government comparison of wages in San Francisco and New York laid out in Table 13. This suggests a falling off in the differential between the two cities in the 1870s, though it is clear that wage rates remained higher in San Francisco than in New York City even in 1880.[11]

Within San Francisco, from the 1850s there were two opposing views about wage rates. One was that of the

Table 13

Comparison of wage rates, San Francisco and New York City, 1870 and 1880

	1870		1880		Ratio S.F : N.Y.C.	
Occupation	S.F.	N.Y.C.	S.F.	N.Y.C.	1870	1880
	$	$	$	$		
Blacksmith	3.81	2.25	3.57	2.68	169	133
Blacksmith's helper	2.34	1.49	2.09	1.53	157	137
Boilermaker	3.38	1.84	3.22	2.17	184	148
Boilermaker's helper	2.24	1.40	1.97	1.50	160	131
Bricklayer	5.00	3.16	4.00	3.12	158	125
Carpenter	3.85	2.88	3.35	3.41	133	98
Compositor	3.41	2.53	3.29	2.98	134	110
Hod carrier	3.00	1.96	2.50	2.03	153	123
Iron moulder[a]	3.72	1.95	3.51	2.21	192	158
Iron moulder's helper[a]	2.46	1.13	2.22	1.22	218	182
Street labourer[a]	2.50	1.49	2.00	1.57	167	127
Other labourer	2.00	1.76	2.00	1.39	114	144
Machinist	3.37	2.27	3.03	2.53	148	120
Machinist's helper	2.25	1.55	1.91	1.70	145	112
Mason, stone	5.00	2.89	4.89	2.50	173	196
Painter, house	3.72	2.44	3.10	3.00	152	103
Patternmaker	3.00	2.45	3.08	3.15	122	98
Plumber	3.66	2.76	3.63	3.39	133	107
Stonecutter[a]	4.14	2.85	3.66	2.49	145	147
Teamster	2.64	1.70	2.68	2.14	155	125

[a] Philadelphia rates; New York unavailable.

capitalists wishing to increase immigration partly to push wages down; the other was held by the workers, who feared just that. In 1867 the dispute was encapsulated in a quarrel between the Pacific Mail Steamship Company and the Mechanics' State Council of California. The Steamship Company would have benefited from any increase in traffic and so emphasised that wages were high in California to encourage migration and the use of its ships. The Company said, for instance, that caulkers were paid $9 a day. The council, however, replied that the average wage was $2.50, and that not even the most skilled worker in any trade could look for more than $3.25 a day and few could expect more than $3.[12] This was in a period in which labour was in relatively short supply.

Individual Irish immigrants would presumably judge the controversy through experience, but their total sense of satisfaction would depend on more than wage rates. Quite as important would be whether the Irish migrant would have been conscious of a rise in his living standards as a result of higher wages. One point would have been clear: food prices were lower than in the east. It was said that whereas easterners consumed 7 lb of coffee, 2 lb of tea and 25 lb of sugar annually, Californians consumed 10 lb, 6 lb and 60 lb.[13] Another contemporary comment was that 'the price of wheaten flour' in San Francisco was about half what it was in Liverpool or New York.[14] Anthony Tollope, overestimating wage rates, said that 'two dollars and a half per day which the labourer earns in San Francisco' were 'as good as three and a quarter in New York', because of local food prices. 'No doubt,' he admitted

> this high rate of pay is met by an equivalent in the high cost of many articles, such as clothing and rent; but it does not affect the food which to the labouring man is the one important item of expenditure. Consequently the labouring man in California has a position which I have not known him to achieve elsewhere.[15]

Many others made this important point, that lower food costs gave the Californian the edge over the easterner.[16]

Food prices were not, however, the only item in an immigrant's budget. In general, outsiders were warned that

It would be a fatal mistake... to suppose that... high wages mean the full measure of competence that appears on the face of them... Everything is dearer—house rent, clothing, and most of the necessaries of life.[17]

A correspondent in *The Catholic Guardian* believed, for somewhat idiosyncratic reasons, that

The day labourers in the city lead hard lives;... running in the rain to catch the Folsom, Mission, or Howard Street cars. In the evening they have to return; rain may be falling or a cold wind blowing; a glass of beer or whiskey at the next grocery store is taken to keep out the cold, and they arrive at home in wet clothes. They pay for rent, five dollars a month; car hire, three; for beer or whiskey 'to keep out the cold' three dollars *at least*, eleven dollars a month, to which we must add the expense of meeting friends at the bar now and then; they may be fairly estimated at four dollars a month.[18]

Even though his view of the hidden social costs of city life may have been fanciful, the message is clear and unobjectionable. That it was widely held can be seen by the action the California Labour Exchange took when issuing its 'Circular to Workingmen'. It felt obliged to deny as 'an erroneous impression' that 'the cost of living in California... is so enormous as to be oppressive to the working man'. Admittedly 'the luxuries of life are, of course, expensive here, as they are everywhere, but the frugal', it was claimed, 'will soon find that they can live here more cheaply than they can in any of the Eastern States'.[19] In fact according to one modern authority the year of the circular, 1869, saw the opening of a fourteen-year period in which food bills fell by nearly 18 per cent.[20] Since food may have made up 40 per cent of the working man's total expenditure, this fall was of obvious importance to Irish immigrants, whose total budget could have benefited by about 7 per cent. Falling food prices were not, however, matched elsewhere, for housing costs, for instance, rose in this period anywhere from 6 to 83 per cent, and these would have made up 15 per cent of a family budget. It has been argued that for most families the rise in rents in these years exceeded the fall in the cost of food by about 2 per cent, while, generally, the decline in wages in some fifteen occupations of twenty-two surveyed was greater than any fall in the cost of living.[21] If these figures are totally trustworthy, which like all drawn from nineteenth-century sources they are not likely to be, they might suggest that after 1870 particularly the acute Irish observer could have sensed a drop in living standards if he was finely attuned to contemporary wage and price movements. Even then, men who were able to calculate the precise changes in their material world would have had no idea whether they were in the midst of a long-term secular trend that would continue to undermine living standards or whether tendencies might suddenly reverse. Observers outside the city could still notice in 1890 that in twelve major manufacturing industries wages were, on average, 12.5 per cent higher on the Pacific coast than in the Middle Atlantic region.[22] There is no evidence of either a massive immigration or remigration, and this suggests that in the end favourable feelings about higher wages may have been fairly balanced by pessimism about higher prices.[23] At the same time, the total judgement on material prosperity was unlikely to be limited to views on wage and price movements. Individuals, as has been seen, could see some upward economic mobility in their generation and were likely to be able to see more in that of their children. For many the fall in living standards after 1870 may have been marginal; for some, standards may have risen.

The precise level of satisfaction for Irish wage-earners would, however, have differed with the economic climate. The evidence suggests that the five-year period from 1863 was in many ways the happiest for them. Trade unions flourished, and between 1863 and 1865 'virtually all the strikes ended successfully for the workers'.[24] Pressure rose for shortening the working day and for securing a more effective lien law. In 1868 Governor Haight approved a Bill establishing the eight-hour day and another giving wage-earners preference in suits against defaulting employers. Unfortunately, though, the period of prosperity was brief. In August 1869, reflecting the new economic climate, partly the result of the opening of the transcontinental railroad and the expectation of a rise in immigration, the California Planing Mills succeeded in re-establishing the ten-hour day. Trade Unions faltered in the face of increased immigration of both whites and Chinese, while the lien law proved quite inadequate in its task of safeguarding wages.[25] In the spring of 1868 several San Francisco capitalists had helped to found the 'California Labour

Exchange', and, by the end of June 1869, had found employment for 6,198 Irish males and 3,101 Irish females. W. O'Connell, President of the Irish-American Benevolent Society, became a trustee, symbolising the importance of the institution to the Irish community. But the Exchange, too, fell victim to the new economic circumstances, producing its last report in 1871.[26] Irish wage-earners could thus well have been experiencing harder times even before the depression of the mid-'seventies made matters worse. At the end of the decade labour was plentiful and wages were correspondingly low. In April 1879 a strike of labourers on the Sea Wall and on Nob Hill failed, as contractors found men willing to work for $1.50, rather than the $2 being claimed by the strikers. Since the Sea Wall was a state undertaking, the labourers on it should have been working an eight-hour day. In fact they were working a ten-hour one, against the letter of the law.[27]

Despite its birth in a Gold Rush, therefore, San Francisco did not prove a land of plenty for all, nor for all its Irish. From afar wages might look high, but nearer at hand so did prices. Normal market conditions prevailed in the city, influencing the amount of social and economic opportunity, Not all San Franciscans, however, fell victim to the hard times; neither did all the Irish. They experienced a variety of fortunes which ran from those of the Donahues and Sullivans, who became steadily richer, to those of the unskilled who lived along the waterfront, more often than not unemployed. Those who were victims suffered both materially and from what a contemporary called 'the general temper of Western society...to make its poorer members feel not only unfortunate but infamous'.[28] They crowded the almshouses, the asylums, the hospitals. Their presence was to be deplored, but was not exceptional in terms of the inegalitarian society in which they lived. In the final analysis it is important that the Irish community also contained the successful, like John Sullivan, who lived in the Twelfth ward with, in 1880, his twelve children, the two sons in the legal profession, and his four servants—all born in Ireland. Here in one household the variety in the Irish community was apparent.

The world of the individual Irish San Franciscan was very much a product of the job he or she followed. Both adult Irish and those too young for employment were also much affected and influenced by the stability of social relationships. The most immediate ties were formed within the family, at school and in church. The quality of these relationships was of the utmost importance in determining the hopefully calm stillness at the psychological centre of the individual life. The following chapter analyses these relationships to discover their vitality and strength. Their success would provide a very definite reason for a general sense of satisfaction.[29]

Chapter V
Family and community

Although the Forty-niners have been traditionally seen as a human tide of young unattached males, they were sometimes accompanied by their wives and children, and sometimes sent for them within a few months, even in the earliest days. The often-quoted statistic that the white population of California in 1850 was 92 per cent male is misleading, since although figures exist for the mining areas of the state for that year, for settlements with few women on the whole, because fire and accident destroyed the census schedules of Conta Costa, Santa Clara and, most important, San Francisco counties they are lacking for areas where the sex ratios were probably slightly, at least, more even. Certainly by 1852 San Francisco's white population was 83 per cent male, while the Irish-born there were 68 per cent male.[1] Irish migration from the eastern United States may well have been largely of single men, but that from Australasia, for instance, differed. Remigrants from there travelled in family groups and were only 59 per cent male.[2] Consequently the Irish community of San Francisco from the beginning contained a sizable number of families, to inaugurate a trend that deepened with the passing years. The image of the anomic, unsettled wanderer will not do to cover the majority of Irish San Franciscans, who showed few signs of having departed from their traditional group social patterns.

Throughout the period the vast majority of Irish San Franciscans lived either in family groups or lodged with others of their own kind. Very few, to judge from the manuscript schedules of the census, lived completely alone in their own separate dwelling. In 1880, for instance, in the Seventh ward, which contained possibly the poorest Irish community, where 41 per cent of first-generation males over sixteen years of age were in unskilled occupations, only twenty-seven of a total 1,232 first-generation Irish males lived alone, while, further, only eight of 520 second-generation did so. Undoubtedly the supply of housing helped produce such low figures. It was virtually impossible in the Seventh ward for men and women to live alone when few dwellings were available to even the wealthy recluse. This is not to suggest, however, that the Seventh ward was totally filled with variants of the nuclear family, for it was not, but, at the same time, the fact that 2·1 per cent of the first-generation Irish employed male adults in the ward lived alone, or that 49·1 per cent of them boarded or lodged, should not be taken as meaning the complete disruption of family life. In the first place, a single set of census evidence cannot say whether the pattern visible in June 1880 was static or changing; in the second place, it is difficult to be sure whether, particularly among the poor, an individual's boarding or lodging was habitual or temporary. It is also unclear whether the boarding or lodging of single men and women should be taken as anything more than *prima facie* evidence of either personal or group dislocation, for, presumably, the connection would be disavowed, for instance, by all confirmed bachelors and spinsters. The pattern of Irish migration, whereby, often, individuals went first to prepare the way for relatives, meant that boarding and lodging habits might well be temporary. Certainly it is true that among second-generation adult Irish San Franciscans in employment living in the Seventh ward only 1·6 per cent lived alone and 24·2 per cent boarded or lodged. The 50 per cent decline from first to second generation here provides one more piece of evidence of the overall improvement going on among the total Irish group.

Yet it is also necessary not to go too far towards seeming to argue that the boarding and lodging houses of the Seventh ward were filled with contented, potential home-owners, only awaiting sufficient funds to set up separate establishments. This clearly would not be true and, for many, sharing a room in a badly built, poorly ventilated and serviced lodging house would have been a depressing experience, particularly if past experience or future expectation would have led the individual to want higher standards of comfort and cleanliness than the situation offered. It is interesting, as Table 14 shows, that in the Seventh ward, regardless of generation, it was the semi-

Table 14

Percentage boarders and lodgers in each occupational status, Seventh ward, San Francisco, 1880, for first- and second-generation employed Irish males

	White-collar	Skilled blue-collar	Semi-skilled	Unskilled	N
First-generation	33.8	50.6	58.6	46.1	605
Second-generation	19.3	21.3	29.1	27.8	126

skilled rather than the unskilled who provided the highest percentages of boarders and lodgers. This was due in large measure to the number of sailors in the ward in lodging houses, comprising 13.7 per cent of the first-generation group and 15.9 per cent of the second-generation group. Had there been fewer sailors the percentage distribution of lodgers and boarders by occupational status would have been linear, increasing towards the unskilled group. The presence of the sailors distorted this pattern but should also act as a brake on a runaway statement about the breakdown of family life in the ward based on too cursory a glance at the total statistics with too little regard for their overall composition. A similar remark could be made of a very different group from the sailors, the white-collar workers. If, by and large, they experienced higher incomes than other groups, it requires an assumption to argue that their boarding and lodging patterns

Table 15

Percentage distribution of total first- and second-generation employed male Irish boarders and lodgers, by occupational status, Seventh ward, San Francisco, 1880

	White-collar	Skilled blue-collar	Semi-skilled	Unskilled	N
First-generation	7.8	19.6	33.9	38.7	605
Second-generation	12.7	34.9	34.9	17.5	126

can be added unthinkingly to those of other groups, or that they provide irrefutable evidence of the breakdown of family life in the ward under the stress of urban poverty. Table 15 sets out the percentages of the total lodging and boarding Irish male population that fell into the various occupational statuses[3]. It shows that whereas seven out of ten first-generation lodgers and boarders were in semi-skilled and unskilled occupations, only five out of ten second-generation were. The fact that five out of ten second-generation were not is important, again, in preventing an unqualified argument from the figures on boarding and lodging that they inescapably reveal the total amount of dislocation in social patterns.

The Seventh ward has been given detailed coverage, as it was an extreme case, likely to reveal most acutely any strains affecting Irish family life.[4] In other wards with fewer Irish in unskilled occupations there was less evidence, in boarding and lodging, of communal strain. In the more middle-class Eleventh ward 65 per cent of a sample of 1,082 Irish households were made up of nuclear familes, while the vast majority of Irish adults lived with people to whom they were related. Only 5 per cent of Irish boarders lived with non-related families and only 3 per cent of Irish adults boarded with non-Irish families. It has been calculated that, in this ward, only 27 per cent of Irish men of both the first and second generations were boarders.[5]

In neither the Seventh nor the Eleventh ward does the census suggest that the Irish family was particularly failing to enfold and support its children, though the census would by its nature be unlikely to include the peripatetic homeless child or young adult. As far as it is reliable the census does not support the view that the Irish were in any disproportionate fashion likely to be supplying recruits to San Francisco's very own version of the juvenile delinquent, the 'hoodlum'. The appearance of these gangs in the mid-1870s worried San Franciscan and visitor alike, and could be taken as evidence of the partial collapse of family life. According to one observer the 'hoodlums' were regularly organised gangs of boys and girls, aged between fifteen and twenty or twenty-five, 'their business being to waylay unoffending citizens during the hours of the night and get as much as they can out of them, and when found necessary, speedily despatch them to happy hunting-grounds by means of knives or revolvers, with which they are well provided'. A further 'employment of the young vagabonds' was 'to follow people and annoy them by telling them lurid stories'. There were, it was said, some twenty or more gangs comprising 500 to 550 members, in 1875 described by the incoming mayor as appearing 'to be fast taking possession of the city'.[6] It is highly unlikely that there were no Irish among them, since there were Irish in the Industrial School drawn from the same constituency of the uncontrollable young. But there is no evidence that the hoodlum was particularly Irish or that the phenomenon could be directly attributed to the weakness of the immigrant family.

On the contrary there is stronger evidence that the Irish family did exist to act as a consequential stabilising agency for nearly all San Francisco's permanent Irish population who could be expected to live in family groups. This was important, because the anxieties and threats of an unfamiliar external world would be diminished and mediated by close familial ties that provided a supportive, structured network of relations. Family life strengthened and encouraged the individual by giving him or her a familiar and immediate role and a level of self-confidence that could be useful elsewhere when that role was successfully filled. Family life appears strong quantitatively from census data; qualitatively, if sometimes only negatively, from evidence available in the columns of the short-lived organ of the Irish middle class in the city, the *Catholic Guardian*. This newspaper took pains to lay out its conception of familial roles directed towards the improvement and consolidation of family life. Its philosophy was one of coherence and mutual support, of both rights and duties within the family, intermingled in what may now seem a claustrophobic and destructive way, but which the paper then clearly felt to be normative and successful. 'The wise wife,' said the *Catholic Guardian*,

> should always bear in mind that although the husband is the oak of the family, he is largely sustained by the little tendrils of conjugal sympathy, encouragement, and praise; by these he is made brave and strong and persistent in the prosecution of his business, whether it be the tinkering of a tin pan, the mending of a shoe, or the building of a steamship.

With such a view it is not surprising that the paper felt further, for instance, that woman's suffrage was argued for only by 'silly females' controlled by advocates of 'Free Love', and that the education of women must have a strong domestic content. 'Educating girls for household duties,' it said, 'ought to be considered as necessary as instruction in reading, writing and arithmetic, and quite as universal.' Though the idea of the wife as inferior consort may not sound attractive to modern ears, it did not entail female passivity in the family. The paper preached active if separate familial roles for husband and wife to strengthen their joint domain.

The *Catholic Guardian* also had advice for the father directed towards improving his familial role. It warned against the danger of authoritarianism and against the corruption of power that so easily turned into the destruction of tyranny. It suggested that

Many a father keeps his children so at a distance from him that they never feel confidently acquainted with him. They feel that he is a sort of monarch in the family. They feel no familiarity with him. They fear and respect him, and even love him some... but they seldom get near enough to him to feel intimate with him... they approach him through the mother... In this keeping-off plan, fathers are to blame. Children should not be held off. Let them come near... It is wicked to freeze up the love foundations in the little ones' hearts—fathers do them an injury by living with them as strangers. This drives many a child away from home for the sympathy his heart craves, and often into improper society. It nurses discontent and mistrust...

This clearly should not be the case. The opposite should be true, whereby children, secure in their parents' love, would be immeasurably aided in their struggles in the wider world, as well as benefiting from a constantly exhibited and educative series of parental values.[7]

A very high degree of endogamy in Irish families ensured that Irish values would be reinforced by being shared and passed on by both partners and also diminished the possibility of strife between two differently derived patterns of values within one family. Most Irish children grew up in solidly Irish families, as the census and other evidence shows. Table 16 demonstrates that among first-generation Irish, some of whom appear in all three years 1852, 1870 and 1880, there was no growing tendency to look outside the Irish-born group for a spouse and, perhaps, even the contrary tendency among Irish-born females who were married in the 1870s. In nearly thirty years the pattern of marriages changed in only one apparently significant respect, the increasing choice from the American-born. Before seeing this process as an example of the melting pot at work it is wise to look more closely at exactly which Americans the Irish were marrying.

Table 16

First-generation Irish marital patterns, San Francisco, 1852, 1870, 1880 (%)

	Spouses				
	Irish	British	Native-born	Other	N
1852					
Irish males	87.6	7.7	3.1	1.6	640
Irish females	85.6	8.6	4.3	1.5	655
1870					
Irish males	88.1	4.5	7.1	0.3	6,273
Irish females	73.2	7.8	11.0	8.0	7,547
1880					
Irish males	84.1	4.3	10.9	0.7	8,035
Irish females	74.4	7.8	10.3	7.5	9,072

In 1880 875 Irish-born males had American-born wives in the city. In 573, or 65.5 per cent, of those cases the American herself had two Irish-born parents; in another eighty-four, or 9.6 per cent, of the cases she had one. In only the remaining 218, or 24.9 per cent, of the cases was there no Irish blood immediately visible on the census schedule, from which this information was obtained. A parallel, though less striking, state of affairs was true for Irish-born females. In their case, 293, or 31.2 per cent, had chosen husbands with two Irish-born parents, and fifty-two, or 5.5 per cent, had chosen mates with one. The remaining 63.3 per cent had married husbands without Irish-born parents.

The same picture emerges from a closer examination of those Irish-born who had chosen to marry seemingly British-born partners. Irish-born males had chosen 349 British-born females: 138 of these, or 39.5 per cent, had two Irish-born parents, and twenty-nine, or another 8·3 per cent, had one. Only 52·2 per cent of the British-born spouses had no apparently immediate connection with Ireland. Among Irish-born females married to British-born males there was, again, a lesser but similar Irish presence hidden among the British: 125, or 17·7 per cent, of the husbands had two Irish-born parents, while twenty-five or another 3·5 per cent, had one. The vast majority, 556, or 78·8 per cent, had had none, suggesting that here females did melt comparatively easily into the British-born and native-born communities.

Table 17

Marital patterns, American-born of two Irish-born parents, San Francisco, 1880 (%)

	Spouses				
	Irish	British	Native	Other	N
Male	30·7	7·3	60·6	1·3	967
Female	33·4	14·0	50·2	2·3	1,716

The second generation provides better evidence of progress towards exogamy, as it can be assumed that this group married, by and large, within the United States, not in Ireland, as perhaps the vast majority of the first generation had done. Table 17 deals with the central sector of the second generation: those Irish San Franciscans not born in Ireland but with two Irish parents. This table reveals a continuing preference for endogamy. Immediately striking is the fact that close to one in three marriages of both men and women in this group were to Irish-born spouses. There was thus a strong and very visible force pulling the second generation back into the ethnic community. The percentage marrying native-born spouses is also immediately apparent, but once again the surface figures hide unexpected facts. Only 124 of the 586 wives, or 21·1 per cent, had no Irish-born parent, and 402, or 68·6 per cent, had two. The first choice of the male second-generation Irish was clearly one of his own kind. Irish females of the second generation differed again, in degree, in their attachment to the community. Some 398, or 46·2 per cent, had a husband with no Irish-born parents, but even here, consequently, over half had married spouses of some Irish descent. Very few of either sex chose partners from the first generation of other ethnic groups.

Further corroborative evidence of the strength of endogamy comes from the marginally Irish group that was born outside Ireland with only one Irish-born parent. Among males, 29·1 per cent chose an Irish-born mate of double Irish-born parentage; another 33·1 per cent chose either an Irish-born mate with one Irish parent or a non-Irish-born mate with two Irish parents. Some 15·1 per cent had chosen a non-Irish-born mate with one Irish-born parent, and only 22·9 per cent had chosen one with no Irish connections whatever. Among females of this marginal group, the percentages for the four categories were 20·8, 19·0, 7·7 and 52·6 respectively. Once again, females were less likely to be married within the Irish community, but it is notable that, even among them, just under one half did so to some extent. It has been suggested, working from a sample of Irish in the Eleventh ward of San Francisco, that as far as the second generation was concerned males tended to marry later than females, on average perhaps ten years later.[8] If the drive among males for a partner from the same group was as strong as the evidence suggests, it was also tempered by a willingness to wait on opportunity rather than marry outside the group.

If a melting pot had been at work it would have shown itself in a large number of marriages between the Irish and other immigrant communities. Had large-scale intermarriages taken place it would have been remarkable. Equally remarkable, however, is the paucity of such matches. The full range is laid out in Table 18.[9] It suggests that Irish-born females, and, proportionately, Irish-born males, had chosen German-born spouses most often when marrying outside the native- or British-born group.[10] The number of marriages with Swedes and Danes may show either apostasy on the part of Catholics or the choice of Irish Protestants. Either way, Catholic Europe appears well represented in Table 18.

Table 18

Marital patterns, Irish-born with non-British foreign-born, San Francisco, 1880 (Irish-born distinguished by number of Irish-born parents)

Males Irish-born	N	Wives born
No Irish parents	2	Germany 1, Sweden 1
One Irish parent	3	France 2, Germany 1
Two Irish parents	49	Austria 2, Chile 2, China 1, Denmark 2, East Indies 1, France 7, Germany 24, Italy 1, Mexico 5, Norway 1, Spain 1, Sweden 1, South America 1
N	54	

Females Irish-born	N	Husbands born
No Irish parents	1	Sweden 1
One Irish parent	8	Austria 1, Denmark 2, France 1, Germany 2, Italy 1, Spain 1
Two Irish parents	661	Austria 27, Belgium 10, Chile 4, Denmark 49, Finland 6, France 84, Germany 317, Greece 3, Holland 15, India 1, Italy 30, Malta 1, Mexico 2, Norway 11, Poland 7, Portugal 14, Russia 4, Spain 3, Sweden 52, Switzerland 17, Venezuela 1, West Indies 2, South America 1
N	670	

Second-generation marriages with the non-British foreign-born provide the figures in Table 19. The pattern is not distinctively different from that of the first generation, with the German-born providing a majority of the alliances. These figures in Table 19 understate, however, the non-British foreign-born element in second-generation marriages, because they omit marriages with ostensibly native-born spouses who, on closer inspection, turn out to be second-generation members of other immigrant groups. To ignore these is to give a falsely small impression of the amount of intermarriage between immigrant groups, and to inflate the amount of intermarriage between the native and Irish stocks, to suggest wrongly that where the Irish melted they flowed into a broad, indistinguishable river of native stock. A more precise

Table 19

Marital patterns, second-generation Irish with non-British foreign-born, San Francisco, 1880 (distinguished by number of Irish-born parents)

Males	N	Wives born
U.S.-born, two Irish parents	10	Denmark 1, France 3, Germany 3, Italy 1, Russia 1, Sweden 1
U.S.-born one Irish parent	3	Denmark 1, Germany 1, Sweden 1
British-born, two Irish parents	1	Mexico 1
N	14	

Females	N	Husbands born
U.S.-born, two Irish parents	134	Austria 5, Belgium 2, Cuba 1, Denmark 9, Finland 2, France 12, Germany 72, Holland 2, Italy 9, Luxemburg 1, Mexico 1, Norway 1, Poland 2, Portugal 3, Russia 2, Sandwich Islands 2, Sweden 6, Switzerland 2
U.S.-born, one Irish parent	20	Austria 1, France 3, Germany 8, Holland 2, Italy 3, Sweden 1, Switzerland 2
German-born, one Irish parent	2	Germany 2
W.I.-born, two Irish parents	1	Germany 1
N	157	

measurement of the melting pot here is given in Table 20. There the birthplaces of the parents of 1,246 couples in San Francisco in 1880 are analysed. Couples were included in the group if either partner was in any way of mixed descent, visible in the census schedules. Thus this group would not include any Irish couple that had four Irish-born parents between them, but would include those that had only one. Because the group is so defined it provides a useful benchmark to measure not only the progress of the melting pot among couples, but also among groups of decreasing Irishness.

From Table 20 it is possible to establish that in these marriages of mixed ancestry 49·4 per cent of parents had been born in Ireland, over twice the percentage provided by the next most important area of origin, Germany, with 23·3. The only

Table 20

Parental birthplaces of Irish couples, San Francisco, 1880 (where one, two or three parents Irish-born)

No. of couples	Other parents born in
92 with one Irish-born parent	Austria 3, Britain and Empire 56, Bohemia 1, Chile 1, Denmark 13, East Indies 1, France 18, Germany 92, Holland 6, Italy 7, Mexico 4, Norway 1, Panama 1, Portugal 3, Spain 6, Sweden 8, Switzerland 6, U.S.A. 48, South America 1. N 276
1,090 with two Irish-born parents	Africa 1, Austria 70, Belgium 26, Britain and Empire 39, Chile 10, China 2, Cuba 3, Denmark 131, East Indies 2, Finland 18, France 308, Germany 1,048, Greece 6, Holland 41, Hungary 2, India 3, Italy 85, Luxemburg 2, Malta 2, Mexico 22, Norway 26, Paraguay 1, Poland 23, Portugal 44, Russia 18, Spain 21, Sweden 135, Switzerland 41, U.S.A. 37, Venezuela 2, West Indies 1, South America 9, unknown 1. N 2,180
192 with three Irish-born parents	Austria 2, Britain and Empire 1, Chile 1, France 21, Germany 21, Italy 6, Spain 4, Sweden 4, Switzerland 3, U.S.A. 1. N 64

other significant sources of marriage partners were France, which provided 7·0 per cent; Sweden, 2·9 per cent; Denmark, 2·9 per cent; Italy, 2·0 per cent; Britain and the Empire, 1·9 per cent; the United States, 1·7 per cent; Austria, 1·5 per cent; and Switzerland, 1·0 per cent. Intermarriage between second-generation Irish and other second-generation immigrants, except for Germans, and, to a lesser extent, French-Americans, was remarkable by its absence. Also noticeable is the failure to marry into the native stock.[11]

The factors bringing about this state of affairs in San Francisco in 1880 for the Irish were both natural and cultural, natural in the sense that they followed to some extent from the demographic patterns of the city or, in the case of marriages that had taken place in the east, from demographic factors there; cultural in the sense that they reflected choices made by individuals educated by their families, and by group norms, including religious values. The high proportion of German marriages followed in part from the fact that the German-born made up 51·9 per cent of the white non-British foreign-born of the city. The French-born were the second largest component of this group, 10·8 per cent, but no other nationality provided over 5·0 per cent save the Italians, who made up 6·5 per cent. It was no wonder that intermarriage did not happen very often, for it could not. Numbers available, however, were not the only determinant. The lack of a single marriage with the Chinese community, which comprised 33·4 per cent of the non-British non-Irish foreign-born of the city, gives the lie to that.[12] Where cultural feelings, in this case on race, were less strong, other factors played an important part. One that did so was the white sex ratio of the age group over seventeen years of age, which stood at 1:1·19 in the women's favour.[13] This produced a situation wherein the Irish female had a wider choice than the Irish male and one where other non-Irish males found Irish females the more valuable and attractive from their scarcity value. The unequal sex ratio helped produce the differing patterns of intermarriage for Irish men and women already discussed.

Cultural pressure for endogamy began in the family. The Irish press supported the Irish family, but the most important institution acting to maintain the homogeneous Irish community was the Roman Catholic Church, whose strictures against marriage with Protestants, if ignored by Irish Protestants, did much to add to language and cultural barriers between the Irish and other groups and establish an extremely strong defence against exogamy.

The Catholic Church in San Francisco was clear from the outset that 'Matrimonia Clandestina inter Catholicos et Acatholicos non sunt valida'. The problem of mixed marriages was given equal priority with that of finances at the first Ecclesiastical Synod of California, held in the city between 19 and 23 March 1852.[14] In 1864 Thaddeus Amat, Bishop of

Monterey, produced *A Treatise on Matrimony, According to the Doctrine and Discipline of the Catholic Church*, giving the Church's case in full and extreme form. According to the bishop, 'In case of any opposition between the laws of the church and those of the prince, or of the state, those of the church would stand, as to the validity or invalidity of the marriage contract before God, whatever might be the opinion and judgement of men to the contrary.' Thus civil marriages and divorce were forbidden, the latter 'as coming from Judaism'; also mixed marriages, for 'the Catholic church has always abhorred and detested ... mixed marriages, and prohibited them ... being prejudicial to Christianity'. Particularly as 'from such mixed marriages, even the most fortunate ones, proceed infidel children; neither Catholics nor Protestants; loving no religion at all, if not hating every religion'. Such strong official feeling would necessarily act as a brake on those to whom it had value, leading them to acknowledge the truth that such marriages 'besides committing a mortal sin, cause great scandal to religion and do great injury to themselves, living in a state of degradation, their matrimony being nothing else but a palliated concubinage, which will surely bring them to eternal condemnation, unless they repent and repair the scandal by redressing their steps'.[15]

Eight years later, in 1872, the Catholic hierarchy, in the persons of Archbishop Alemany of San Francisco, Amat, and Bishop O'Connell, sent a letter to the Catholics of the Province of San Francisco expressly on the subject of mixed marriages, restating that 'the Church abhors, and has ever abhorred, mixed marriages; she does not allow them to be celebrated inside of her temples, nor with her sacred vestments, nor with the imparting of any blessing'. The circular letter containing these remarks was to be read on the first Sunday in Advent every year to encourage the faithful to, at least, religious endogamy. The ecclesiastical leaders admitted by implication that some Catholics ignored the teaching of the Church: they, 'almost abjuring their faith, apply for the celebration of their marriage to a civil officer or Protestant minister, not only exposing themselves thereby to make a contract which has no force before God, and, consequently, does not prevent their intercourse from being a horrible concubinage, but, also, committing really a sin of sacrilege—partaking of the enormity of a sacrilegeous communion received at the hands of a minister or magistrate'.[16] The frightening strength of such language was surely another prop for endogamy.

The Church did not disallow all mixed marriages, even though it disliked them so intensely. The Ecclesiastical Synod of 1852 petitioned the Pope to extend to the diocese 'privilegium concessum Belgiae, et Canadae, scilicet ut Matrimonia Clandestina inter Catholicos et Acatholicos in hac Diocesi sint valida'.[17] Between 1853 and 1863 the entire archdiocese, however, only granted some 1,366 dispensations for mixed marriages, presumably where there was 'the free exercise of the Catholic religion to the Catholic party' and 'the Catholic education of the children of such marriages, both male and female'.[18] Both conditions would have led to the strengthening of Catholic values and consequently to a reinforced feeling that future marriages should be endogamous. The Church's eternal vigilance was as marked for marginal Catholic families as for mainstream ones, thus damming up some possible outflow.

Despite the Church's attitude to mixed marriages and to birth control the resulting Irish families in the city appear to have been relatively small. The 1852 census reveals an average of 2·1 children per Irish family; the 1870 census 2·3; and a sample of the eleventh ward in 1880 shows 3·1 children, if the wife were Irish-born, and 2·1 if second-generation—though it should be remembered that these figures will not be entirely accurate, as they will not include the widow or widower with no children, nor the complete family from which death, ambition, mutual or individual disgust and age had removed members.[19] In such small families parental authority would have been easily and directly felt. If authority was an integrating and stabilising force, then the size of families could have been related to their successful reintroduction and growth at the heart of the Irish community.

The Roman Catholic Church was thus an integrating force for the Irish community, though not only in determining marriage patterns. It functioned daily as well to meet the needs of the Irish, and its ever-outward growth with the expansion of the city was a sign of its success.[20] Leaving aside as a special case the Mission Dolores, inherited from Mexico, the earliest Catholic churches began close to the waterfront: St Francis of Assisi on Vallejo, organised in June 1849, and St Patrick's on Market Street, founded in September 1851.[21] In July 1853 the cornerstone of St Mary's Cathedral on California and Dupont was laid. None of these buildings proved immune to the later flow of population. In March 1860 St Francis moved west to a new building on Vallejo between Dupont and Stockton, while in 1872 St Patrick's moved slightly south to the north side of Mission between Third and Fourth.[22] The Cathedral remained a breakwater against the rising tide of Chinese in its vicinity until 1881, when it too took its marching orders, though ten years were to pass before they were implemented.[23] While old buildings were closed new parishes also reflected the need and urge to construct. In December 1861 the Church established St Joseph's on the west side of Tenth Street between Folsom and Howard, and St Bridget's on the south-west corner of Broadway and Van Ness in February 1864; while in 1880 St Ignatius', originally dedicated in 1855, marked the settling down and the expansion of the Irish community by moving to a new structure on the north side of Hayes, west of Van Ness. By then further peripheral parishes had been set up: St Rose's on Brannan near Fourth; St Peter's on the north side of Columbia between Twenty-fourth and Twenty-fifth; and St John the Baptist on the north side of Eddy, between Octavia and Laguna.[24]

The visitor who remarked in 1872 that 'The Catholics, of course, are everywhere and very rich; fat lands have descended to them from the Spaniards and Mexicans, fat revenues flow to them now from the Irish' was only partly right.[25] It was not until 31 January 1877 that the Mexican government paid the Catholic Church any money due to it from the Pious Fund of the Californias, and meanwhile in 1855 the United States Land Commission had given the Church only the titles to missions, cemeteries and very limited acreages of adjacent land and gardens.[26] One result of this despoliation of the Californian Church was to kill any possibility of continuity between its Mexican and American periods. The position of the Church in San Francisco in November 1848 showed that incoming Catholics would have to rebuild their Church from the foundations. In that month Lieutenant James A. Hardie reported that

> the Catholic congregation of the town, among whom there are some Americans of standing, have to divide their pastor with two other large parishes on the other side of the Bay of San Francisco, and he has to spend a large portion of each month in the saddle. And, when the priest celebrates Mass in San Francisco, he does so at the mission three miles from town, there being no chapel in the town, so that, during the rainy season (and, in fact, during the whole year, for the poor) it is a matter of difficulty to get to Church even when Mass is celebrated.[27]

The need to construct new ecclesiastical institutions gave the incoming Irish the opportunity to be among the first patrons of the new Catholic Church and helped give them their unshakable hegemony within it, one that lasted for the remainder of the period. Men like Jasper O'Farrell and John Sullivan, women like Mrs Catherine Sullivan, gave lands and funds for new buildings, from schools to the cathedral.[28] John Sullivan gave land not only for the cathedral but also six fifty-vara lots off Larkin for St Mary's College; $5,000 to the fund for the Presentation Convent on Powell and Lombard; land on which the church at Mountain View was built; and funds for building this church and towards St Patrick's; as well as $12,000 to the Presentation Convent on Taylor Street and the same amount to the Sacred Heart College.[29] Mrs Richard Tobin, the wife of one of the founders of the Hibernia Savings and Loan Society, likewise gave the first building to the Holy Family Sisters of San Francisco.[30] The importance of Irish support became even greater once institutions had been set up. For instance, when the Holy Family Sisters bought their second Day Home at 1413 Powell 'The purchase price of five thousand dollars was guaranteed by the Hibernia Bank and through the kindness of Judge Robert Tobin the Sisters secured easy terms of payment'.[31]

The Church depended not only on the rich. The Day Home, for instance, was greatly helped by the free services, skills and materials donated by a number of individuals. The McDonalds, Reileys, Gallaghers, McPheeleys, O'Connells, Quiglys, Noonans, McMillans, Flahertys, Dalys and O'Connors who participated all bore witness to the value and strength of the Irish connection with the Church, as did the list of names of Irish ladies who gave their services to a fair to raise money to build a permanent convent. The bountiful included Mrs Richard and Mrs Robert Tobin, Mrs C. D. O'Sullivan, Mrs B. O'Connor, Mrs P. Donahue and Mrs Myles D. Sweeny, whose husbands were among the political and financial elite of the city. These men were unlikely to mingle socially with the plumbers, painters or carpenters whose skills built the Day Home, but both groups united in support of the Church, which flourished directly as a result.[32]

The financial relationship was a major one. Once founded, Church institutions needed a continuous injection of funds from the pious to survive. By and large the Irish provided them. In May 1868 the San Francisco *Irish News* reported the heavy debt hanging over the cathedral and the Irish response.[33] In May 1872 the *Catholic Guardian* reported that the debt was still a problem but that 'The Ladies' Fair, to liquidate the debt of St Mary's Cathedral, at Platt's Hall, has, we are happy to learn, proved a brilliant success'.[34] Later events, however, continued to prove that trying to finance a cathedral was often a case of running to stand still, though the Irish continued to sprint as vigorously as any.

The Irish community extended its financial patronage in other directions, too. In December 1870 Miss M. Nunan even edited a special newspaper for the Roman Catholic orphanage, *The Fair Messenger*, 'A Journal Devoted to Literature, Amusement, and the Advancement of the Cause of Charity'.[35] The advertisements in it for Catholic prayer books, for *The Irish Brigade and its Campaigns,* for *A History of Irish Saints* and the lack of corresponding works for other ethnic groups reveal the almost single relationship between San Francisco Catholicism and the Irish. Miss Nunan was not over-pleased with the results of the fair, but her discontent was not unusual. Two years later the *Catholic Guardian* remarked of an allied event, 'Patronage has not been so liberal as should be expected from a Catholic population so large and wealthy as San Francisco contains.'[36] Perfect charity being rare in any community, these grumbles do not provide strong evidence that Irish San Franciscans did not take their charitable obligations seriously. Their upper class certainly did in the main, making it, once again, difficult to see the Irish San Franciscans merely as impoverished refugees from the Famine.

The Church supported Irish life in its turn in a number of ways. It was performing an integrative and reinforcing role when, for instance, in February 1868 the Archbishop administered the sacrament of confirmation to about three hundred persons, including over fifty adults, or three months later repeated the sacrament at St Rose's Convent, Brannan Street, near Fourth, for about fifty 'young ladies'.[37] Critics of San Francisco Catholicism assumed that the Church played a role in the life of the Irish which was more than merely spiritual. The Reverend F. E. Jewell of Howard Street Methodist Church delivered a sermon in December 1874 in which he pronounced: 'You know that while Patrick has his nose, perhaps, in the sewer all through the week, when he comes on Sunday he is just as big a man as enters the temple? He is surrounded with objects of beauty and with the incense of worship, and these things are as much for him as for the richest man in the parish.'[38] Here the Church was seen as psychologically supportive. Less understanding yet equally significant evidence of the relationship between the Church and the Irish was given by the *Jolly Giant*, a paper given to noisy if ineffectual nativist outbreaks, in March 1874, when it complained querulously that

> respectable American people... from time to time, have been subject to annoyance and inconvenience in passing in front of the Jesuitical Roman Catholic Church on Market Street by a crowd of vulgar men who stand in front of that place every Sunday after last mass. This custom of vulgarity is practised in every Catholic country of the world. But this being a Protestant country, we object to this Irish show, for the sake of decency and civilization.[39]

These crowds of Irish showed the Church functioning as meeting place and community.

The Church itself recognised its social roles that ran beyond its religious one and symptomatically became the centre of a system of associations that revolved round it. Through these the Irish maintained another supportive connection with their Church, while the Church set up societies that recognised a duty beyond the sacramental. In December 1861, for instance, it established the long-lasting Sodality of the B.V.M., which in

1880 had 600 male and 250 female members. In February 1874 the Church Society of St Francis' Parish was organised, which by 1880 had 2,500 members meeting at St Francis' Church 'to promote the spiritual and temporal well-being of the parish, and to cooperate with the clergy in all matters in which they may require assistance of the laity'. Given the strength of the Irish presence in the Church, it is not surprising that Myles D. Sweeny was president and Robert J. Tobin vice-president of the organisation.[40]

Such societies were directed towards the better internal functioning of the Church but were by no means the only ones through which it wielded influence. During the period many societies in the city, secular and religious, Irish as well as other, were established to deal with the challenges of urban and everyday life, but some problems were beyond the scope of small voluntary agencies and required institutional attention, which the Church was willing to give. It lent its authority, personnel and funds to provide urgently needed social services, though it relied on both private and state aid to complement its own. Fortunately sectarianism was not dominant in the state, so that the legislature could support institutions like the Female Catholic Orphan Asylum or the Little Sisters' Infant Shelter and the work of the Sisters of Mercy with public money. In 1880 there were at least seven societies in San Francisco offering social services under the aegis of the Church—the three already named, the Magdalen Society, the Mater Misericordiae, the Society of St Vincent de Paul and the St Boniface Orphan Asylum.[41] State aid was too limited and too infrequent to be continuously relied on, so that there was plenty of room for private activity. Not surprisingly, the Irish were very evident in providing support.

The Irish role in helping the Church to provide social services was well illustrated in the case of the earliest of the Church-run institutions, the Orphan Asylum that dated back to February 1851, being taken over by the Sisters of Charity in 1852. It was the orphanage that happily received the fruits of the ten-day fair organised by the city's upper-class Catholics in December 1870 and those of the less successful one in December 1872. Through continuing private support the orphanage was able to move in 1854 to a brick building on

Market near Third that cost $45,000. In 1864 a second brick building was built to house an attendant school that grew to have several hundred scholars. In 1862, marking its general development, it bought a farm at Bay View in south San Francisco for very young orphans. In February 1872 the orphanage itself moved to Mount St Joseph. Considering the contemporary controversy about public moneys being given to Catholic schools it is significant that state money was forthcoming for the school established with the orphanage.[42]

By 1880 a second institution had been founded, the St Boniface Orphan Asylum, on the north side of Grove between Polk and Van Ness. It was reported in 1880 that this orphanage had been founded 'a few years since by Miss Catherine Gross, for the reception of those poor orphans of every nationality and religious denomination for whom no home could be found in other asylums'. It was also said that Miss Gross still considered the asylum her own private property, but 'as a Roman Catholic ... considers herself subject to the jurisdiction of Archbishop Alemany'. She had room for some twenty-seven orphans at this date.[43]

The Magdalen Asylum was founded in January 1864 under the charge of the Sisters of Mercy. In February 1868 it had 217 inmates; by 1 January 1870 it had given refuge to 417 penitents since opening; in 1880 it had 200 and had received over 600 since its founding, 'only about six per cent.' of whom had 'proved refractory'. At this date seventy-four young girls were maintained in the Industrial School from the asylum 'at the expense of the city', where 'separate apartments' were provided for them, again showing the close relationship between Catholic institutions and the social services of the city.[44] The Little Sisters' Infant Shelter, incorporated in March 1874, existed 'for the purpose of taking care of the young children of working women during the day, thus allowing the mother to perform a day's work'. It had a building at 512 Minna Street in 1880, where it was reported that the rooms were 'pleasant and spacious, and fitted up with all the articles necessary for a nursery'.[45]

The Church also had a very close relationship with the Mater Misericordiae or House of Mercy at 23½ Rincon Place, next to St Mary's Hospital and run by the Sisters of Mercy. 'This,' it was said, 'is for the protection of young women of unblemished character—none others admitted. Some remain waiting for a situation, and others are employed in the sewing school, where dressmaking and all kinds of machine sewing is neatly done at short notice.' In 1880 there were about fifty inmates. The institution was supported by inmates and by donations.[46]

The Society of St Vincent de Paul, which existed 'to relieve distress wherever found', had two branches in 1880, the St Patrick's Conference, organised in 1866, and meeting every Wednesday evening in the basement of St Patrick's Church, and the St Peter's Conference, organised in 1870 and meeting every Sunday after last mass in the library attached to the church. Despite the meeting places the Society claimed not to be sectarian: 'Though a legitimate offspring of the Catholic Church, and principally supported by members of the same', so its advertisement went, 'yet its charities are extended to all worthy persons who are in distress'.[47] It is not known how well the boast reflected the fact.

These societies were quite clearly dominated by the Church and supported by the Irish. Yet by no means all the societies established and run by the Irish in San Francisco had primarily religious ends. Secular societies provided both companionship and social welfare, and combined protective, benevolent and fraternal aims. Men were afraid of dying in poverty and obscurity and of being put in an unmarked pauper's grave. They therefore formed societies that had as one task that of organising the funeral and seeing to dependants, if any. Men were also afraid of sickness and unemployment and the effects of both on the living standards of themselves and their families. They therefore also banded together both to provide funds for emergencies and to form protective unions to prevent others from undercutting their wages. The need to save to provide the social security not guaranteed by any state authority led the fortunate to support financial institutions, savings and loan banks, where they could expect, if they were lucky in their capitalists, to see their money grow with interest. Societies which dealt with the basic problems of loneliness, the need to belong and provision for the future were many and the most successful. But they were not the sum total. Irishmen also supported societies that looked to the re-establishing of the glory of Ireland, or the establishing of Ireland in San Francisco politics. They joined the militia, in their own companies, for the status it gave them in the community. In 1880, according to *Langley's Directory*, over 7,500 Irish men and women could have been members of Irish and Catholic societies in the city, and an unknown number of Protestants members of the two lodges of the loyal Orange Institution.

It would be wrong to interpret the great network of Irish societies solely as evidence of a defensive community cowering behind their associations in a feeble attempt to deal with the problems of dislocation and the attacks of a hostile environment. The multiplicity of groups is also evidence of the exuberance and vitality of the Irish, of the spirit of optimistic adjustment that led to the creation of a wide range of group activities in the city. Consequently the pragmatism shown in the founding of protective societies should not be confused with pessimism. Associations were centres from which the Irish could sally forth to take what they wanted from urban life, within the bounds of possibility set by a pluralist society, secure in the knowledge that their bases were well established and an excellent starting point from which to foray into San Francisco life. One road led from these societies to the Church; a second to social intercourse; a third to political life. The combination of the private stability of the family, the institutional strength of the Church and the functional vitality of associationalism was very important in producing Irish satisfaction. The following chapter explores Irish associationalism more fully.[48]

Chapter VI
Irish associationalism

The first distinctly Irish societies in the city were founded in 1852. The first Irish celebration in the city had taken place on 17 March 1851 for St Patrick's Day, but the participants do not seem to have wanted to create a permanent institution from the event, possibly because too many regarded themselves as transient.[1] On 3 February 1852, however, a group of Irishmen came together to form the Hibernian Society, with Dr R. K. Nuttall as president.[2] By March 1852 the group had attracted some fifty to sixty members to their celebration of The Day and also, significantly, A. Bartol, who had been president of the Board of Assistant Aldermen.[3] The society was still in existence in 1859, with about fifty members, now with the stated purpose 'to perpetuate generosity by extending relief to Irish immigrants', but it appears to have dissolved very soon afterwards.[4] The second society founded in 1852 was the Sons of the Emerald Isle, which came into being on St Patrick's Day. It quickly ran short of steam, and needed reorganising in April 1856. In 1880, however, the revived body still comprised 274 members, having developed a 'benevolent arm' in 1868.[5] These all-male societies were secularly orientated, towards benevolence and fraternity, whereas the first all-female society, the St Mary's Ladies' Society, founded by the Sisters of Mercy in 1859, had avowedly religious aims to begin with, though these changed with time. In 1880 it was said that 'the purpose of promoting piety among the Catholic females has recently been converted into a Mutual Benevolent Society' with 1,100–1,200 members who met in St Mary's Hall, next to St Mary's Hospital, but for nigh on twenty years the association had existed to draw Catholic Irishwomen together with social and religious bonds.[6] Generally the first ten years of American San Francisco saw very little permanent Irish commitment to associations, possibly owing to the transience of the community.

The years 1859 and 1860 were marked by the foundation of a number of Irish institutions in the city with widely divergent aims. The cluster of incorporations at this point suggests strongly that the Irish community was now settling very firmly into the fabric of city life, within ten or twelve years from the beginning of the American period. The most important of these bodies was the Hibernia Savings and Loan Society, founded on 12 April 1859 in an upstairs room on Jackson, above Montgomery, with John Sullivan as president and John McHugh as vice-president. The Society originally took deposits of $2.50 or more, remaining a stock company until 29 August 1864, when it became mutual.[7] By 1869 the Society had 14,544 depositors and deposits of over $10 million, over twice as much as its nearest rival.[8] The institution was, as its name suggests, very much an Irish one and its success was often seen as symbolic of the Irish story in the city.[9]

In December 1859 another significant associative event occurred when both the McMahon Grenadier Guard and the Montgomery Guard were founded as the first Irish military associations in the city. By 1869 the former had sixty-eight members, the latter 116, but by 1880 both had experienced a slight decline in membership to fifty and sixty-five respectively. By 1880 there were, however, a total of six Irish companies making up the Third Regiment Infantry of California Guard, including the later foundations of the Shields Guard, founded in December 1860 and reorganised in February 1870, the Wolfe Tone, founded in February 1862, the Meagher Guard, founded in May 1862 and the Emmet Life Guard, founded in November 1862 and reorganised in May 1868. The total membership in 1880 stood at 352.[10] There were other more short-lived military associations that had disappeared by 1880, for instance the Hibernian Rifles, founded in January 1871, the Jackson Dragoons, founded in 1863, the Sarsfield Rifle Guards, founded in 1867, the California Rifles and the Legion of St Patrick, both in being in 1871.[11] There had also been a branch of the Irish Republican Army, organised in February 1868 and having 120 members in 1869, but this had disappeared soon afterwards.[12]

In May 1860 Irish San Franciscans moved forward on a third front by setting up the Irish-American Benevolent Society, probably the first of their associations to describe itself as a benevolent society from its inception. It was, it said, 'a volunteer association ... formed in the City and County of San Francisco, of individuals residing in said City and County, for the relief of its sick members, the interment of its deceased members' and also for 'the propagation of general intelligence, unity, friendship, and brotherly love amongst all its members'. Thus it had a social aspect, and its members were under the obligation to be ready to parade at any given time. To guard against some dangers of disruption it had a rule that 'Any member introducing any political or religious subject into the meetings of this Society shall be fined $5.00 for every such offence'.[13] By 1869 the Society was in such a flourishing condition that it could afford a new meeting-hall 'on the northeast corner of Harvard St. and Harvard Court, between Third and Fourth Street', while, it was said, so many were applying to join that it was in the fortunate position of being able to think of raising the fees for initiations. Its popularity was shown by the numbers attending its outings. 'So great was the crowd that attended the Irish-American Benevolent Society's picnic on Sunday,' said the *Irish News* on 8 May 1869, 'that the steamer had to make two trips to take them.' Eventually, however, decline set in and in 1889 the Society was disbanded[14].

The same year of 1860 also saw the founding of a second benevolent society, the St Joseph's Benevolent Society. 'The objects of this society,' it was said, 'are to extend assistance to each other in time of sickness, by corporeal aid and spiritual consolation; for providing their deceased brethren with a decent and Christian interment in accordance with their Holy Faith; for the relief of the families they may leave after them; as also for stimulating each other to a more constant observance of the duties of religion, and the general promotion of moral and intellectual improvement.' Whereas the Irish-American Benevolent Society met in the Irish-American Hall in the 1870s, the much more religiously orientated St Joseph's met every third Sunday in the basement of St Mary's Cathedral. That it was an Irish society can be gathered from its officers of 1880, including James R. Kelly, its president, and Michael Dolan, its secretary. In 1869 it had 200 members; by 1880, 450, again revealing the continuing need for such institutions among the Irish of San Francisco. It did good business, too: in January 1873 it was reported that it had received $4,500 in the past six months and paid out $1,500.[15]

The fraternal, benevolent and social institutions so far described were common throughout immigrant America. But in March 1860 the San Francisco Irish founded a very unusual and, not surprisingly, short-lived body, the 'Irish Fine Arts Aid Society', which gave evidence that they felt ready, if prematurely, to lift their eyes from the mundane to the more sublime, in short to provide funds for no less a body than the Royal Dublin Society. Such funds were to be used to maintain students on the continent of Europe while they completed their studies in the fine arts. The infant San Francisco Irish community was seemingly ready to patronise the Dublin Irish, and on 14 June 1860 sent £50 to Dublin with the promise of £100 annually.[16] But no further funds arrived, for the subscribers' enthusiasm diminished when they realised they had to find $1,500 over the next three years. The moral of the story seemed to be that they should patronise their own community first and give up their plans for burnishing Old Ireland's intellectual glories. By 1863 the project was but a bitter memory among those who saw that Irishmen could afford to send money to Ireland for political but not for cultural purposes.[17]

The political association that drew San Francisco Irishmen together at the end of the 1850s was, inevitably, the Fenians. Their branches were most valuable in binding Irishmen together through weekly meetings and through what many Irishmen considered the most rightful of causes. Though the Californian Fenians receive comparatively little mention in the standard work on the subject, they were as strong and vital as any.[18] Their San Francisco origins are a little obscure, but by 1871 it was claimed that the three Circles then organised in the city, the Thomas F. Burke, the Erin's Hope and the Emmet, dated back to 1856, 1858 and 1859 respectively.[19] In 1864 the claim was that the Brotherhood had organised in September 1859 'for charitable purposes and the redemption of Ireland', but a year previously it was claimed that the San Francisco State Centre dated back to 1857.[20] Certainly the Brotherhood was in existence in January 1861, when San Francisco Fenians were the organisers of the journey that Terence McManus's body took across country to New York. Colonel M. D. Smith and Jeremiah Kavanagh from San Francisco were also two of the six American Fenian representatives at McManus's funeral in Ireland.[21] The California Fenians did not hold their first 'General Convention' until September 1864, when thirty-four of them met, very appropriately as far as the revolutionary aspirations of the movement were concerned, in the armoury of the Second (Irish) Regiment in San Francisco.[22] The movement grew steadily in the city, from two circles in 1865 to six in 1869, but was always in danger from three directions.[23]

First, there were Irishmen outside the movement who disagreed with its aims, maintaining that it perpetuated divisions among the Irish community in San Francisco, as in America, by separating those who had come to settle permanently in the country from those who intended to return, as well as sustaining provincial Irish rivalries. 'Even here,' said one critic, 'on the far-off shores of the Pacific do we not see and feel the effects of the deep-rooted bigotry, intolerance and prejudice that too many of them exercise toward each other? It does appear strange that the Irishmen in San Francisco do not fraternise with each other, as the Germans, French, Italians or Scotch.'[24] This was to exaggerate disunity, for no fewer than eleven Irish societies had taken part in the Anniversary Celebration of the St Patrick's Brotherhood the previous year.[25] But the outburst is a measure of the hostility to the movement from within the Irish community.

The second danger to the Fenians came from within. They splintered in San Francisco as they did in the nation and by 1869 were divided into the Savage and Hamill wings, with the Hamill wing claiming one centre in San Francisco.[26] The third hostile force was the native American. At first there was sympathy in San Francisco for the Fenian cause. In May 1866 the *Alta* described the Grand Fenian Demonstration at People's Park, San Mateo, in friendly language: 'comely looking, finely dressed, and orderly to a degree; chubby-cheeked urchins and beautiful girls; hearty youngsters, all the way from baby-class upward, were there. We have never mingled with a more decorous company, and must confess that the congregated beauty of the "daughters of Erin" warmed our heart.'[27] But a year later, with the 'Battle of Limestone Ridge' as history, the mood was different, for the Fenians had ceased to look colourful and now appeared dangerous. The *Alta* said, 'How desperate that cause is need not now be argued; but every true friend of Ireland will be glad when their futile organisations and exhaustive schemes are abandoned, and Irish-Americans become a plastic element in the Great Republic.'[28] The failure of the second invasion of Canada in May 1870 finished the movement effectively throughout the nation, but while it lasted its organising ability and its Irishness were attractive focuses for most Irishmen, in San Francisco as elsewhere. The balls and picnics gave a chance for outings, meetings and gossip on the grandest scale.[29] In May 1868 it was reported that 8,000–10,000 Savage wing Fenians went on a picnic to Belmont Park on the Peninsula by rail. Their line of carriages stretched for half a mile and was 'headed by three or four engines, puffing and blowing like so many thousand savage Fenians, eager for the fray'.[30] As late as May 1870 12,000 people attended the Fenian demonstration in Redwood City, San Mateo County.[31] Feminine interest was kept up by an annual ball for the Fenian Sisterhood.[32] Successful drives for Fenian funds drew Irish San Franciscans together, too. In October 1865 Californian Fenians had sent $5,000 east.[33] In July 1867 the Pioneer Emmet Circle of San Francisco alone sent $1,000 for the aid of Fenian prisoners in England, having raised the money through a picnic at San Mateo.[34] In August 1868 the New York meeting of the Brotherhood received a gold draft of $1,000 from California, which was reported to be 'the biggest sum the organisation received for more than a year past'.[35] San Francisco Fenianism lingered on in the Knights of the Red Branch, founded in 1869, into possibly the late 'seventies. But after the late 'sixties it never again achieved its dominating position in the Irish community.[36] While it lasted, even in its years of division, it did a man no harm to be a member. In 1868 the president of the Savage wing was elected street superintendent of the city.[37]

There was no hiatus in the foundation of Irish societies as the Fenians fell apart. The late 1860s saw further developments on three broad fronts. First, the growing consciousness of the

Irish received further expression in the immediately successful Ancient Order of Hibernians. Second, the continuing success of the Hibernia Savings and Loan Society began to spawn a number of imitators, and, third, the labour shortage in the period before the opening of the transcontinental railroad gave great impetus to a number of labour organisations, many staffed by Irishmen.

The Ancient Order of Hibernians was first thought of in San Francisco in February 1869 and organised in March when some 'eight or ten young Irishmen' came together.[38] By 1871 there were six divisions in the city claiming 1,735 members; by 1873, eight; by 1880, ten divisions, meeting in the Hibernia Hall once a week.[39] The Order played both benevolent and social roles, often necessarily simultaneously, as when, in company with members of other Irish societies, its members joined a committee to make arrangements for a ball for the benefit of the widow and family of the late David J. Hynes, or when members of Division No. 2 attended the funeral of James Callaghan, reportedly producing a procession of 'fully one thousand persons'.[40] In 1878 the Order revealed itself to be politically conservative when its State Convention 'unanimously adopted resolutions denouncing members of Orders which have for their object to antagonize the peace and good order of this glorious Commonwealth', proposing rather 'to put down their feet on any semblance of Communism'.[41] In the interim members' attention turned to less serious matters, to balls, excursions and to the celebration of the Fourth of July and of St Patrick's Day, when the Order was very much to the forefront.[42]

The growing wealth of the Irish community was sensed by Irish capitalists, who also knew the necessity for saving against a rainy day in the absence of state-run insurance schemes. Broadly speaking, the financial institutions that grew up in the 'sixties were of two kinds: those in which Thomas Mooney had a hand, and those in which he did not. His greatest construction was the California Building Loan and Savings Society, dating from May 1861. James Shields was the first president, but Mooney was the organiser and presiding genius. By 1867 he said assets were over a million dollars and he was lending money on 'city real estate, houses, ships, factories and merchandise'.⁴³ Unfortunately Mooney's luck and skill did not hold, and he failed on 13 September 1870. According to those who did not like him he attracted support from working men by attacking the Chinese and 'monopolists' and by being a conspicuous ally of labour movements. He was said 'to have wept for joy when they appeared to have triumphed'.⁴⁴ His connection with the Irish community was, in his heyday, as strong as it could be: he delivered the oration on St Patrick's Day, March 1868, in the Metropolitan Theater, when his message was that Napoleon III would 'drop'; Europe, including Great Britain, would fall into revolution, republicanism and anarchy, and Ireland would gain her freedom.⁴⁵ One financial obituary emphasised Mooney's Irishness: 'He was conspicuous as a spotless Irish patriot, a historian who penned the wrongs of Ireland as no other man could do. He corresponded with Savage, Dr. O'Brennan, and others, and by all he was considered worthy.'⁴⁶ Mooney also had connections with the Builders' Insurance Company, which reportedly led to the California Savings and Loan Society losing $27,000; his son was a director of the Celtic and Teutonic Farm Association; while shortly before his final fall he was engaged on his own behalf in floating the Celtic Insurance Company. An unfriendly contemporary described Mooney's Builders' Insurance Company as 'the most insidious insurance trap that had yet been laid for gulls in California' but pointed out that 'appeals to political and religious prejudice wrought wonders among the numerous Irish Catholics in bringing him business'.⁴⁷ Mooney's unfortunate end did not mean that the Irish lacked money to invest, for they did. Yet his schemes were not the only Irish ones to go under.

In 1868, for instance, two short-lived societies were founded, the Hibernia Provident Association, 'To make comfortable and ample provision for the widows and orphans or other heirs or devisees of deceased members of the association; to encourage industry; to foster charity; to strengthen the ties of friendship among its members and to cultivate and reward provident forethought'; and the Irish American Mutual Association, 'To secure to the heirs of deceased members a cash payment of as many dollars as there are members'.⁴⁸ Neither association survived the 'seventies, but there were others to replace them, even though the same year of 1868 saw the disincorporation of the Hibernia Savings and Land Association and the division of its profits.[49] Two societies founded in 1873 were still surviving in 1880: the Celtic Protective and Benevolent Society, which had 175 members in that year, meeting every third Wednesday of each month at the Irish-American Hall, multifariously 'To extend aid and assistance to members in case of sickness or accident, to bury the dead, to afford mutual protection in business, and to elevate the character of its members'; and the St Patrick's Mutual Alliance of California, which had slightly fewer aims, namely 'To unite in a mutual union, Irishmen and their descendants of all creeds and classes, to protect and extend charity to the widow and orphans, to strengthen, foster, and promote, fraternal feelings of friendship and charity among its members'. The second society seemed to be flourishing in 1880. It had added a second Alliance in 1878 and, in 1880, claimed a total of 310 members.[50]

Beyond them were other benevolent societies which put more accent on a religious dimension, for instance the St Joseph's Benevolent Society of St Francis' Parish, founded in March 1872. By 1880 this had 300 members who met on the first Sunday of every month in St Francis' Church and were agreed 'to visit the sick, bury the dead, and provide for families of deceased members'. In 1867 the Church must have had a hand in the founding of the St Mary's Benevolent and Library Association, possibly finding it easier to maintain a close relationship because the aims of the society were not connected with the financial matters in any way. Rather, as its advertisement stated,

This association has been organised for the purpose of protecting the Catholic working man against the moral and social evils usually attendant upon a life of arduous and precarious labour. A large reading room has been fitted up for the accommodation of the society in the basement of St. Mary's Cathedral. It has a carefully selected library, numbering at present over one thousand five hundred volumes, consisting of all the Catholic works published in America, to which will soon be added those of Irish and English publishers. There is also a good collection of other useful and instructive works.

In 1880 the sixty members included Martin Murray (Secretary and Librarian) and James H. Nolan (Treasurer).[51]

The difficulty of establishing the precise relationship between the Church and the Irish-dominated societies is illustrated in the matter of temperance. The connection was not simply a matter of the Church approving more strongly those that accentuated religious ends and being more lukewarm towards those that did not, for there were some areas where the correct religious attitude could be in dispute. The Catholic Church was generally considered to be on the side of the saloons and did not give much support to temperance in San Francisco.[52] Perhaps reflecting this, the St Mary's Benevolent and Library Association had begun life in 1867 as the St Mary's Temperance Benevolent and Library Association, but later dropped Temperance from its title: it had always been moderate in its views on drink, offering a choice of two pledges to its members, either that of total abstinence or that of restraint from drinking in saloons, and only taking liquor as a medicine or article of diet.[53] Either because of such faint-heartedness or because the group lacked dynamism generally, it disappeared and was superseded by the Father Mathew Total Abstinence and Benevolent Society, founded in May 1869 and incorporated in the following January, and by the Catholic Total Abstinence Union of the Archdiocese of San Francisco, founded in 1874.[54] The Father Mathew society was in favour of total prohibition but not of legal compulsion, preferring to rely on the individual conscience.[55] It advertised its aim as 'To encourage all persons to abstain from the use of intoxicating liquors; also to afford relief in case of accident, or sickness, and assist in the burial of deceased members', and claimed 300 members by 1880. Its officers in that year were, as far as can be judged, Irish to a man. It met twice a week, showing its independence of the Church by the choice of venue, the Irish-American Hall.[56]

The Catholic Total Abstinence Union met generally once every three months in St Joseph's Hall. Its venue and its president in 1880, the Reverend J. B. McNally, showed its closer connection with the Church. But while the general body met infrequently its six subordinate agencies met bi-monthly in the churches of St Bridget, St Joseph, St Patrick, St Peter and St John, and in the Cathedral of St Mary, further underlining its religious connections.[57] Despite such a number of subsidiary groups there was little support on the whole among the Irish of San Francisco for the cause of temperance. In February 1880 a third society was founded, the Catholic Total Abstinence Mutual Beneficial Association, 'To provide for the family of deceased members' and levying a 'per capita of $1' upon 'each member on the death of a member', but this was a weak plant from the start that never grew, symbolising the poverty of the soil in which all Irish Catholic temperance societies were planted.[58]

Just as the precise relationship between the Irish associations and the Church is difficult to work out, so is that between the Irish and the labour associations of the city in the period. There are signs of early combination on a religious and ethnic basis. In February 1854 the Catholic Labourers' Union Association, composed of Irishmen, donated $500 to the Roman Catholic Orphan Asylum, but in general labour co-operation at this time was *ad hoc* and ephemeral even when unions did grow out of it', and there were more failures than successes.[59] If this was so, it is not surprising that such co-operation as there was among working men grew to be based very firmly in the ethnic group and that, since the Irish made up a large proportion of the workforce, so many labour associations seem to have been Irish.[60] The purpose of these associations was more than merely protective: they also had benevolent functions, as well as a social dimension. One way of gauging which Irish-dominated ones existed at a given time is to look at the celebrations for St Patrick's Day. In 1862, for instance, the only labour organisation in the procession was the Labourers' Protective Benevolent Society.[61] In 1868 when a convention met to plan the celebration of St Patrick's Day, representatives attended from the Labourers' Benevolent Society and the Labourers' Protective Society.[62]

The favourable conditions of the late 'sixties led to union growth and, equally, to Irish commitment to unions.[63] In 1870–71 Irish names were apparent among officials of the House Painters' Eight Hour League; the Improved Calkers' Association; the Journeymen Boot and Shoe Manufacturers' Co-operative Union; the Knights of St Crispin, Golden City Lodge No. 190; the Labourers' Eight Hour League, the Labourers' Protective and Benevolent Association; the

Plasterers' Protective Association; the Plumbers' and Gas Fitters' Eight Hour League; and the Stone Masons' (Journeymen) Association.[64] But the early 1870s were years of depression that both destroyed existing organisations and made new ones as necessary as they had ever been. Irish San Franciscans were not surprisingly to the fore in the difficult tasks of stemming the tide of disruption and establishing new defences, particularly against the flood of Chinese labour. By 1880 they predominated in a number of protective associations: in the Boot and Shoemakers' Union, incorporated in March 1878; in the Cigarmakers' Association of the Pacific Coast, organised in April 1876; in the Pavers' Union, reorganised in November 1878; and in the Stonecutters' Protective Association, a body that had, unusually, survived since May 1863.[65] The United Workingmen's Co-operative Boot and Shoe Manufacturing Company, incorporated in 1868, was similarly dominated by Irishmen, but since it claimed a capital of $79,000 and only thirty members was not strictly a labour organisation.[66] Its area of concern was, however, one of the three that seemed to lead Irishmen most strongly to organise in the late 1860s and 1870s—the boot and shoe industry, cigar making, and construction.

The variety of Irish San Francisco was shown in the way in which it threw up exclusive societies. In March 1869 the St Francis Literary Society was founded, though it soon disappeared.[67] More long-lived was the Ignation Literary Society for graduates of St Ignatius College. This society reorganised in 1877 under Jesuit supervision and in 1880 had twenty-five members.[68] There were also Irish societies for physical recreation. As early as May 1853 there was an Irish hurlers' club, and, reflecting the city-wide interest in baseball in the late 1860s, the Hibernia Green Baseball Club.[69]

With so many societies in the city, increasingly marking a maturing and accommodated Irish community, and, around 1870, the development of a feeling that there was an important permanent Irish group in the city that would benefit from further and more rigorous organisation, which could promise much, attempts were made to represent it, nominally at least, in a single society. Irish societies were accustomed to acting together on 17 March or 4 July but Irish society remained split for the remainder of the year, except on extraordinary occasions as when an Irish Relief Committee was established to aid families of Irish political prisoners; it gave at least one concert, and by the time it had disbanded had raised $7,267 in all.[70] However, in January 1869 it was proposed to start the St Patrick's Society of San Francisco to help all Irish immigrants in the city find their feet, unfortunately with little immediate result.[71] Nevertheless in November 1870 a St Patrick's Society was founded 'to uphold the national character, to promote progress, fraternal feeling and good citizenship among its members' which soon had 120 members, among whom were the most prestigious names in both the Irish community and the city. The Hon. Eugene Casserly was president; Eugene L. Sullivan, Joseph A. Donohoe and P. H. Canavan were vice-presidents; C. D. O'Sullivan was treasurer, T. N. Cazneau recording secretary, and Charles F. Smyth corresponding secretary.[72] Sadly, again, early enthusiasms produced no long-lasting results, but on 5 July 1871 the Irish Confederation was founded, which made its mark on the Irish community and the city by erecting the Irish-American Hall, a 63 ft × 46 ft building seating 1,000 persons, on Howard between Fourth and Fifth. According to one report it was 'the first instance in which a body of Irishmen have purchased a piece of real estate in this country, and erected a building on it for their own use, at so high a figure', put at about $50,000.[73]

The Confederation does not appear to have been strongly knit, for the March 1872 convention of Irish societies saw Mr O'Leary calling for action on a resolution introduced by him at a previous meeting for a special convention of all Irish societies in the city 'for the formation of an Irish National Union in San Francisco'. O'Leary was successful and the appropriate resolution was unanimously adopted.[74] Possibly before the special convention, the committee that organised arrangements for the St Patrick's Day celebrations proposed raising an 'Irish National Fund' in future, by means of contributions of ten cents per month by each member of all the Irish societies in San Francisco, 'the fund to be controlled by a Directory to be appointed by delegates from each society'.[75] Later circular calls were issued for a convention of delegates of the several societies for 3 June 1872, but once again enthusiasm seems to have ebbed before practical steps could be taken toward a general society for Irishmen.[76] Nonetheless the idea remained, and at last in January 1875 such a society was founded, under the title of the Knights of St Patrick. The reason why it succeeded in passing the planning stage where other schemes had failed was that its object was not so much the knitting together of the San Francisco Irish community as 'The elevation of Ireland to her place among the nations'.[77] 'None,' as the Society itself pointed out, 'can be admitted to membership of whose fealty to the cause of Ireland's independence there can be a doubt.'[78] In 1880 the Society claimed only 350 members and in the previous year only eighty had attended the annual banquet, possibly suggesting that its aims were either too exclusive or too high-flown for many San Franciscans.[79]

But it did have one point in common with its predecessor of 1870: it did attract Irish and other politicians. At the 1879 banquet the Hon. Thomas Beck, Secretary of State, the School Superintendent, A. L. Mann, Judge M. H. Myrick, ex-Senator Philip A. Roach, the Hon. William Broderick, Sheriff Matthew Nunan, Tax Collector William Mitchell and Superintendent John Foley came as invited guests. Supposedly Governor William Irwin would have come as well, had he not been attending a celebration of St Patrick's Day in Sacramento.[80] Local politics as well as Irish nationalism thus sustained what Hugh Quigley in 1878 ranked as one of the most important Irish-American institutions of the city.[81] As previous support for Fenianism in the city had shown, Irish nationalism, perhaps because distance lent enchantment or took away meaning, was a strong force in San Francisco. Perhaps it was not so surprising that the first Land Reform League in the world was founded in California with both president and secretary Irish-born.[82]

All societies so far mentioned, even the more secularly orientated, were, if they were anything, Catholic in their religious tone. The Protestant Irish of the city are elusive, but during the mid-1870s they were numerous enough and felt it necessary to coalesce and found two branches of the Loyal Orange Institution of the United States, first organised in the city in April 1875. By 1880 the California True Blues, No. 118, the first lodge, met at 909½ Market Street, on the first and third Wednesdays of each month, while Harmony No. 127, the second lodge, met on the second and fourth Saturday of each month 'at the Potrero'. The size of the membership is uncertain but the existence of the two lodges suggests that perhaps over one hundred Irish Protestant males needed the Orange Institution as a focus for their affairs.[83]

The existence of so many societies devoted in part to protecting the individual from the ill winds of fortune should not lead to the assumption that this was their primary use for him. On the contrary, the Irish used their societies even more when days were fair, in both the literal and the metaphorical sense. By the late 'sixties seldom a Sunday went past without one or more Irish societies bearing their members off north or south on a picnic or an excursion. Perhaps newspaper reporters exaggerated the numbers taking part, but they could hardly inflate the number of occasions when expeditions left the city. Military companies might go out by day to picnic and to shoot at targets; benevolent societies to enjoy themselves and to try to raise money; the Fenians to hear rousing speeches, take collections and enjoy the crowds; the Sons of the Emerald Isle to compete in their 'Grand National Games'.[84] In the city, of an evening, societies met to elect their officers, plan and give balls, take part in competitions and probably drink convivially.[85] It might be unfortunate that plans had to be made to give a ball for the orphans or 'for the Benefit of Mr. John O'Brien, an old member of the "Sons of the Emerald Isle", who has been under great affliction for the past three years, by the complete loss of his sight', or that an Irish Music Festival was needed on behalf of the family of Mr Martin O'Brennan, and such episodes might reflect the ever-threatening dislocation of urban life, but there was no law that forbade members from enjoying themselves while doing good, or even demanded that they should not enjoy themselves first and keep the wolf from the door but incidentally.[86]

The major date in the calendar for Irish societies was St Patrick's Day, when they marched their concerted forces through the streets of the city, before breaking up into their individual units to enjoy the evening as they wished. The planning began well before the day, often in late January, and increasingly involved representatives of all societies wishing to take part. In 1868, for instance, the organising 'convention' included representatives from the Sons of the Emerald Isle, the Irish-American Benevolent Society, the Labourers' Benevolent Society, the St Joseph's Benevolent Society, the St Mary's Temperance, Benevolent and Library Association, the St Joseph's Temperance, Benevolent and Library Association, the Emmet Circle of the Fenian Brotherhood, and John Hamill 'representing the State Centre of the Fenian Brotherhood'.[87] The convention produced a committee and the planning began.[88] The first celebration, held in March 1851, was without such detailed planning. Later the Sons of the Emerald Isle took charge of organisation, but as the number of the societies increased, and the city and its Irish community both grew, they came to share the burden with others.[89]

With the years, support for the celebrations grew ever stronger in the city. In 1869 the day was celebrated 'in a manner far surpassing that of any preceding occasion'.[90] In 1872 'All the Irish military and other organisations participated, the procession reaching nearly two miles, and numbering six thousand people in line, and was witnessed by 50,000 people along the line of march, on the streets not including the many thousands in windows and roofs. It was almost a 4th of July in attraction and numbers and not a discordant ripple occurred.'[91] No greater distinction could be given to the 17th than to compare it with the 4th. In 1876 a slightly hostile witness reported that 'a very large and numerous procession passed through the streets; it took rather more than one hour to march past my window', he said, going on to report that it 'was conducted in the most orderly manner, the people in the streets quietly ranging themselves on the sidewalks to allow it to pass; and, whatever their sentiments might be of the Irish, keeping them within their own breasts'. But, he continued, 'I cannot say much for the getting up of the procession; it appeared to be something between a funeral and a military display, more of the former than the latter perhaps.'[92]

As both the references to 4 July and to the military air about the procession suggest, the celebration of the day rested in part very much upon the sense that it marked a national Irish occasion, when the unachievable temporarily took form and content, and aspiration became reality for a short time. San Francisco, however, was in the United States, and the British flag flew in Dublin. The Irish recognised it simultaneously as they indulged their nationalism. In 1858 the procession followed a banner with the words 'Erin go bragh: we'll never forget thee', a sentiment that seemed to recognise permanent separation.[93] At the same time the day demanded strong anti-British feelings and equally strong pro-Catholic ones. Thus it must be marked by an official oration or sermon castigating the British government. In 1858 the Reverend J. A. Gallagher produced one; twenty years later the Reverend Father Rooney was still doing the same.[94] In a large sense these were exercises in mythology, designed to relieve some of the tensions of resettlement and therefore containing much comforting falsehood. 'It is a well-known fact,' said Father Rooney, 'that our pagan ancestors were not steeped in any of the degrading practices to which Greece, Rome and Egypt were addicted. Our noble land never offered human sacrifices, nor did she pay homage to the low animals; she adored only the sun, moon and stars, as figures and representatives of light.'[95] After the march, the orations and sermons came the balls and the dinners of the evening, where the sense of being poised between two worlds could be reflected in the toasts and the speeches, though this perception need not only disturb, but could lead to a desire to take the best of both. In 1858 the focus of toasts swung back and forward across the Atlantic: first 'St. Patrick's Day'; then 'Ireland'. Next 'The United States'; and then 'The Shamrock'. Fifth, 'The People', and sixth 'James Buchanan, the President of the United States'. Staying in America, the seventh toast was to 'California and her constituted Authorities', but then the eighth went east to 'The Poets and Dramatists of Ireland'. Back again went the ninth to 'The Memory of Washington'; and yet back again to 'The Memory of the Illustrious Dead of Ireland'. Then followed 'The Press', 'The Army and Navy', 'The Ladies', and 'Robert Tyler of Philadelphia', 'for his advocacy of a transcontinental railroad'.[96]

All over the city by the end of the 'sixties balls and dinners took place, not always without complaint. In 1869 a 'Poor Celt' wrote to the *Morning Call* about the way in which some 'rich' Irish had retired to the 'Occidental' while the poor had to make do with the 'Brooklyn'.[97] Each society prepared its own programme. An advertisement for 'The Twentieth Anniversary Ball of the Sons of the Emerald Isle Benevolent Association' at La Grande Armory Hall gives a flavour of what was expected. 'Alpers' full quadrille band,' said the insertion, 'will furnish the music. John Blake, the celebrated Irish piper, has been secured for the occasion, and those who do not feel inclined to trip "the light fantastic" can enjoy themselves by dancing reels and jigs, at intervals during the evening, to their favourite tunes on the Bagpipes. Tickets, admitting a gentleman and ladies, one dollar.'[98]

The 'Poor Celt' was not, however, alone in having a complaint about the way in which St Patrick's Day was observed. A letter to the editor in the *Monitor* of 23 January 1869 argued that processions should be given up and the money spent more wisely.[99] In 1870 the editor of the paper himself argued that the money normally spent on parades should be used to alleviate the sufferings of the families of the Irish martyrs.[100] It was not possible, however, to change the form of celebration, for it expressed too strongly Irish San Franciscans' feelings. They must march and they must eat and drink, whether it be at the Irish National Banquet with Mayor McCoppin and the Hon. Eugene Casserly, senator elect, or with the St Mary's Temperance Society.[101] Celebration must be public, social and convivial; that was what it was for.

Just as the St Patrick's Day celebrations became more complex and more embracing at the end of the 1860s as the new Irish societies came into being and were ready to take part, so the Irish acknowledgement of the Fourth of July also grew simultaneously. In 1867 the fourth division of the march was composed 'chiefly' of Irish societies. It was led by the Irish Battalion, Companies A, B and C; followed by the Sons of the Emerald Isle, the Irish-American Benevolent Society, the St Mary's Temperance and Library Association, the St Joseph and St Francis Societies, the Labourers' Protective Union, and the Labourers' Union Benevolent, the McMahon Grenadiers, and finished with the Fenians.[102] In 1868 the line of march was very similar, with the additions of Companies A and C of the Irish Republican Army.[103] In 1870 these were no longer able to take part, but the Irish contingent had been strengthened by the Ancient Order of Hibernians. The Labourers' Unions had disappeared, but five avowedly 'benevolent' societies attended, the Father Mathew Temperance and Benevolent, the St Mary's Temperance, the St Joseph Benevolent, and the St Joseph Temperance and Benevolent, together with the Irish-American Benevolent Society.[104] Thus it continued year by year, giving good indication of the health of the Irish societies, for none would miss the celebration if it could make the requisite show. According to an observer of the Fourth of July procession in 1875, its military bands played 'Fenian music', while in 1877 another reported, after seeing the procession of that year, that 'Among the most numerous were a band of "The Ancient Order of Hibernians" carrying a green flag with a harp on it, and so large that the unfortunate standard-bearer could hardly stagger'.[105] Both incidents show how the Irish used the national day for their own equally national ends. It was no accident that the Fenian Sisterhood, in 1868, held its annual ball on 4 July.[106] Irish nationalism was created in America in part through association with American nationalism.[107]

The Irish societies existed not only to protect their members, or to take part as a body in the great national festivals, but also to allow the individual to express his feelings through them when he wished to do so but, alone, would have been unheard. The first occasion when this occurred was a melancholy one: the San Franciscans' procession in honour of Abraham Lincoln. Then the Irish societies marched, but not as a group. The St Joseph's Benevolent Society was in the eighth division, the Irish-American Benevolent in the ninth and the Fenian Brotherhood in the tenth.[108] In 1871 a less unhappy procession celebrated the twenty-fifth anniversary of Pius IX; some 14,000 participated, including thousands of Irish, marching with the Sons of the Emerald Isle, the Irish-American Benevolent Society, the Labourers' Protective Association and the Hibernian Rifles, all in the second division; with the Ancient Order of Hibernians in the third; in the Legion of St Patrick in the fifth; and in the Meagher Guards in the sixth.[109] In 1876 the Catholic population of San Francisco celebrated the city's own anniversary with a march to the Mission. The Irish turned out in force in their societies, as well as providing the major officials of the day. Thirty-two Irish, or Catholic groups with largely Irish membership, marched in all divisions from the fifth to the fourteenth. The crowd would have noted 'The American colours, carried in a line of some six thousand men, with the Irish and Mexican flags', and, if reflective, would have realised that the Irish colours' presence represented the dominance of the Irish in the Catholic Church and the overwhelming importance of the group in city life.[110]

The extraordinary variety of Irish associations in San Francisco in the period suggests a settled, organised community with a deep commitment to both the present and the future. There was no reason why any Irish immigrant should feel lonely or isolated in the city, for there were these many societies willing to welcome him, and to permit the individual to express his feelings while developing, too, a sense of group identity and solidarity. These societies acted not only as an economic but also as a psychological safety net, breaking, at least, any downward fall into despair and alienation. At the same time they were the bricks that built up the public Irish community, and in consequence had another dimension needing discussion, one of political importance. As has been seen, politicians wooed members for their votes and used the Irish societies in their campaigns because they knew that through them they could reach direct into the heart of the Irish community. Since the city boasted this largely stable, generally expanding network of societies, it is not surprising that Irish politicians were successful in organising the Irish vote and acquiring political power. That power was also highly satisfactory to the Irish, for through it they were able to order their civic universe. The extent of their political success is the subject of the following chapter.

Chapter VII
The politics of adjustment

On 30 June 1879 Louis Kaplan, Registrar of Voters for San Francisco, reported that exactly 10,000 of the city's 37,915 electors had been born in Ireland.[1] Thus nearly 27 per cent of the city's voters were Irish-born when, according to the census of the following year, only 20 per cent of the total non-oriental labour force was Irish-born.[2] Greater permanency of the Irish community or a greater predeliction for politics may have been responsible for the difference between these two percentages, but either way the importance of the Irish vote in city politics was clear, if not equally acceptable to all.[3] Nor was the Irish vote an entirely new phenomenon in San Francisco politics. The first report of the country clerk, after the new registry law, showed that on 1 July 1867 3,579 of the 16,550 registered electorate, or close on 22 per cent, had been born in Ireland.[4] The late 'sixties and the decade of the 'seventies saw a continuous stream of declarations of intention to be naturalised, and the granting of certificates of naturalisation to Irish-born immigrants in the city. Between 1866, when records begin, and the middle of 1880 close to 7,500 of these certificates were granted to the Irish-born. The number varied by year: in 1874-75 only 102 were given out; in 1876-77 1,502; but generally, during the period, over 40 per cent of the total went to the Irish-born population of the city.[5]

The Irish-born were the most significant of the foreign-born voters of the city, with their importance increased by the further presence in the electorate of second-generation Irish-Americans. Their party preferences were to have great impact on the political history of the city. Apparently there was no exclusive support for the Democratic Party. Reflecting the special conditions in the city, the spread of the Irish through all levels of occupation and the inability of the native-born to establish exclusive control over the distribution of resources, the Irish had no pressing need defensively to identify with it. Thus those in the higher-status groups were able to respond to other pressures than ethnic hostilities when making up their political minds, and some consequently responded to the voice of their class, though the Protestant Irish probably responded to ethnic pressures when, as it was said, they supported the Republicans.[6] Even so, since the main part of the Irish community was not in the happy position of belonging to one of the city's elite groups, as say the directors of the Hibernia Savings and Loan Society were, it is also true that the majority of the Irish in San Francisco did reply to social, economic and political conditions by joining the Democratic Party. Hostile outsiders could believe, wrongly, that all Irish were Democrats, but when in September 1865 the *Alta* said, 'The Irish citizens, as a rule, went for the Democratic ticket,' the paper was correct in implying that some did not.[7] There were traditional attempts to try to separate the Irish voter from the Democratic Party, but what was unusual was that there was a chance of success in attempts to keep the entire Irish community from voting for Democratic candidates.[8] In crucial elections, such as that of 1867, it was not surprising therefore that an element of hysteria crept into discussions as to which way the Irish would vote. Irish voters were reminded that 'thanks to the Democracy' they had rights and offices 'from Senatorship down to Post Office Clerks', while rumours were put about that the Republicans were bragging that they would buy 1,500 Irish and German votes. The Republican candidate for Governor, Charles C. Gorham, was accused of having said that Irishmen were worse than Negroes, and ethnic rivalries were played on by the report that

The managers of the tide-land-Negro-and-Chinese-equality meeting at Union Hall, on Saturday night, had the unblushing effrontery to use the Irish flag among their decorations, notwithstanding it is the open avowal of Gorham and his partisans that they regard a negro [sic] as better than an Irishman. This impudent act is a flagrant insult to the entire Irish people, and is so regarded by all true Irishmen.[9]

Nevertheless it was true that for most Irish voters the health of the Democratic Party was of the greatest political importance. They were unfortunate in that during the period 1856–66 two events weakened the party considerably and so diminished the Irish political impact. First, the Committee of Vigilance in 1856 led to the foundation of the People's Party in the city, a body that controlled San Francisco politics for ten years; second, the Civil War led to the division of the Democrats into two major factions, one of which remained independent, with a debilitating reputation for secessionism, the other fusing with Republicans in the Union party. The combined result was to produce a stagnancy in city politics between 1856 and 1865 which partly reflected the apathy of Irish voters, who had no vehicle for their political ambitions with the decline of their party. In 1856 11,035 city voters went to the polls in an important fight between the new People's Party and the Democrats.[10] Ten years later in 1865–66, despite the growth of the city's population from around 50,000 to nigh on 90,000, only 12,997 voters turned out for the municipal elections.[11] Yet in November 1864 no fewer than 21,024 electors cast their votes in the contest between Lincoln and McClellan, marking the extent of disillusion with city politics.[12] It was not until 1867 that municipal politics recovered some vitality with the resurgence of the Democrats. In that year 9,689 voters turned out in the Second, Fourth, Sixth, Eighth, Tenth and Twelfth wards alone, to vote for the supervisors; 9,759 electors voted in all wards for Frank McCoppin, the Democratic candidate for mayor, as against 7,014 for Thomas Young, the Unionist candidate, and 644 for two other runners.[13] Once the burden of the Civil War was lifted from the Democratic Party's shoulders, and once the People's Party had melted into the Republican Party, the Democrats were given a new opportunity to re-enter city politics to fight for the now vacant ground; simultaneously the Irish began to register to vote with new enthusiasm.[14] In the period between 1 July and 1 September 1867 the number of Irish-born on the Great Register of Voters went up from 3,579 to 5,366, an increase of nigh on 50 per cent.[15] The years between 1856 and 1866 turned out in retrospect to be exceptional. After 1866 the Irish vote became an aggressive reality of San Francisco politics once more as it had been before the formation of the Committee of Vigilance of 1856.

The strength of the Irish vote naturally produced the accusation that Irish were mindless followers of the

Democratic Party, particularly in the Republican press, and consequent denials that this was so.[16] Later, at the end of the period, much play was made of the strong Irish and Roman Catholic element in the Workingmen's Party, in attempts to discredit it.[17] The fear of the 'low Irish' in politics could suggest that the Irish electorate was particularly ignorant, particularly radical, particularly poor and particularly ready to undermine the propertied classes, but such a set of fears, though often in the nativist mind, conflicted with certain important facts.[18] The first of these was that, whatever the outward aspect of the Irish community to the nativist, whether it seemed to consist mainly of unskilled labourers and whether the Irish element at the polls seemed by and large to be drunken, rowdy and badly dressed, there was very little difference between the unskilled Irish and other Irish when it came to naturalisation. In 1870, according to what the Irish of San Francisco told the census marshals, 2,634 of the 3,926 unskilled Irish in the city were naturalised, compared with 5,751 of the 8,245 in other occupations, giving respectively percentages of 67 and 70.[19] When, however, the unskilled came to register they do seem to have been a little more eager to do so than the skilled, perhaps because of the prestige, perhaps because the political bosses found the unskilled more amenable; either way, whereas labourers made up only about 24 per cent of the Irish-born workforce in 1870, they provided over 33 per cent of the registered voters; while in 1880, whereas only about 22 per cent of the Irish workforce were labourers, 26 per cent of the registered Irish electorate were.[20] Further, in 1880, 32 per cent of the registered Irish electorate were in unskilled occupations. But, equally, such figures meant that in 1870 67 per cent of the registered Irish electorate were not labourers, and that in 1880 68 per cent of the registered Irish voters were not in unskilled occupations.[21]

Another important consideration ignored by nativists was that the socio-economic composition of the Irish vote could vary by district. In the Eleventh ward, which had a tradition of voting Democrat and which between 1860 and 1874 was represented by the Irish-born trio of Frank McCoppin, P.H. Canavan and Edward Commins, a sample of some 542 registered Irish voters shows that only about 28 per cent of them were unskilled; that approximately 20 per cent were in white-collar occupations; and that at least half the remaining 52 per cent were skilled rather than semi-skilled workers. This ward comprised most of the southern area of the city. Its boundaries were adjusted from time to time, but in 1880 ran along Ridley to Market to Seventh and then to the Bay. [22] It was an area that went through great development in the 'seventies, was comparatively remote from the downtown area and included many home owners among its population. Towards the other end of the scale was the First ward, in 1880 defined as the area of the city bounded by the Bay, Kearney and Washington, one settled in an earlier period of the city's history. There the picture of the Irish-born voter was more comforting to the nativist. There were 325 Irish voters in the ward's first four precincts, and roughly 45 per cent were in unskilled occupations. Nevertheless even here over half the voters were not, and approximately 20 per cent were in white-collar or skilled occupations. Between these two examples lay that of the Seventh ward, in 1880 defined as south of Market and north of Harrison, between the Bay and Second Street, an area of significant Irish concentration. There a sample of 169 Irish-born registered voters revealed 36 per cent in unskilled occupations and approximately 40 per cent in white-collar or skilled occupations. This is not to say that nativist views had no foundation in fact. What they did reflect was, in the main, the difference between the Irish-born and the native communities, at the extreme. For instance, even in the Twelfth ward on the north-western edge of the city in 1880, whereas 55 per cent of native-born registered voters were in white-collar occupations, only 20 per cent of Irish were, and whereas but 2 per cent of native registered voters were in unskilled occupations, 31 per cent of the Irish were.[23] Such differences coloured the nativist's perception of the total Irish electorate.

The political history of San Francisco between 1848 and 1880 can be broken down into four periods: from 1848 to the 1856 Committee of Vigilance; from 1856 to 1866, the period of the People's Party, and, within those years, the Civil War; from 1866 to the onset of the Workingmen's Party in 1877–78; and the close of the period, during which the Workingmen's Party grew startlingly and then no less wonderfully declined. Irish political life naturally took its quality from the events that characterised these periods.

The political history of the earliest years of American San Francisco had little structure while the population regarded itself as transient, *en route* for the mines or for 'home' in the east, using the collection of tents and shacks by Yerba Buena cove simply as a fitting or refitting station. As 1849 went by, as more men turned their back on the mines, but not on the state, and decided that fortune was more likely to favour them in the city, the need for political organisation developed, to ensure that whatever resources did come to be permanently available by the Bay were put into the right hands. Men arrived with political ambition who saw the city as the probable cornerstone of any career they might erect, and their need for support drove them to political organisation. Such a man was David C. Broderick, a second-generation Irish-American, born in Washington, D.C., but politically matured in New York City, even if he had never been a member of the Tammany Society.[24] His connections initially seem to have been primarily with New Yorkers but his Irish ancestry was an important political asset.[25] Broderick was well enough known in the city by the end of 1849 to win the Democratic primary held on Christmas Eve to decide who the party candidate should be in the January election for the state senate.[26] Broderick's arrival in the state legislature after a massive victory, in which he received all but twenty-eight votes in a total of over 2,500 cast, led to an increasing accent on organisation, seen in the message of the 'Address of the Democratic Members of the Legislature' on 2 February 1850. This, in Tammany style, argued for a tightly knit structure based on country, town, club and precinct meetings.[27] Broderick practised what he preached, and by the autumn of 1850 had established a San Francisco organisation called, significantly, 'Young Ireland' by its foes.[28] He was a natural focus for the Irish voter.[29]

Broderick's power did not mean rapid and complete political success for the San Francisco Irish. Broderick, as a contemporary said, 'aimed to manage men rather than municipal measures', because his overriding aim increasingly became his own election to the United States Senate.[30] Consequently he concentrated on forwarding his own career rather than on the interests of the Irish or any other social group in the city. At the same time there was a strong southern influence in the city Democratic Party which produced almost as much intra- as inter-party warfare, dissipating political energies. This is not to say that Irish office-holders did not appear as the Democrats began to tighten their hold on city politics, but that they were hampered by nativism both within and without the party. 'The Chivalry', as the southern wing was known, was, as events in 1854–55 were to prove, not above abandoning the party in the hopes of destroying the Irish threat to its domination, and in many ways the battle, during the 'fifties, between the two groups for the control of their party antedated by some seventy years the struggle for the national Democratic Party between southerners and immigrants.

Broderick's inability to establish unchallenged control over the party in San Francisco permitted even further rivalries than the simple one between southerners and immigrants. Some Democratic politicians belonged to neither of these groups and pursued their own courses, producing a bewildering kaleidoscope of alliances from election to election. Men who might seem indistinguishable to the nativist were extremely hostile political bedfellows. One of Broderick's greatest enemies in the city was Pat Canney, a Roman Catholic Irishman in the Customs House.[31] When two of the victims of the 1856 Committee of Vigilance, James P. Casey and Edward McGowan, first met, Casey wished to fight a duel over the defeat of a candidate he fancied by a candidate supported by McGowan.[32] James O'Meara supported not Broderick but Gwin in the extremely turbulent struggle for control over the Democratic Party in 1854.[33] Such confusing wrangles among the politicians help to explain why it is very difficult to descry a definite Irish presence in city politics before 1854. Irish Democratic energies, like those of Democrats generally, were too dissipated in factionalism, it would seem, though it would be unwise to press the point too finally, as the evidence is by no means compelling in any direction. Such signs as there are, including, in these years, the lack of any sustained invective against the Irish vote, suggests that it was taking its character from its surroundings. These were fluid: society was open;

there was no need for a tightly knit defensive political stance.

Comparatively speaking, the Irish enjoyed a large measure of political freedom in the early years. The onset of party politics, however, was bound to reactivate political attitudes brought to the west coast from the east, and among these was anti-Irish feeling, which was probably always present but of low intensity to date. The April 1851 elections did produce the story that 'At the [Whig] primary election in the third ward on Wednesday night, a wild Irishman was brought in to vote a ticket, when his vote was challenged, on the ground that he was not a citizen. At this he became very indignant, and said that they were not gentlemen in that ward, for they never challenged his vote in the second ward, from which he had just come, and where he had just voted.'[34] But this was an election won by the Whigs; consequently tempers need not be frayed too far; humour, not invective, could rule. Politics was generally in these first years of American democracy a fairly violent game in many ways, and those who took part could not be gentle to be successful. The danger for the Irish here was that hostile opinion could quickly forget that violence was often purely political and see it as culturally endemic if it needed to do so. It was an easy step to arguing that a group like the Irish was innately violent and so could not take part in ordinary political intercourse without harming those with whom it came into contact, and thence to arguing that it should not be permitted positions from which it was likely to do harm. Unfortunately in a society largely male, poorly policed, and without a network of inherited institutions which could be used to bear down on the unruly, physical force was often evident and went unchecked. The close connection between law and politics did not help. For instance, when Charles Duane, one of Broderick's henchmen, appeared before the Hon F. Tilford, one of Broderick's associates, in the Recorder's Court and answered three different charges—'Firing a pistol within the City limits, contempt of Court in not appearing to answer a citation yesterday, and lastly for assaulting an officer'—the subsequent events could lead an observer to doubt the value of his courts. Duane was excused on the first two charges, as it appeared he fired at a dog which had just bitten him, and was then attacking a Mr

Fenno, and that he had torn up the citation without knowing what it contained, and 'some mitigating circumstances appearing in the case of the assault, he was only fined $1'.[35]

If there was evidence that those with friends in high places could escape the penalties for violent behaviour, then it was not surprising that society turned its back on its own legal institutions when it felt that the level of violence had risen to dangerously destructive levels. Similarly it could be expected that those who feared that political violence might be punished by a less political legal system opposed the substitution of a Committee of Vigilance for the regularly constituted courts. Aside from the theoretical arguments against the surrender of sovereignty to an *ad hoc* body were the more practical ones as to what limits such a body would observe to its actions and the potential danger to its political enemies in its organisation. The creation of the 1851 Committee of Vigilance in San Francisco on 9 June by political enemies of Broderick ensured his attitude to it, beyond whether he would have opposed it on grounds drawn from his political theory.[36] Broderick's view of the committee is encapsulated in a letter he wrote about Samuel Brannan's disinclination to accept any responsibility for the action of the Committee of Vigilance in hanging its victim, Jenkins, for what he said of Brannan showed what he felt of the body to which he belonged. 'Of that gentleman,' wrote Broderick, 'it is unnecessary for me to say anything further, notorious as he is for his violence and contempt of law. He is widely known as a turbulent man, ready to trample upon all laws that oppose his private opinions or his private ends.'[37] For Broderick the committee ignored basic legal rights. It was hardly surprising that his Irish and other supporters who could expect the committee's hostility were consequently far from friendly: Charles Duane, for instance, pursued a highly obstructive course towards it.[38]

It has often been noticed that the committee turned its attention to the immigrants from Australia.[39] What needs adding to the traditional account is that many of these Australians were in fact Irish, who had come to California from the antipodes.[40] In pointing out that there was an ethnic and political dimension to the work of the 1851 Committee of

Vigilance, there is no suggestion that it did not also have other goals, directed towards reforming and strengthening law and order in the city. Those whom it punished seem, by and large, to have deserved their fate, and there is no evidence that they would have met it had the committee not taken its stand. Yet it is undeniable that the committee had its political ends, which became more articulated in its latter days, though, unlike the outcome of the 1856 committee, these aims were not shared even by all members of its movement. Independent nominations, drawn from both Whigs and Democrats, were made by the committee for the elections of September 1851 for county and township offices, and they were in the main successful.[41] Because of the dispute between Whigs and Democrats over whether an election was necessary for city offices, no nominations were made for them by the Whigs, who might have used the committee for party purposes, and consequently the character of politics did not change.[42] Broderick's position in the Democratic Party remained strong, and Irish voters were not likely to have felt barred from politics.

The period between the 1851 Committee of Vigilance and the rise of the Know Nothings in 1854 was not, however, one in which large and successful political machines based on immigrant or other voters could have been constructed. The population was far too transient for permanent relationships. The Boards of Aldermen changed composition almost monthly.[43] It was said in 1855 that the city's population was less than it had been in 1853.[44] The Democratic Party, potentially the best ground for the growth of a machine, remained riven between its many factions.[45] Democratic and Whig primaries were reported to be both violent and corrupt, suggesting the inability of politicians to control the results as they would have liked.[46] On 16 March 1852 the *Alta* reported that in the election for members of the Democratic General Committee and Ward Committees 'several persons were guilty of carrying bricks in their hats'; while in the October primary elections in the Seventh ward 'a band of rowdies seized the ballot box and scattered the ballots to the four winds'.[47] Because the political situation was so chaotic San Franciscans had little sense at this time of a steady increase in the influence of the foreign-born in affairs, but, at the same time, in remarking on the prevalent corruption and violence they were preparing themselves for an easy shift into nativism, should it be argued that the evils in the system were the exclusive responsiblity of the foreign-born.[48] By October 1852 there was complaint that the Democratic Party particularly, but also the Whigs, had become the victims of spoilsmen. 'Has it come to such a pass,' asked the *Alta* rhetorically, 'that respectable Whigs and Democrats are used as mere things of wax?'[49] In November 1852 it was claimed that the Democrats had not served the city's best interests in accepting Peter Donahue's gas contract, for it was 30 per cent more expensive than another 'equally advantageous and responsible'.[50] No mention was made, however, of Donahue's Irishness. Belief in political corruption, however, was widespread.

In this situation, too fluid to give much of a perception of group differences, personality was given greater importance. Broderick remained a target of abuse and continued to be accused of organising violence at the polls, as the following verse suggests:

> Hail to the chief who in triumph advances,
> Noted for playing political 'roots',
> Who has broken the points of the chivalry's lances,
> And 'lam'd' all the Roman men 'out of their boots'.
> Then the victor's wreath twine for him,
> Go the whole swine for him
> Who maketh our leaders his tools or his toys;
> We'll all go of course for him,
> And shout till we're hoarse for him,
> Broderick, the chief of Bowery bhoys.[51]

Once again, though as yet no explicit connection was made between the immigrant voters and the political boss, the possibility lay there ready to be exploited should the need arise.

Nevertheless, on the eve of the Know Nothing movement there was, beyond continuing argument over the place of denominationally run education, little deliberate sectarianism in politics. On 26 May 1854 the *Alta* remarked that 'Without yielding one jot or tittle in their peculiar doctrines to each other, the religious associations of San Francisco have ever exhibited toward each other a kindliness of feeling, proceeding from an acknowledgement of the right to differ in opinion, even upon what might be considered cardinal points'.[52] On the very next day the same paper remarked of Know Nothingism, 'We do not believe there is a State in the Union where the proscriptive and sectional principles of Nativeism [sic] would be apt to meet with so little favour as in California.'[53] When the party triumphed in the September elections the paper argued that it was its promises of reform and the desire for clean elections that led to its victory, a view shared by other observers.[54]

With the Know Nothing victory in seven of the eight wards, however, matters changed considerably. Whatever the reasons for the Know Nothing triumph in San Francisco, one of its important planks nationally was its nativism, and victory gave nativism a sounding board.[55] As the May 1855 elections approached the issue of the foreign-born began to emerge, for it was inseparable from the existence of the Know Nothing party. At first editors denied that nativism was an issue—though it was a sign of changed conditions that they needed to do so—but later it was stated, 'The issues, it was generally understood, were to be between the Know Nothing, or American party, and the Anti-Know Nothings, comprising the foreign-born population of the city and the entire strength of the two wings of the old Democratic Party.'[56] Perhaps reflecting the emergence of the nativist issue and the opposition to it, the Democrats took four of the eight wards on this occasion, including the Second, where Irish-born R.H. Tobin defeated the perennial nativist Frank Pixley.[57]

A youthful coalition of nativism and reform can be seen in *The Political Letters of 'Caxton'*, published in San Francisco during 1855.[58] Letter VIII established a connection between despotism and corruption and linked both with Broderick. Californians, said the author, 'bolt at the very idea of despotism. They can distinguish no difference between the serf of Nicholas and the slave of Broderick ... between that banded clique which unites to plunder the Treasury and monopolize public offices, and that gang of midnight thieves, who, with sling-shots in their hands and stilletos at their sides, fraternize with ruffians, for the purposes of robbery and assassination.'[59] The author married political corruption and the foreign-born, attacking the 'poor foreigners and ignorant exiles... stuffing the ballot-box and violating the right of suffrage'.⁶⁰ Five years was not sufficient to learn self-government.

> Where one man emerges from the mass of debased and down-trodden exiles who annually flock to America, thousands prove unworthy of the privileges which our law extends to them, and becomes [sic] dangerous elements in our government. The complaint which John Mitchel made of the Irish citizens, applies with equal force to all our foreign population. By immigration they do not cease to be Irish... they do not lose all nationality except that which they assume. They band themselves together in cliques and coteries, and vote in solid phalanx for favourite men. They go up to the ballot boxes as 'the Irish vote', or the 'German vote', and not as Whigs or Democrats, or States' rights men, or nullifiers or abolitionists. They possess no individual opinions. They follow their ringleader, and as he jumps so precisely do they all jump.⁶¹

Once nativism and reform had been combined as issues, those who opposed both became doubly suspect. Unfortunately there was evidence that supporters of the Democratic Party were corrupt. Edward McGowan, soon to play a major role as a fugitive from the second Committee of Vigilance, was accused in the 1854 elections of trying to stuff ballot boxes, doing the dirty work in part in the banking house of Palmer Cook & Co., bankers to David C. Broderick.⁶² In August 1855 another to become a prominent victim of the Committee of Vigilance, Wooley Kearny, 'was tried... before the Mayor for interfering with an officer while striving to quell the disturbance at the corner of Kearny and Commercial streets. Kearny insists,' said the report, 'that he was only actuated by the laudable desire for peace-making.' Violence reappeared at the Democratic primary elections, involving other soon-to-be-famous figures. James P. Casey was reported as shooting and wounding J. W. Bagley, also to be a fellow victim in 1856, at the Sixth ward polls; also of stabbing Mr Cushing. Martin Gallagher, it was reported, was involved in three fights.⁶³ Simultaneously those who had hoped to see the Know Nothings as a permanent vehicle for political reform and/or domination were being disappointed. Whereas in the aldermanic elections in May 1855 the Democrats polled 5,641 to the Know Nothings' 5,577, in September the Democratic candidate for Governor, John Bigler, received 6,435 votes in the city against the Know Nothing candidate J. Neely Johnson, who received 4,874.⁶⁴ It was among such darkening political horizons that the second Committee of Vigilance was organised in May 1856.

Although William T. Coleman, president of this committee, as he had been of the previous one, wrote, 'The personnel of the committee were men above the average. They were selected for their worth, integrity, and good standing in the community... Politics, creed, nationality, or profession were not considered, nor thought of,' he did admit that 'The largest element of the committee was of northern and western men, chiefly representing the mercantile, manufacturing, and vested interests'.⁶⁵ Further, he accepted that James King of William, whose death at the hands of James P. Casey gave the committee its main impetus, 'had aroused a Roman Catholic influence hostile to himself by ill-advised strictures on one of their clergy'.⁶⁶ Traditionally the view of the committee has been similar to that put forward by Thomas G. Cary in 1877, that it grew from the situation where 'For some time the corruption in the courts of law, the insecurity of the ballot-box at elections, and the infamous character of many of the public officials had been the subject of complaint'. Further, King had been 'a man of good education... much respected', whereas Casey had been 'well fitted to act as champion of the political gamblers in San Francisco, for he had spent two years in Sing Sing prison before coming to California, and he had the reputation of being the most accomplished stuffer of ballot-boxes in the city of San Francisco'.⁶⁷ Whatever the characters of the two men—and there is reason to believe that Cary may have been kinder to King than necessary—when the dust cleared in the aftermath of the committee's work, it was discovered that it had performed a very neat surgical operation on the body politic and removed by hanging, imprisonment and exile some twenty-nine presumably cancerous members, who were, however, very noticeably Democrats almost to a man, to a large degree of Irish extraction, Roman Catholics in religion, and sometimes, but not always, friends of David C. Broderick. Nor were the victims unimportant politicians. Edward McGowan had been a J.P., an Associate Justice of the Court of Sessions of the city and Commissioner for Emigration; J. W. Bagley had been a member of the Assembly in 1853; Charles P. Duane was Chief Engineer of the San Francisco Fire Department; James P. Casey had been Deputy County Treasurer for two years, a member of the Board of Supervisors and an Inspector of Elections; William Mulligan had been Collector of State and County Licences, Deputy Sheriff and Jailer; Billy Carr had been a member of the Charter Convention, General Inspector and manager of the First ward polls; Martin Gallagher had frequently been, along with William Lewis, Judge of Elections in the First ward; Terence Kelly had been Judge of Elections at the Presidio; James Cusick had been similarly employed at the Sixth ward.[68] Such a roster suggested the extent of the corruption perceived in the system, and why it was thought necessary to cleanse it of certain elements by non-political means, for political ones would have been insufficient.

That the political system was altered by non-political means cannot be doubted. The justification came through a confusion of the concepts of politics, law and morality. Political action was cloaked by arguments drawn from political theory, even from religion, and given a significance far beyond its desserts. According to an apologist, 'One of the most marked features of the present movement in this State, is the unanimity with which the clergy have approved of it and the churches have engaged in it . . . of all the ministers of this State, we know of only one or two who have not expressed themselves favourable to the action of the Committee; and nearly every one of these has preached upon the subject. And the Catholic priests, if not in favour of the Committee, are not advocates of armed opposition against it.'[69] The Catholic clergy were quiet rather than approving, but the general widespread support for the movement showed that the majority of San Franciscans accepted the self-justifications of the committee, some perhaps because of the quasi-military excitements unleashed, some perhaps because they believed society to be in peril, and some because they felt the same rules need not apply to aliens as to themselves.

In the light of the nativism which was part of the force propelling the committee, it is not surprising to find that the Irish of the city opposed its works. It was rumoured that the committee even considered arresting Broderick, but it was not given the opportunity, and probably lacked the ability to do so directly, though indirectly it was successful in what John S. Hittell called its 'main purpose and its most valuable results', that is, 'to drive from power the tricksters by whose help he held control of the Democratic organization in San Francisco'.[70] Consequently, and not surprisingly, Broderick opposed the committee; so did his Irish supporters, who joined him in a Law and Order party, whose rank and file, it was said, were 'without exception, natives of Ireland'.[71] By contrast, the French, English, Scots and Germans supported the Vigilance Committee, so that the opposition to it rested on the Irish alone.[72]

Among those who kept themselves aloof from the committee were the Jackson Guards, who had a heavily Irish membership. They made the grounds of their opposition clear in a letter to the *Herald*, publicising the fact that they had refused to take an oath to support the Vigilance Committee, for, as they said, it was 'an oath, composed of sectarian insolence and intended to wound religious feelings'. The wording was as follows: 'I do solemnly promise and swear in the presence of Almighty God and these witnesses—by the hope of a future state—by the blessed Virgin Mary and all the Saints in the calendar, that I will not bear arms against the Vigilance Committee of San Francisco. So help me God and the blessed Virgin.'[73]

The Irish were in the minority, however, by comparison with those who supported the committee. Broderick left the city and was soon involved in his eventually successful bid for the United States Senate. The absence of 'his portly frame, rowdy swagger, and face of vulgar aspect' was remarked on by his enemies, who continued to attack him to maintain their momentum and control of city affairs.[74] There was a moment of doubt when it seemed that Broderick had used revulsion from the Vigilance Committee among Democrats to enlarge his hold upon the party in the city, but this vanished in the triumph of the People's ticket in the November elections. The People's ticket received 6,834 votes, against 4,001 for other candidates, and elected eleven out of twelve supervisors.[75] Not all those who voted for the People's Party were nativists, but the result was sufficient to depress those like Eugene Casserly who were both Irish and Democrats. Writing to Isaac

V. Fowler in New York in May 1857, he commented, 'Three years or four ago, you would have liked this country; but now, the people are sadly demoralized by Vigilance Committees, a licentious and cowardly press, and an almost universal passion for defamation.'[76] He would have been further depressed in the following year had he read what was now being passed as a true history of San Francisco politics in the past six years. According to the English publicist Ernest Seyd, after 1851:

> The gamblers and murderers' party managed to keep uppermost some few years. Political tricksters of some talent appeared in the country, and managed to organise a party that long reigned supreme, and may be styled the *Irish democracy* party, consisting of a great number of the foreigners out here, but mostly of Irishmen, who voted, whether citizens or not, under the guidance of a gang of meddling politicians, Jesuits, demagogues, and ballot-box stuffers ... Matters were brought to a crisis in May, 1856, when the inhabitants ... rose in a mass to shake off the yoke—not of the fellows in office, because they had been elected, whether rightly or wrongly—but of the murderers, ballot-box stuffers, gamblers, etc."[77]

The nativist view could now emerge naked and unashamed. Even if the committee had never decided explicitly to proscribe the foreign-born in general, and the Irish most particularly, the results had been in that direction, so that for some years many Irish Democrats appeared to turn their backs on city politics to wait for more favourable opportunities.

The situation was not, however, one of unrelieved gloom for the Irish. Even during the period of the People's Party they could draw comfort from political developments in three areas all of which suggested that the loss of initiative in 1854–56 did not mean a permanently secondary role in San Francisco politics, nor the complete exclusion of the group from all political life. First, reflecting the diversity of position and political feeling among the Irish in the city, certain of them took office in the People's Party, revealing that class rather than ethnicity or religion had the greater say with them. In 1858 Thomas Young was elected Supervisor on the People's ticket for the Fifth ward; being succeeded in 1860 by Dominic Gaven.[78] In 1861 Gaven was joined by Myles D. Sweeny, the prominent Irish banker, who was elected from the Second ward, though he was defeated for re-election in 1863.[79] Gaven resigned in May 1863, when the mayor, H. F. Teschemacher, a member of the People's Party, nominated E. C. Kennedy, also an Irishman, to succeed him. Kennedy retired in February 1864, thus leaving the People's Party without an Irish-born Supervisor for the last two years of its life.[80] But the party could not be accused of a totally proscriptive anti-Irish bias.

At the same time Irish-born San Franciscans appeared among the Supervisors of the Democratic Party. In 1858 William McKibben was elected for the Ninth ward, though he remained in the office for but a year.[81] In 1859 John Lynch was elected from the Twelfth ward for a term of two years.[82] In 1860 he was joined by Frank McCoppin, beginning his political career in the city, who won election from the Eleventh ward, which he was to represent until 1867.[83] In 1863 M. Cody recaptured the Twelfth ward for the 'Citizens'.[84] One quarter of the Board of Supervisors in the period 1860–63 was thus born in Ireland, though by 1865 only McCoppin remained. Nevertheless in the interim the Irish community could not complain of its representation on the Board.

Even if such triumphs were local and limited and did not include, for instance, nomination to the mayoralty, there were a third set of heartening political signs in state-wide politics. Broderick won his Senate seat, and though his victory soon turned to ashes he did raise others a notch or two along with himself. Men like John Conness and Eugene Casserly advanced in the Democratic ranks behind him. At the same time non-Broderick Irishmen like John G. Downey were making their way up within the general Democratic organisation.[85] Casserly remained in the regular party when the Democrats split over the Lecompton constitution, but Conness was nominated for the Lieutenant-governorship by the Anti-Lecompton Democrats in the elections of 1859. Conness's opponents were Downey for the regular Democrats and J. F. Kennedy for the Republicans. Kennedy ran well ahead of his running mate, but Conness and Downey ran behind theirs in San Francisco, not suggesting strong ethnic interest in the election.[86]

In the summer of 1861 the Union Democratic State Convention met to nominate a candidate for the gubernatorial elections in the autumn. Conness received the nomination on the fourteenth ballot, after strong opposition from the supporters of both Downey and Casserly.[87] Ironically, however, it was agreed that the Irishman would probably drive away about six thousand of the Irish in the state who had voted for Stephen A. Douglas the year before.⁸⁸ As far as San Francisco was concerned, there, it was said, it would be remembered that 'Conness was an active opponent of the Montgomery School bill, a measure which zealous Catholics desired to pass'. Consequently 'The *Monitor,* the Catholic organ,' it was said, 'is bitterly opposed to him, and no doubt chiefly for that reason,' and its hostility could lead to the loss of a thousand Irish votes in the city.⁸⁹ Indeed, whereas Douglas electors had received 3,573 votes in the city in a total poll of 13,593, Conness received 3,177 in a total poll of 15,154.⁹⁰ He also ran behind the Union Democratic candidates for Congress and for the Lieutenant-governorship.

But Conness's day was yet to come. On 10 February 1863 it was reported that he had been elected on the sixty-ninth ballot to the United States Senate by the state legislature.⁹¹ Conness, it has been said, did not want the Douglas Democrats to fuse with the Unionists, but he did profit from the fact that when the two Union factions destroyed each other's chances of the Senate seat, in a welter of recriminations over bribery, he seemed, in the end, acceptable to the main body of the legislature.⁹² Opinion was very divided in the state over his suitability.⁹³ The San Francisco *Evening Bulletin* thought

> Though he is not the best, it must be granted that he is not the worst man in the world for the position... His canvas had been conducted decently and in order. Nobody has charged him with buying, bribing or bullying anybody... His lack of money has been paraded as a virtue, and if he has made a slate contingent on his election he has been shrewd enough and his friends obedient enough to keep it quite concealed.⁹⁴

The *Alta,* however, asked simply, 'Is there cause for wonder that we are at war today, and that disintegration threatens the nation?'⁹⁵ In the future he was to be called 'the little renegade Irishman' by those who did not approve of his having snatched so high a political prize from those who presumably had more right to it.⁹⁶ But he was the first Irish-born United States Senator of the post-Famine years.

In September 1863 Downey was nominated by the Democrats for the governorship but was outpolled in San

Francisco by 9,271 votes to 5,450 and lost the election in the state at large.[97] The approach of the 1864 presidential election, however, heartened the Democrats in the city and the Irish among them. Their opponents were riven by faction, reportedly over the plans to redistrict San Francisco, but also over the possibility of Negro suffrage.[98] The city was also given the unusual sight of two Irish-born political generals attacking each other over what was becoming the increasingly delicate question of post-emancipation America. Conness, it was reported, denounced Casserly as

> the head and front of the disunion party in California. He called upon God to take Irishmen out of the power of such men as he, and make them apostles of liberty. O'Connell had denounced slavery. The greatest bard of Ireland had written paeans to liberty. He inveighed against the *Monitor*, which had attacked him as one unworthy to address Irishmen. He insisted that an Irishman was ennobled by becoming an American citizen.[99]

In return Casserly indignantly repudiated the charge of disloyalty.[100] An editorial pointed out to Catholics that since the anti-slavery bull of Pope Gregory XVI in November 1839 'We do not see how zealous Catholics can make their enmity to emancipation appear consistent with their religion'.[101] The Unionists held firm and the Lincoln electors carried the city and the state, but 8,321 voted in San Francisco for McClellan against 12,667 for Lincoln.[102] According to a foreign observer at the time, 'The great majority of Irish votes in California ... were cast, not for Lincoln, the apostle of liberty, but for M'Clellan [*sic*], the Copperhead or Democratic candidate.' However, 'the majority of North-of-Ireland men in America voted for Lincoln'.[103] The *Alta* suggested that Catholics and Jews had been assailed in the election campaign and had therefore voted Democratic to provide McClellan with such a good showing.[104]

As the war ended Casserly moved to the forefront of San Francisco Democratic politics.[105] His roots lay deep in the Irish community there and he found it easy to articulate Irish views. In September 1865 he made a speech revealing that two sources of discontent were emerging, first from the lack of a specific contract law and, second from the problem of race. Echoing John C. Calhoun, Casserly maintained, 'The

Democratic Party had always held that our institutions contemplated only the white race'.¹⁰⁶ When the Freedmen's Bureau Bill was vetoed, San Francisco Democrats endorsed Andrew Johnson by resolution and by torchlight processions. Casserly was well aware that the Irish were coming to feel threatened from two directions, by the Chinese as well as the black. The Chinese threat produced anti-coolie clubs which were linked with ward clubs, thus producing a new source of political impetus. Labour organisations with an Irish membership and an anti-Chinese bias helped to revitalise the Democratic Party.¹⁰⁷ By the middle of 1867 there was dismay among even those who supported the People's Party at the way in which the Union Party primary elected more candidates nominated by the Workingmen, who had previously been reported as indulging in 'coarse invective and out of place vituperation' against the People's Party, than did the People's Committee.¹⁰⁸

It was, however, the Democrats who benefited most from what the successful candidate for Governor, Henry H. Haight, was to say was 'a protest against... populating this fair State with a race of Asiatics—against sharing with inferior races the government of the country'.¹⁰⁹ Haight received 10,461 votes in San Francisco, against 6,363 for the quite widely unpopular George C. Gorham.¹¹⁰ Whereas the state legislature had contained thirty-one Union and nine Democratic senators, sixty-one Union and nineteen Democratic assemblymen in the sixteenth session, 1867–68, the seventeenth saw twenty-one Union and nineteen Democratic senators, and fifty-two Democratic and twenty-eight Union assemblymen.¹¹¹ The Democratic triumph reached a conclusion in December 1867 when forty-four of the Democratic caucus, on their fifth ballot, voted that Eugene Casserly should become the next United States Senator from California.¹¹² On 2 December 1867 the Irish Democrats of San Francisco enjoyed their finest hour so far. Senator-elect Casserly arrived in the city to be greeted by the mayor, Frank McCoppin, and five of the military bodies making up the Irish Battalion.¹¹³ McCoppin had also scored a resounding victory in the September elections and presided over a Board of Supervisors containing P. H. Daly, of the First ward, Edward Nunan, of the Tenth, and P. H. Canavan of the

Eleventh, all Irish-born San Franciscans.[114]

No group could succeed as the Irish had now done without there being ripples of resentment. The important point is the magnitude of the hostility which accompanied the accretion of political power. Tension there was: some disguised in humour. In the May 1861 elections the story went that 'The general order which reigned everywhere was a matter of surprise to a recent importation from the Emerald Isle, who, having hoisted in more than his share of whiskey, was much incensed that it was "twelve o'clock and not a blow struck yet!" to the great amusement of the crowd'.[115] In 1863 William H. Brewer wrote: 'A friend tells an election anecdote, which he says is true—true or not, it is good. Two Irishmen meet at the polls, one accosts the other:

No. 1: 'Mike—hev yer vowted?'
No. 2: 'Yes.'
No. 1: 'Vowt agin fur Downey, for the damned Yankees are staleing the counthry away from us.'[116]

At the same time however, importantly, the Irish could laugh at themselves, exhibiting a level of political self-confidence as well as literary ability and a sense of the variety of feeling within their community. In 'A Goose Pie, and How It Was Cooked' F. McC———n, a candidate for mayor, was characterised as a trimmer who courted the Irish vote though he scarcely deserved it. One crony asks him, 'By the way, in your little message to the Mayor of N.Y. the other day, what the d———l did you mean by our being all of "one religion and blood", you know? It is a little mixed, my boy, and, coming from you, smacks too much of the Anglo-Saxon, you know.' Another remarks, 'The boys say you prefer English to Irish, and Republicans to Democrats, and d———n my eyes if it don't appear so ... Ireland is not enthusiastic over you. The Fenians entirely repudiate you on account of that little office you held under the Queen. They say you were for Peel, but not for Repeal.' To which McC———n's answer is: 'Can't we talk race and religion, and strike a responsive chord in the Irish heart? Train has been stirring them up by telling them they have not their proportion of officers—(you needn't press this much)—can't you arouse their pride?'[117]

If Irishmen could be satirised for their pursuit of the Irish vote, it is hardly surprising that ridicule was extended to those who had no right to call themselves Irishmen but did so on the necessary occasions. In *A Political Stew* the *dramatis personae*, '(All Italians)', discuss the candidacy of H. B——d, who wishes to be mayor. B——d remarks, 'Boys, stir around; say I was born in Ireland—Coleraine—a nephew of Sir John B——d's ... and that I am a Catholic—that is, in sentiment—and intend to be baptized as soon as Mrs. Senator C——ly returns ... Say, M——d, that was a clever dodge, telling those boys in the Tenth that I was born in Ireland. Good thing that some of them cannot read. Damn old Hawes. But for his Registry bill, no one would be wiser. Wonder if any of them have looked in the Great Register?' To which M——d replies, 'The Irish vote is indispensable to you. Without it, success is impossible.' B——d: 'Well; trust me for that. I can play upon the harp and the *lyre* too. By the way, M——d, I hope none of them remember the time when you were a Know-Nothing Alderman here, and a candidate for the nomination of that party for Mayor'. M——d: 'O, well, those things must be forgotten sometimes; besides, I am a Catholic now, and that you know condones a heap of sins.'[118]

The third side of the satirical triangle, hostile attack on the Irish by their political enemies, was exemplified in *Bribery; or, The California Senatorial Election. A Comedy. In III Acts*. Here a collection of characters including Handerly, a Senatorial candidate, McQuintin, a candidate for Harbour Commissioner, Father Cotton (S.J.), Eugene Castle, Pete O'Dunup 'the ironmonger', and Father Stealthy, a Jesuit priest, discuss political affairs in a generally awkward and obvious dramatic piece. Castle also wishes to be chosen to be United States Senator. It is his actions that are the main vehicle of the satire. At one point he remarks:

Already, I begin to clutch the glittering prize. I fancy I already tread the Senate Chamber; and, Irishman as I am, in all the pride of an American Senator. The moneyed interests I am connected with have come down gloriously with the sinews of war. The Irish clans are mustered on my side, and the Jesuits, the cunning Jesuits, with their secret, stealthy ways, will strain every nerve on my behalf... The end justifies the means: so says the Holy Father Cotton. He vainly thinks that, after my election, he can control my course. I understand him. But in the end he will learn, that I can out-Jesuit all such Jesuits as he. Eugene Castle is no 'sardine'. My faith is a rational faith, so long as the Church and the Irish contribute to my ambition and profit.[119]

The force of the satire was, however, blunted by the apologetic 'Addendum by the Author'. 'It is proper to add,' he hastened to say,

that in this piece no reflection is intended on the Catholic Church, whose conservative course is appreciated by no one, more than the Author. Nor is any imputation intended on the Catholic Clergy as a body. It can boast of such men as the good Arch-Bishop of San Francisco, illustrious for piety and virtue. They are the last men to sanction corruption. But, as for political Jesuit Priests, any more than other political priests, the Author does not disguise his detestation.[120]

As far as Jesuits went, the Archbishop himself exhibited less than Christian patience, so that he and the author would have enjoyed some common ground.[121] The addendum in itself helps to explain why there was resort to political satire in San Francisco: there was, happily for the Irish, little likelihood of recourse to the political riot.

Satire could reveal and release tensions by distorting reality and attempting to put Pat back in the place he had come from. The practising politician like Leland Stanford, however, was well aware of the reality of the Irish vote, which, it is instructive to note, the railroad magnate courted rather than ignored or attacked. When the St Patrick's Brotherhood held their celebrations in San Francisco in March 1862 Governor Stanford attended the gathering at Hayes' Park. Back in Sacramento other politicians showed they shared his political sensitivity. Both branches of the legislature gave the day its value by adjourning at an early hour, while in the city the Board of Supervisors did likewise 'in honour of the day'.[122]

Such political behaviour gives the context into which attacks such as that made on McCoppin for voting no on a patriotic resolution have to be set.[123] Although it would be difficult finally to disentangle ethnic relationships from politics it is possible to argue that in San Francisco many such attacks were primarily party political because, paradoxical as it might sound, the native-born were neither so defensive nor so confident as to indulge in all-out communal warfare. The outbreak of violence on the news of Lincoln's assassination is instructive in this respect. Crowds attacked the building in which the *Monitor* was housed and did a large amount of damage. At first sight this could seem a typically aggressive move against a minority group. But there were special circumstances in the case: the crowds were attacking the paper as a Copperhead, not as an Irish, organ. They went on to attack the *Democratic Press*, the *Newsletter*, the *Occidental*, *L'Echo du Pacifique* and the *Franco-Americaine* for their Copperhead sympathies too.[124] In fact the Catholic authorities, in the person of Archbishop Alemany, had long since disavowed the *Monitor's* policies, in August 1863.[125] In later years when the editor at the time of the riots, Brady, claimed $5,000 for the damage he had received and a Bill went to the state legislature to permit the Board of Supervisors of San Francisco to pay compensation, the *Monitor*, by then under new editorship, thought that the claim should be looked at very carefully before the Bill was passed.[126] There was no automatic closing of ranks, for there was no feeling that a community insult needed avenging. Part of the relative ease of atmosphere was due to the archbishop, who, as fair-minded men accepted, always preached political moderation. In November 1864 his circular to Catholic priests put his attitude into words. 'I have,' he said,

> deemed it proper to request of you, to warn your flocks against . . . deceits and commotions, and to instruct them to continue to join with their reverential submission to civil authority, their calm, quiet, peaceable and independent conduct.
>
> Princes may sometimes make war, but private individuals cannot. The company of seditious men can do no other service than to drag the incautious into excesses, quarrels, enmities, blows, and not unfrequently into an untimely and unprovided death.[127]

The archbishop's call for peaceful politics could be heeded because the situation was not one in which violence was needed. The Irish community did not feel political frustration; the opposition was psychologically too weak for successful aggression.

Such continued to be the case, in the main, for the ten years after Casserly's and McCoppin's triumphs. The Irish community achieved equitable if not overwhelming political representation in the city, as befitted a large yet minority group. As far as the Board of Supervisors was concerned, Irish presence was strongest in 1869–70. In 1869 Richard Ring represented the Seventh ward for the Democrats; James F. Adams the Tenth ward, having defeated, on the Independent ticket, Edward Nunan, the sitting and Irish-born Democratic Supervisor; P. H. Canavan represented the Eleventh ward and M. J. Kelly the Twelfth, both as Democrats. The Irish press pointed out that both Edward Flaherty, of the Third ward, and T. McCarthy, of the Fifth, though born in New York City, were Irish-Americans. Interestingly both sat as Republicans. Other Irish-born politicians in high places in the city included M.C. Smith, superintendent of streets, John F. Meagher, a school director, Michael Cooney and Charles Corkery, Justices of the Peace, Charles Mayo, a pilot, and J. P. O'Reilly, a port warden.[128] But, partly reflecting the fact that city politics were not so controlled as to provide any candidate with an inevitable majority, McCoppin failed to be re-elected in September 1869 by a matter of 126 votes. The campaign had not been the cleanest: McCoppin had had to go so far as to send to Ireland for evidence that he was not a bastard. Opponents tried to smear him with accusations of violence and corruption.[129] It was suggested after the election that his 'liberal use of the power of political ostracism', or the policy of rewarding supporters, had been partly responsible for his defeat.[130] In fact he had increased his vote by almost a thousand over 1867; unfortunately his opponents increased theirs by over three.[131]

After 1870 the Irish presence on the Board faded slightly, partly because the rules were changed so that from 1873 all Supervisors were elected at large. This was done, ostensibly, because the voting populations of wards had become extraordinarily unequal in number and redistricting was too thorny a solution, and because, it was said, a general ticket would stop 'repeating' or 'colonising', that is, men voting illegally in a succession of wards on polling day. In this way, the importance of the Eighth ward with its 'steady voters and vast wealth' would be increased against that of the 'transients' of the Fifth.[132] Strictly, class, not ethnicity, was behind the change, though both factors were at work. Thus, whereas in 1870 the Irish-born Robert Goodwin and Edward Commins came on to the Board for the Fifth and Eleventh wards, the elections of 1873 ended with not a single Irishman among the Supervisors.[133] In 1875 Thomas Bryan won election as an Independent from the Third ward; in 1877 John Foley and J. W. Farren appeared from the First and Third.[134] Yet, if a contemporary view is to be followed, such men marked only the tip of the iceberg of Irish presence on the Board. According to one account, five of the Supervisors elected in 1877 were 'Irish-Americans', namely John Foley, Mangles, Roundtree, Smith and Farren, and further there was a marked Irish presence in the Board of Education, the judiciary, among law officials, and in the post office.[135]

Judging from the way in which, in the 'seventies, San Francisco increasingly sent Irish-born citizens to Sacramento, the appearance of fewer first-generation Irish on the Board of Supervisors was not evidence of a weakening political presence. By contrast, the numbers of Irish in the San Francisco delegations to the state capital were evidence of the opposite. Only one Irish-born legislator was sent to the Assembly from San Francisco before the fifteenth session, 1863–64, reflecting the stalemating factionalism in the Democratic Party before then and the victories of the Republicans and People's Party. Thomas Gray was elected to the seventh session of 1856 as a Democrat; and then as a Republican to the ninth in 1858. John Lynch and T. W. McColliam in 1863, however, were the forerunners of the Irish breakthrough that produced at least one Irish-born Assemblyman from San Francisco in all sessions of the legislature from fifteenth to twenty-third, bar the nineteenth, though, as might be expected, they were not all Democrats. In 1865 David Dwyer was elected to the sixteenth session as a Unionist; in 1867 Mathew Canavan, Frank Mahon and J. J. O'Malley went to the seventeenth as Democrats. H. W. Fortune, George R. B. Hayes and William O'Connell represented the city Democrats in the eighteenth session from 1869 to 1870. The Republican resurgence of 1871 left the Irish without representation to the Assembly of the nineteenth session; John Hamill, Independent, was the sole Irishman in the delegation to the twentieth. The massive Democratic advance in 1875 produced a delegation from San Francisco containing no fewer than seven Irish-born Assemblymen: William Broderick, James G. Carson, John O'B. Kennedy, Michael McCarthy, Thomas McInery, William O'Connell, and D. C. Sullivan, all Democrats. In 1877 five Irish, four Democrats and a Republican, went to the lower House from San Francisco. The lone Republican was William K. Forsyth; the Democrats, William Broderick, James E. Connelly, Charles Gildea and John J. Tobin.

The Irish assault on the upper House came after that on the lower, reflecting the accretion of power over time. Only one Irish-born state senator appeared from San Francisco before 1875, David Mahoney, the follower of Broderick, who sat in the fifth and sixth sessions of 1854–55. But perhaps reflecting the pressure that built up during the early 'seventies which was not permitted expression then because of the temporary decline of the Democrats, there was a sense of opening floodgates after 1874. Philip A. Roach was the only Democrat among five state senators from San Francisco in the twentieth session, but four of the newly enlarged delegation of ten were Irish-born in 1875, M.J. Donovan, Frank McCoppin, Edward Nunan and Roach, while Timothy McCarthy, born in New York, made a fifth. Donovan, McCoppin and Nunan held over to the twenty-second session and were joined by John Boyston. McCarthy also held over and was joined by John C. Murphy, born in Massachusetts.[136]

Such political advances could not come without organisation, and such organisation was bound to bring the charge of bossism from those who felt that the concept of party regularity based on ethnic affinity conflicted with the idea of the free and rational political choice. Unfortunately for both nativist and purist, corruption was evident not merely among the Irish, nor was it confined to Democrats. In the 'sixties Conness seemed to some to have stepped into Broderick's shoes. 'If,' said a critic,

a popular citizen is suggested as a suitable person for a certain office, he cannot be nominated without having been first chalked out on Conness's slate; he must express his readiness to pack sand and eat dirt for the Great Senatorial Manipulator. If we require a member of the legislature, he must be a friend of our 'only sober senator'. If we want a sheriff, the Great Western Prestidigitateur pours him out of a magic bottle. If we desire a justice of the peace, the Great First Cause creates one directly. If we would have a head schoolmaster, that eminent scholar sets his traps and catches one. If a special policeman be required Senator Conness springs his rattle and presto! we have one of his friends.[137]

At the end of 1867 Monroe Ashbury, a Supervisor, claimed that a caucus of six members, by no means all Democrats, governed the Board of Supervisors.[138] In the elections of 1869 McCoppin, up for re-election as mayor, was charged with controlling them.[139] McCoppin's defeat led to the exultant view that 'The "Ring" is certainly smashed to pieces' but later second thoughts saw that it survived unharmed.[140] Its survival showed that strictly party politics could not rule in the city, where no group could aspire to overall control.[141] Party was factionalised, too, to bring continual struggles among competing groups for success, particularly at primary elections.[142] In some ways the days of the 'fifties seemed to have returned; even to be surpassed. 'Never,' said an editor, of the Democratic primary of 1870, 'was corruption so open and unblushing.'[143] The bosses emerged to try and bring order to the chaos, but for the moment they were unsuccessful.[144] In the anarchy any group that had number and a degree of organisation would advance: here lay the basis for Irish successes. And in such conditions ballot reform alone, as was tried in 1869, was bound to be a failure.[145]

The Irish improved their position also by becoming brokers for other ethnic groups in familiar fashion. This was the meaning behind the remark 'The grand Italian Democratic procession of last Saturday night was composed of seven Italians, born in Italy, and eleven gentlemen from Limerick'.[146] Philip A. Roach seems to have been well aware of the possibilities of interethnic co-operation. In his speech of 19 September 1872 for Horace Greeley before the Tenth ward wigwam, a key sentence told how Greeley had 'electrified the world by the enunciation of great principles in social science, and the electric cable', Roach said, had 'carried them through the depths of ocean... to sainted Ireland, to heroic Poland, and to liberty-loving Germany'.[147] In 1877 Roach was invited by the Italians of San Francisco to give an address on the three hundred and eighty-fifth anniversary of the discovery of America by Columbus, He mixed nationalism with cultural pluralism, pronouncing that 'National Spirit will achieve national greatness and elevate character, when the people, on occasions like the one which has brought together this intelligent audience, assemble in their native or adopted homes, to honour the memory of their countrymen distinguished for the performance of deeds beneficial to humanity'.[148] Sometimes interethnic relations were not so easy. The German-born elements were not the natural followers of the Irish, though some, as Catholics, and all as foreign-born, had common ground. Germans and Irish disagreed over the 1856 Committee of Vigilance. In 1871 some Germans threatened to vote Republican because they believed that the Irish had sympathised with the French in the late war. The *Monitor* sternly advised them that 'in every way, public and private, social and political, we can do far better without German support than they can without the Irish'.[149] In 1872 the same paper, however, praised Judge Louderbach for 'utterly setting aside the prejudices of race' and sentencing A.J. Plate, a German who tried to break through a St Patrick's Day procession, though it had nothing but scorn for Judge Stanley, who held that Plate could not be indicted for his action because the Board of Supervisors could not regulate common law through their ordinances. 'His Conduct,' said the *Monitor*, 'in ignoring the people is unparalleled in the history of the nation. It is a direct insult to them and to their representative.'[150]

As such an episode showed, regarded by some Irish as 'an attack on the Irish people in this city; their inalienable rights and prerogatives as citizens', there were those always ready to look out for danger signals heralding a return to Know Nothingism.[151] In 1873 the *Monitor* touchily defended the 'Irish' senator who, in its opinion, had properly defended California's interests when he was attacked by the *Alta*, the *Bulletin*, the *Bee* and the *Record*.[152] Three years before, a single issue of the paper had contained a sharp attack on the *Sacramento Union* for its attitude to the Irish and sent a hostile shaft in the direction of the *Bulletin* for saying that McCoppin was too partial towards Irish nominees.[153] In the same month the *Monitor* maintained: 'The truth is there is a Know-Nothing spirit rampant in this city today. Neither party is exempt from its influence.'[154] Yet other Irish were less pessimistic and less thin-skinned. When rumours were heard of an anti-Catholic society, the Crescent, to defeat Catholics at the polls, led, it may be added, among others by two Protestant Irish, the *Catholic Guardian* passively, if a little sardonically, remarked, 'We do not believe it can succeed; we believe there are too many in this country who belong to no Christian organisation and who are well enough informed to know that the clamour against Catholics had not foundation, to permit the success of the crusade.'[155]

Once again it was possible for the level-headed to distinguish political party rancour and nativism. It may well have been true that Casserly and McCoppin so controlled the Democratic Party in San Francisco that they could order it to replace a candidate for Supervisor, and it may have been a fact of political life that it was necessary for the Taxpayers' Committee to nominate 'the O'Sullivans, Murphys, Patricks and Kirkpatricks', while the observer would 'look down the list of Democratic nominees in vain for a single name of similar omen'. But the important point was, as this paper went on to ask, 'What does it mean? Is it an effort to take the wind out of the enemy's sails?'[156] If it was, these events hardly showed the proscription of the Irish from political life. Such moves rather evidenced the impossibility of doing this, and the consequent political accommodations.

This is not to say there was no continuing nativism in the community, for there was nativism in the national culture, ready to be transplanted from the east. When William Minturn visited San Francisco from New York in the mid-1870s and wrote his account, he told the following story:

> I was introduced to one of the chief city officials of San Francisco,—a very insignificant Irish-looking creature. To this person I had a letter of introduction, which I had sent to his house in San Francisco, and had waited four or five days for an answer, refusing other invitations, so as to be able to accept any politeness he might show me. On being introduced I said,—'I had a letter of introduction to you, dear Mr. ——, which I sent to your house in San Francisco; I suppose you did not get it, being out of town?' 'Oh no,' he said, 'I got it four or five days ago, but you understand, not being at home ——.' I did not understand at all. Just think on an Irish creature like this representing the society of a city like San Francisco.[157]

What Minturn's remarks reveal is the potential danger of nativism, not its actual progress in the city. Consequently it would be unwise to take too much notice of the extremist press, for example the accusation in 1877 by one newspaper that

> The selection of our municipal officers has fallen into the hands of bad, ignorant, and, we fear, vicious men. Two foreign-born whisky dealers are accredited with controlling the Democracy, and the Democracy controls the town... The result is a Board of twelve Supervisors, of whom not more than three are claimed to be honest, or believed to be competent.[158]

Read quickly, this might appear a call for action against the immigrant, yet it was not, for, as a later publication of the same paper made clear, such a crusade was bound to fail, and appeals had to be made on grounds of morality, not ethnicity, if they hoped to succeed. Two weeks later *The Argonaut* said:

> We want to hear no more about the German, or the Irish vote, and we sincerely hope we have heard the last of this narrow, selfish, Native-American, Crescent, anti-Catholic, Protestant, secret society nonsense.

There were no political dividends in that. But possibly there were in another direction, so the paper continued.

> To nominate a Superintendent of Schools because he is a German, a Sheriff because he is an Irishman, a member of the Board of Education because he is a Catholic, a Street Superintendent because he is a Democrat, a Chief of Police because he is an American, or anybody simply because he can catch a class vote, is pandering to base, narrow, and mean prejudice.
>
> The present incumbent of the Sheriff's office is a Brady-Mannix figurehead. Sheriff Nunan makes good beer. The Hibernia Brewery is an excellent institution, but Mr. Nunan is not a good sheriff.[159]

These were not the words of confident, aggressive nativism, nor yet those of a battered, defensive Protestantism. The recourse to humour and the failure to play up the religious issue, the accent on the need for unprejudiced and able men were the signs of an attempt to shift argument away from narrow sectarianism to higher ground. Certainly nativist prejudices were part of the call for unprejudiced men, but, perforce, they had to play the part of a minor theme. Success in city politics would have been impossible for any group that made their prejudices too plain.

Such common sense was, however, the order of the day in normal conditions. The onset of the Workingmen's Party produced abnormal ones and consequently great changes in the tone and character of city politics. As the 'seventies progressed, fear of radicalism grew. The appearance of the Workingmen's Party crystallised it, and anxiety gave free rein to a host of irrational prejudices. In these conditions it was not surprising that opponents of the new movement increasingly turned to nativist arguments to attempt to discredit it, for it was quite true that many of the rank and file of the Workingmen were Irish-born. At the same time, however, it was also true that the Irish community was itself split by the movement. The most instructive examples of this were the appearance of Eugene Casserly among the Non-Partisans opposing the Workingmen, and, symptomatically, the temporary destruction of the Democratic Party in the city, through collapse into factions, said to be 'the Irish under the lead of Dennis [sic] Kearney; the chivalry, under the lead of Charles De Young; and the balance, embracing the Broderick or Northern Democracy, under the leadership of Andrew Jackson Bryant', to be interpreted as those who joined the Workingmen, those who joined the Non-Partisans, and those who remained independent and powerless.[160] The Regular Democrats tried to keep their position in city politics partly by continuing to appeal for Irish support, using traditional arguments, as when their organ the *Examiner* advised that none should support J. McM. Shafter for Non-Partisan delegate to the Constitutional Convention, as he had 'publicly declared that he could throw a lasso in a crowd in this city, and catch with it more Chinamen worthy of citizenship and suffrage than he would of Irishmen'.[161] Four days later, after the election for delegates to the convention was over, the paper again attempted to discredit the Non-Partisans in Irish eyes. 'An examination of the vote on the Non-Partisan ticket in this city,' it said, 'shows that the candidates who have names indicative of Irish blood were generally the most scratched. The fact shows the deep-seated, ineradicable prejudice which lurks in the hearts of many against that race, and proves that the spirit of Know-Nothingism, now apparent in the Crescent organisation, and in the Order of United Americans, is rife in this community.'¹⁶² Such manoeuvering suggests at least the hope that some Irish voters would remain unattracted by the Workingmen and available to support the Democrats.

By the middle of 1879 the *Examiner* had to admit that 'The [Workingmen's] organisation is largely composed of adopted citizens, of whom the Irish constitute the mass... the Irish greatly predominate and of the men of that race who now support the candidacy of Mr. Kalloch [for the mayoralty], at least eight-tenths are Roman Catholics'. Apart from the small glimpse of the socio-economic basis of the Workingmen's Party, and the tantalising implication that both Protestant and Catholic Irish supported it, however, the paper ignored this aspect and concentrated on the ethnic factor, trying to prove that Kalloch as an ex-editor of a Baptist newspaper was both pro-Chinese and anti-Catholic, clearly considering this to be the most important.¹⁶³

Other evidence suggests the close connection of the Workingmen in the city with the Irish population, though, obviously, not all members were Irish, though the vast majority, it was felt, were foreign-born, including a good-sized German group.¹⁶⁴ When the Workingmen met, it was often in the Irish-American Hall or the Hibernia Hall.¹⁶⁵ When they marched they 'had a quantity of Hibernian green ribbon bound about their hats and coats'.¹⁶⁶ When Will P. Johnson composed his poem 'Kearney's Request', lines 1–4 of verse three ran:

> Remember the 'Sand Lot', our native soil,
> It's like the dirt of the dear green Isle;
> Bury a few handfuls of the sand with me,
> For it kills all Snakes and Reptiles.¹⁶⁷

When extremists wished to attack the movement they declaimed: 'Take from the sand-lot Dennis Kearney, and from the Workingmen's party its Irish, and there would have been no agitation... Take the Irish from Kearney's municipal ticket, and nothing would be left but the anomaly of a howling Hard-Shell Baptist Republican Protestant preacher to represent a party, whose inspiration and rank and file are foreign-born Irish, Catholic, and Democratic.'¹⁶⁸

The vehemently hostile could have been attempting nothing more than a smear campaign, but they seem to have been describing the party accurately. If the Irish did not comprise the bulk of the membership, it is difficult to see who did. Likewise when the same enemies attacked the Irish leadership of the party they were also on firm ground and were logically emotional: 'Mr. William F. White,' said *The Argonaut*, 'of Santa Clara, is an illiterate person of Irish birth, who had been long enough in America to be fairly entitled to any of the political honours of our country, if residence has any special claim for consideration. His candidacy rests solely upon the fact that he is of Irish birth... It is because he is Irish that he is the nominee of an Irish party... If he was not Irish, he would get neither nomination nor votes.'[169] Kearney was not the only Irish leader of the Workingmen's Party; his subordinates Thomas Donnelly and John P. Dunn were too, as well as his arch-enemy within the party, Frank Roney.[170] The Irish presence among the thirty Workingmen elected to the Constitutional Convention from San Francisco was unrepresentatively slight: only six were born in Ireland, namely John D. Condon, Patrick T. Dowling, Joseph C. Gorman, Peter J. Joyce, James O'Sullivan and Patrick M. Wellin, though three others, Bernard R. Kenny (who died before the convention opened), Luke D. Doyle and Thomas Harrison, claimed Irish blood.[171] In the twenty-third session of the legislature, however, Thomas Kane, Martin Kelly and Joseph C. Gorman sat in the senate, representing half the party's strength from the city, while J. J. McCallion, Michael Lane, John Burns, P. T. Gaffey and Garrett Pickett were the five Irish-born out of the thirteen Workingmen's Party representatives in the lower House from San Francisco.[172] Kearney may himself have created the conditions whereby the Irish were not as prominent among the visible politicians as they might have been, since in May 1878 he introduced the highly controversial resolution before the state central committee of the party that officers of the party should be ineligible for nomination to public office. As the *Alta* said, it was strange that his original power 'emanated from his Irish following', yet his recent declaration was equivalent to saying that 'no one with a "Mac" or an "O" before his name should go to the Constitutional Convention' or, presumably, hold any later office.[173]

Nevertheless, when on 1 September 1879 the same paper published an analysis of the 'names, nativities, age, occupation and dates of naturalisation' of the candidates in the two main tickets for the imminent city elections, it found that of the whole Workingmen's ticket 'forty-one of the candidates are foreigners, and twenty-four come from Ireland'.[174] The party was running an Irish candidate for sheriff, for auditor and for coroner, six Irish candidates for Supervisor, from the First, Second, Fourth, Seventh, Ninth and Tenth wards; three candidates for Justice of the Peace, and two for school director as well as a number of Irish on the legislative ticket.[175] At the end of the day the party found it had had a mixed success, but among those who triumphed were Irishmen Thomas Desmond, for sheriff, John P. Dunn, for auditor, and J. D. Connelly for Justice of the Peace.[176]

The Irish complexion of the party was a godsend to its opponents, who played up the ethnic character of the Workingmen, possibly in part to undermine the socio-economic threat that their reforms might bring. According to the editor of the *Alta* the Kearneyites were 'enemies of the free school system, [for] such of them as are able, send their children to the Church schools, to the Convents and clerically directed institutions of their Church. That party has declared,' the editor said,

its purpose, if successful, of abolishing the Board of Education. They have declared that they would turn our school system over to the care of the Supervisors. And see how they have prepared for such an event. They have nominated for the Board of Supervisors, ten of the twelve, foreigners by birth, nearly all of them Irish. If they get power they intend the Supervisors shall rule the schools, and so have been careful to nominate, almost exclusively, those who are opposed to our public school system, to fill the positions of Supervisors, who are to supercede the Board of Education. There is evidently a power behind Dennis Kearney, which has had the manipulating of their ticket.[177]

Similar sentiments were voiced by San Francisco's premier anti-Catholic, who was, it should be carefully noted, a Northern Ireland Presbyterian who was not an American citizen. John Hemphill delivered a sermon at Calvary Presbyterian Church on 'The Election—Our Duty'. He took as his text Exodus xviii. 21: 'Moreover thou shalt provide out of the people able men, such as fear God, men of truth, hating covetousness; and place *such* over them, *to be* rulers of thousands, *and* rulers of hundreds, rulers of fifties, and rulers of tens' In the words of the *Alta*, Hemphill said:

In his wise counsel, Jethro, on whose words the speaker dwelt at length, did not advise Moses to go to Ireland or Germany or France for men to carry out the law laid down for the people of Israel by the Divine ruler, but he told them to select able and honest men from among his own people, free from corruption or covetousness. The speaker was not against any man because he was a foreigner—for he was of foreign birth himself—but when a political party set up for its candidates Supervisors and School Directors, twenty of whom out of the twenty four were
FOREIGNERS AND CATHOLICS,
It was time for Americans to inquire whether it was safe to put such a party in power. Would not such men use their offices to make out of this State a second Spain or a second Ireland . . .
SUPPOSE TWENTY THOUSAND AMERICANS
Should go to the city of Cork, he said, and attempt to run its Government; should parade the streets with transparencies bearing revolutionary emblems, and threaten in case they could not succeed by the ballot, to adopt the bullet, what would the citizens of Cork say? He thought they would say a great deal, and that somewhat effectively.[178]

In point of fact the fourteenth plank of the state platform of the Workingmen's Party of California read, 'We pledge this party to maintain, in its purity, the public school system authorised by the Constitution'.[179] Furthermore, none who had seen Archbishop Alemany's pastoral letter, read in all Catholic churches on 7 April 1878, and Kearney's reply of 12 April 1878, would have agreed that the two were working hand-in-glove. Alemany was somewhat disingenuous in his remarks when, having stressed the need to distinguish licence and liberty and the threat of groups that failed to do so, he continued, 'Although we do not know of any Catholic belonging to such associations or countenancing their sentiments, (and we know at the same time that Catholics are, by principle and practice the most obedient to authority and law) yet, in the presence of the wild agitation caused mainly by seditious declaimers, we feel it our duty to warn all Catholics in particular, and we will venture to add, all classes of society in general, to discountenance, and frown down all seditious designs, and evil plotters.' Kearney's reply to this was outright.

'I do not acknowledge,' he said, 'the right of the Archbishop to interfere with the political sentiments of any person, much less if that person is true to his country and his fellow men. As a Catholic I have openly rebelled against his assumption . . .'[180]

What both the archbishop and Denis Kearney would have agreed was that the Workingmen's Party was primarily a movement of the economically disadvantaged and only incidentally one whose membership was largely Catholic. The thrust of the movement was in two directions, against the rich and against the Chinese. As one of the party's own contemporary apologists said, the Workingmen were 'between the aristocrat and the Chinaman'.[181] Some saw 'the cry' as 'The Chinaman must leave the State of California'; others stressed 'the rule of plunderers' whose 'hellish and impoverishing power' was about to be overthrown.[182] For most the two crusades were one and the same, for, as was said at the time, the 'monopolists' whose 'blighting hands, in their greedy struggle for gain, have fastened upon every industry, levied tribute upon every element of prosperity, and made all classes of labor subservient to the machination of their rapacity' were 'not content with thus degrading to their own selfish avarice all the material and natural prosperity of the State' but had also 'fostered the introduction among the people of an alien class to compete with the intelligent labour of the land, regardless of all principles of humanity, progress, and civilisation'.[183] It was 'Pat' who bore the main 'mortal grudge against the Chinaman'; consequently he was the mainstay of the party that opposed the oriental.[184]

The failure of the Workingmen to found a permanent political party, having, however, thrown political life in San Francisco into turmoil, left a vacuum into which moved a new generation of political boss as the period closed. Owen Brady and Jack Mannix were the nominal heads of the Democratic machine, organising a party to which the bulk of the Irish working men had perforce to return. But around 1880 Christopher A. Buckley, born in Ireland, 'which country, unfortunately, he left in his early youth', proceeding to California via New York City, began to exert his 'malign and debasing influence'.[185] He built his machine partly on ethnic loyalties and was especially kind to his fellow countrymen. His hand was to lie heavily on the city for a decade or more.[186]

The debacle of the Workingmen's Party therefore did little to shake either the importance of politics for the Irish or Irish importance in political life. The very full involvement of the Irish community in San Francisco politics from the beginning of the city's American period was one aspect of the level of integration they achieved. In one sense such political activity was a further form of associational building. Again, it showed the sense of confidence that here permitted the Irish to make a strong, often successful bid to control the distribution of resources in their new society. At the same time Irish political activity could sometimes mark a defensive group reaction to the possibility of nativist attack. Both roles were possible, although the first predominated. Political activity also demonstrated the high value placed by the Irish upon politics as the medium between them and society. Their involvement in San Francisco politics was far from unusual and was part of their well known national tendency to attempt to control the politics of big cities where they were present in sufficient numbers.[187] The Irish in San Francisco fought their way up the political ladder in the usual fashion and met with the normal nativist response. But their success was more complete by 1880, even by 1870, than that of their group in other major cities like New York, Boston or Philadelphia, and the opposition was proportionately weaker. Their large numbers and possibly their lower degree of transience, added to their predilection for politics and their willingness to be organised by their own kind, brought outstanding political strength. Consequently, just as the San Francisco Irish could not complain of the progress of their Church in 1880, so they should have been satisfied with the Irish advance in the State. Their political record was a good measure of their adjustment to San Francisco.

Chapter VIII
The limits of satisfaction

The very fact that the entire Irish population of the United States had not crowded into San Francisco by 1880 suggests that there were some limits to the Irish sense of satisfaction with the city and that the advantages of life there were not overwhelmingly compulsive by comparison with conditions in all other American cities. The ordinary, everyday strains of living, the tensions of urban life, the dislocation of migration, the problems of accommodation, the potential threat of nativism, the accident of unemployment and the possibilities of disease and death were not magically interrupted on the Pacific coast. Misfortune fell differentially on individuals and heavily on some. Life could not be all sunshine and laughter for all the Irish all of the time.

The Irish naturally appeared in the city's statistics of dislocation. At first sight they might indeed seem to be over-represented in them, to suggest a high level of communal dysfunction. For instance, the *San Francisco Municipal Reports* for 1879–80 included a report by the health officer that 622 Irish had died in the city in the previous year, making up 14·3 per cent of total deaths. The Hospital Report showed that Irish patients, 958 in all, provided 32·4 per cent of admissions. The Almshouse Report recorded 255 Irish inmates, or 35·7 per cent of its unfortunates. The county clerk noted that 138, or 31·9 per cent, of those examined for insanity had been Irish. The chief of police reported that 224 of the commitments to the House of Correction, comprising 23·9 per cent of the total, had been of Irish men and women.[1]. These figures referred to the first generation alone. According to the United States census of 1880 this group made up only 13·1 per cent of the city's population.[2] Clearly there would not be much satisfaction to be gained from so depressing a list of misfortunes, which suggested that the Irish were experiencing a far higher level of dislocation than their numbers warranted.

Two points need to be made, however, before accepting this judgement. It does not take into account second- and third-generation Irish whose youth would make it unlikely that they would appear among these statistics. Properly, the statistics should be related to the entire Irish community, which made up 33 per cent of the city's population and 37 per cent of its white inhabitants. To do so is to make the figures far less alarming evidence of communal disruption. At the same time, however, it is also necessary to add statistics for the later generations, to give the complete picture. This, unfortunately, is difficult to do, save in one instance. It is possible to use both the census of 1880 and the Municipal Reports of that year to give an idea of the total Irish presence in the city's institutions for the unfortunate. The Municipal Report for 1880 showed, for instance, that 32·4 per cent of admissions to the City and County Hospital during 1879–80 were Irish-born. This percentage was below that of the Irish community in the white population of the city, but it clearly needs adding to. In June 1880 the census revealed that 34 per cent of the hospital's patients were Irish-born, but also that another 8·2 per cent were native-born of Irish parentage. Two of this last category of patient had only one Irish-born parent, but even their inclusion as fully Irish does not give a percentage of Irish inmates wildly different from the percentage of Irish in the total city population, particularly considering that the hospital did not admit Chinese. Table 21 sets out statistics drawn from the Municipal Reports over a twenty-year period.[3] It can be said, roughly, that during that period there were at least as many second- and third-generation Irish in the city as first-. Consequently, the Irish presence in the institutions listed hardly appears extreme. Although the percentage of 'Irish' seems high, the true value for the Irish community as a whole is only half the apparent one.[4]

Similar considerations should be borne in mind in examining the city's criminal population in 1880. In June the House of Correction contained 261 prisoners, of whom thirty-seven had been born in Ireland and sixty-five with two Irish parents. A further sixteen had one Irish parent, making a

Table 21
Number and percentages of Irish-born appearing in various of the San Francisco *Municipal Reports*, 1859–80.

Year	Admissions to hospital			Coroner's cases			Health Officer's report: deaths		
	Total	Irish N	%	Total	Irish N	%	Total	Irish N	%
1859–60	861	239	27.7						
1860–61	Not published								
1861–62	1135	351	30.9						
1862–63	1411	465	32.9						
1863–64	1397	450	32.2						
1864–65	1462	610	41.7						
1865–66	1439	460	32.0	176	31	17.6			
1866–67	1429	454	31.8	207	30	14.5	2,522	330	13.1
1867–68	1,796	578	32.2	213	42	19.7	2,577	333	12.9
1868–69	2,323	850	36.6				4,093	479	11.7[a]
1869–70	2,942	1,173	39.9				3,243	431	13.3
1870–71	2,737	983	35.9				3,214	472	14.7
1871–72	2,388	812	34.0				2,998	457	15.2
1872–73	2,854	973	34.1				3,641	502	13.8[b]
1873–74	3,232	1;125	34.8				4,013	588	14.7[c]
1874–75	3,915	1,308	33.4	297	56	18.9	4,163	601	14.4
1875–76	3,375	1,156	34.3	321	57	17.8	4,791	666	13.9[d]
1876–77	3,012	897	29.8	400	63	15.8	6,170	760	12.3[e]
1877–78	3,007	948	31.5	400	75	18.8[f]	4,977	693	13.9
1878–79	3,174	964	30.4	386	81	21.0[g]	4,493	663	14.8
1879–80	2,955	958	32.4				4,337	622	14.3

	Commitments to Insane Asylum			Inmates of Almshouse			Commitments to House of Correction		
1867–68	169	56	33.1	268	86	32.1			
1868–69	198	60	30.3	229*	87	38.0			
1869–70	229	72	31.4	396	138	34.9			
1870–71	225	79	35.1	331	117	35.4			
1871–72	208	71	34.1	326	134	41.1			
1872–73	249	82	32.9	414	122	29.5			
1873–74	282†	92	32.6	408	146	35.8			
1874–75	366	112	30.6	498	197	39.6			
1875–76	431	145	33.6	491	150	30.6			
1876–77	454	138	30.4	801	228	28.5			
1877–78	187	49	26.2	610	175	28.7			
1878–79	389	126	32.4	625	249	39.8	975	210	21.5
1879–80	432	138	31.9	715	255	35.7	939	224	23.9

*Admissions

†Examinations

grand total of 118, or 45·2 per cent of the whole. The city prison contained seventy-two prisoners, only fifteen of whom had been born in Ireland, but a further twenty-three had two Irish parents and two others had one Irish parent, making a total percentage of 55·6 of all inmates. The separate city and county jail had 241 in its cells: thirty of these had been born in Ireland; another forty-six had two Irish parents and a further seven one Irish parent, giving a grand total of eighty-three and a percentage of 34·4. These percentages were not unusually high considering the size of the adult Irish community as a whole in San Francisco.

The feeling that the quality of the Irish social performance, among adults, as shown by such statistics was little poorer than could be expected is paralleled in considering the numbers of largely second-generation young Irish in the city's asylums, recalling as the bench mark that 38 per cent of all children between four and seventeen belonged to the Irish community. The 1880 census shows that although none of the 190 children being looked after by the Ladies' Protection and Relief Society was born in Ireland, seventy-two had Irish parents and five one Irish parent, a total percentage of 40·5. Again, 168 of the 327 'boarders' in the St Joseph's Infant Asylum had Irish-born parents, as did 199 of the 369 orphans cared for by the Roman Catholic Orphan Asylum, only one of whom did not have two Irish parents, giving percentages of 51·4 and 53·9 respectively. Twelve of the twenty-five children in the St Boniface Orphan Asylum were Irish: seven had two Irish parents, five had one. Juvenile crime and misfortune met in the City and County Industrial School, where only one inmate had been born in Ireland, but where a further forty of the total 100 inmates had two Irish parents and eleven others one.

Part of this sizeable Irish presence in city institutions was clearly the result of Irish poverty. This can be seen, at one extreme, in the case of the almshouse, where 64 per cent of the 116 Irish inmates of the first and second generations had been in unskilled occupations; 8 per cent in semi-skilled; 22 per cent in skilled; and 6 per cent in white-collar. Men in unskilled and semi-skilled jobs were most unlikely to have savings to draw on in hard times. The sizable percentage of inmates who had had skilled or white-collar jobs, however, suggests that dislocation was no simple respecter of status and income. The percentage of men from skilled occupations in the almshouse was very similar to the percentage of skilled Irish in the work force as a whole, 22·4 per cent as against 23·2 per cent. Poverty perhaps motivated the Irish in their serious crime. In 1855 and 1862 the state prison reported that of its Irish-born inmates from San Francisco, eight of nine, and twenty-one of twenty-six, respectively, had been sentenced for grand larceny, burglary, or robbery. Although the statistics are so small as to be of doubtful significance, the occupational breakdown of the nine prisoners of 1855 may be of passing interest. They included two labourers, two stewards, two sailors, one porter, one sailmaker and a cooper—none of very high occupational status.[5]

There were other factors influencing the numbers of Irish that entered institutions. The age and sex structure of the Irish community was important. As has been seen, the first-generation Irish became decreasingly male as the years passed, inevitably also ageing. The community as a whole, however, was continually reinforced by the birth of children, to counteract the effect of first-generation ageing. The normal sex ratio among the second-generation children helped to give the whole community an ever larger percentage of females. Considering the demographic changes within the Irish group, it is surprising that the percentages provided by the Irish-born, in the various institutions listed in Table 21, show few signs of change as the years passed. Increasing wealth may have counteracted the influence of advancing years, as far as institutions like the hospital, the almshouse or the insane asylum were concerned. The relatively unchanging Irish-born percentage of recorded deaths was due partly to the fact that even by 1880 the city's first-generation Irish, who had left Ireland largely in their youth, were not yet near the grave, approaching the end of their allotted span, the 50·16 years that the three-year-old San Franciscan could expect to live[6]. Generally the lack of fluctuation suggests that the social performance of the Irish was related in a complex way to its age and sex structure, and to prevailing economic conditions.

Even as the Irish-born community aged, it was also becoming, at least up to 1870, materially better off. Age might increase infirmities, but better material conditions would keep down the calls on public institutions like the almshouse and the hospital. At the same time the rise in the proportion of females, generally employed in less physically destructive occupations and also far less likely to break the law, would diminish, proportionately, the numbers in hospital and prison. The bad times after 1870, however, would put a new strain on the community. Thus the statistics of dislocation do not show a secular decline in the number of Irish in the various institutions but reveal instead that the effects of economic conditions were tending to cancel out the effects of demographic changes, as far as the first generation alone was concerned. The second generation was also ageing, however, and came, during the period, to the ages where poverty and crime had to be dealt with institutionally and socially. Whereas, on the whole, the second generation were upwardly mobile, to diminish the effects on the group of poor economic conditions, that proportion of its members that did become a social burden was newly added to the demands on institutions being made by the Irish community as a whole. Consequently, by 1880, after a decade of economic trouble, the Irish were still appearing in large numbers in the city institutions.

One further point needs to be made. The proportion of Irish appearing in institutions was not simply the result of group dislocation. The control of the almshouse and the orphanages, for instance, was in Irish hands. Their authorities could be more favourably disposed towards admitting Irish than members of other groups. Where there was a shortage of institutional places and care, a group like the Irish would be well served. The city was well disposed to respond to their needs, from either political or religious considerations. In the Magdalen Asylum in 1880, for instance, thirteen of the fifteen Sisters of Mercy were Irish-born and a fourteenth was a Californian of double Irish parentage. Similarly, all the staff at the Roman Catholic Female Asylum were Irish-born from the Sister Superior down. This argument of preferential treatment does not hold, of course, for commitments to prison, unless, conversely, in that political considerations might incline judges to leniency, nor, strictly, to commitments to hospitals or insane asylums, but it needs consideration. Altogether, though the

Irish appearance in city institutions was marked, the level showed some progress from eastern experiences. In 1860 in Boston, when the foreign-born Irish had made up 18 per cent of the city's population, they had provided 40 per cent of the inmates of the house of correction; in 1880 the foreign-born San Francisco Irish provided only 14 per cent. In 1858 in New York City the foreign-born Irish provided 56 per cent of the prison commitments, having made up, in 1855, 28 per cent of the total population.[7] By contrast, in 1879–80 in San Francisco, they provided 24 per cent of the commitments to the House of Correction.

Very few of the total Irish population of San Francisco appeared in these statistics. All, however, would have been affected to some degree by the twin, linked problems of how exactly to respond to their new cultural situation and to the nativists who seemed, so often, to want nothing more than to consign the immigrants to a limbo where they would have no relation to their new society. These problems were highlighted in a concise way in one question more than any other, and that was in the debate over education. Nativists, and others, felt that public education was linked to the very character and future of the republic. The immigrants had to discover in their attitude to it how exactly they intended to relate to their new environment. Debate over schooling raised the important divisive religous dimension, which marked one of the fundamental cultural differences between a group like the Catholic Irish and the host society. Not all Irish held equally strongly to their religious values; some were therefore less exercised than others over the dangers in the public schools to the souls of their offspring. Officially, however, Catholics were warned of the threat of the schools, and the more devout took notice. At the same time, the San Francisco school system was less aggressively Protestant than some eastern ones, or, to put it another way, less anti-Catholic, which made some of the rhetoric about danger appear unreal. Catholic Irish San Franciscans could therefore feel freer to choose between two coexistent lines of thought, the one, put forward most strongly by the Catholic Church, that the public schools were godless and anti-Christian, the other, that their threat could be safely ignored. This view was shared by many of the laity.

The story of Irish relations with the public school system in San Francisco was complicated by an early departure from eastern experience.[8] When the city passed its Free School Ordinance in 1851 it permitted public money to go to support both public and private schools, which included those attached to and supervised by the Catholic Church.[9] Section 10 of the school law of 1 May 1851 stated that

> If a school be formed by the enterprise of a religious society, in which all the educational branches of the district schools shall be taught, and which, from its private and public examination, the committee ... [think] to be well conducted, such schools shall be allowed a compensation from the Public School Fund in proportion to the number of its pupils, in the same manner as provided for district schools ... [10]

The first Catholic parochial school had already begun in September 1849, connected to St Francis', and this was joined by St Patrick's School, begun by the Reverend John Maginnis in September 1851, together educating 300 pupils by the end of that year.[11] At this point, then, even devout Catholic parents were able to conceive of some of their taxes going towards the education of their children. But in 1852, possibly reflecting the influence of Horace Mann, the state legislature brought this happy state of affairs to a close, by inference, in repealing those sections of the law of 1851 that had allowed the transference of public moneys to Church schools, to replace them with a provision that no funds would be given by the state to schools unless they employed 'duly-examined teachers; employed by proper authorities' and were 'free from all denominational and sectarian bias, control, and influence whatsoever'.[12]

For the moment the Catholics did not despair, and rallied their forces to bring pressure on the legislature and on the State Superintendent of Education. He realised that in the south of the state in particular education was already in the hands of the Church, as there was yet no secular alternative to the system inherited from the Mexican period, and he believed that to deprive Spanish-speaking children in particular of their education by crippling their schools financially would be unfair. He therefore supported moves for a third Act to restore the late *status quo*.[13] This was passed in May 1853 in the last moments of the legislative session and produced the expected uproar, but in San Francisco the Sisters of Presentation took the opportunity of opening a third 'ward' school, as the Church schools were known, in December 1854.[14] By this time matters had also been made easier for Catholics in the city's public schools by the abolition of the compulsory reading of the Bible. The first Board of Education in 1851 had adopted a resolution requiring teachers to open schools by reading the Bible and by prayer. Thomas J. Nevins had drafted such a rule, copying New York City regulations, but when John Swett became city school superintendent he ceased enforcing it, because, importantly, he thought 'that under the conditions of a cosmopolitan city, in which there were large numbers of children of Catholics and Jews, it was an unwise policy to continue the reading of the Bible as a school exercise'.[15] As the years went by fewer schools applied the rule and by 1864 it was in general disuse.[16] In 1874 the president of the San Francisco School Board went even further towards nondenominationalism, ruling that the mere repeating of the Lord's Prayer was sectarian and in violation of the school law, and was sustained by his board.[17]

Meanwhile, however, some Catholic parents had chosen to send their children to the parochial schools, and by August 1854 there were 930 pupils in Catholic schools.[18] It was unfortunate for those whose children attended them that the victory for tolerance in 1853 came on the eve of the triumph of the Know Nothings. Not surprisingly the 1855 legislature repealed the 1853 law and turned the clock back to 1852, where it remained. The three Catholic schools in San Francisco survived the blow of losing public funds, however, and were joined in September by a fourth which began life in the basement of St Mary's and a fifth, St Ignatius' Academy, which opened in October.[19] By 1856 there were 1,421 pupils in 'ward' schools.[20] Catholic discontent with the public schools and consequently Catholic support for Church schools was, however, somewhat muted by the fact that, although the city went along with the state prohibition against passing on local tax money to the Church schools, the San Francisco political situation was too delicately balanced after 1855 to permit a Protestant crusade against Catholic teachers in the public schools. Under the 'Ewer settlement' of that year, named after the moderate Protestant Democrat on the City Board of Education, the city hired some Catholic teachers for its public schools and arranged matters so that Catholic teachers were put into what had been Protestant schools and vice versa, at the same time banning all sectarianism. Some teachers in the parochial schools for boys also passed examination by the School Board and were appointed teachers to be paid from the city School Fund.[21] Partly as a result, Catholic diehards found it difficult to whip up communal support for the re-establishment of the conditions of 1853–55. They became alarmed at the numbers of Catholic parents who sent their children to the public schools. The Ewer compromise and its results illustrated the peculiar conditions in the city that allowed Catholics and Protestants to defuse one of the raging controversies of the day.

This is not to say that both extreme Protestants and Catholics did not try to overthrow the existing situation. Attempts were made in the legislature, particularly by Zachariah Montgomery in March 1861, but these failed partly because even in his case there was an ambivalence towards the parochial school.[22] Montgomery preached a general sermon over the years on the unfairness of a system that taxed the citizen but would not provide him with the schooling he wanted for his children, but what was noticeable was the lack of support that he received from Church officials, and the lack of a wave of public feeling to carry his cause to success, possibly because his main aim was to achieve freedom of choice for parents and not financial support for parochial schools.[23] Even this attitude was too extreme, however, for men like John Conness, eventually to become United States Senator from California, who though Irish-born argued generally that the law of 1855 should stand.[24] Conness's views reveal that it was not necessary to be a supporter of religiously biased schools to be an Irishman or a politician in California. He saw great dangers in the principle of sharing funds. 'In a very short time,' he argued, 'the State of California will be engaged in the interesting business of collecting moneys from various sources for the purpose of education, and dispursing and distributing these moneys amongst private parties, to be by them applied in such a way as they see fit for the purposes of education.' The resulting heterogeneity of standards could only be anti-social. He did not believe that the public schools sowed 'the seeds of immorality and death'; rather, that good Catholics should keep their children at them, for they could thereby ensure that the extremes of Protestant sectarianism would be kept out and they would be able to reform, if necessary, from within.[25]

Conness was not a San Franciscan, but he shared an attitude with many Catholics in the city, as attacks by some Catholics on others for using the public schools also revealed. In February 1872 the editor of the new *Catholic Guardian* tried to wake Catholics from what he called their 'lethargy' on the subject, arguing that too many used the public schools merely because they cost less. He was forced to face up to the situation in the city after the Ewer compromise, which seemed to make Catholic education less urgent, and argued;

> It is urged that many public schools are taught by Catholics, and consequently are as safe for education as denominate Catholic Schools. Such an argument is scarcely pardonable in any one entitled to a respectable name ... Besides, Catholic teachers are no more allowed — even if they would — to introduce religious instruction into the schools than if they were pagans, and the very neglect of professedly Catholic teachers on this point tends to beget a corresponding indifference on the part of the pupils, and even to a greater degree than if the teachers were of a class from whom Catholic pupils might not expect or desire it.[26]

The editor returned to his task again later in the year, but his tone was that of a man facing an obdurate readership.[27] Part of the problem was that the public schools were not aggressively Protestant, and in the absence of extremism material considerations baulked large. The difficulty was to convince Catholics that their 'immortal souls' were in 'fearful danger ... in the present common school system', when the system seemed altogether indifferent to religion.[28] Some were convinced of the dangers of contagion where both parties were passive, but the lack of hostile attempts to proselytise left others able to believe that souls could be safe even in public schools. In 1874 even Montgomery seemed the defeatist, asking a Catholic audience then, 'Do we not, while protesting against [the public school system] ... as opposed to conscience, at the very same time give the lie to our own words by accepting it, on the sole ground that it saves us money?'[29] In such a situation, marked by a refusal to keep to the hard line, communal bitterness was likely to be without a dangerous edge.

It is difficult to establish precisely what proportion of the Catholic and indeed of the Irish population did send their children to the private schools as distinct from the public ones, under pressure from their consciences or their preachers, secular or religious. By October 1861 2,777 children were reported as attending private schools, according to the Board of Supervisors, but when the officials gave the reasons for this they did not stress religious compulsion. According to the official view in the city, the reasons why so many children were in the private schools were first that 'children under six years of age [were] not entitled to admission to the Public Schools [so that] the parents of children thus debarred from the privilege of public instruction, are compelled to patronise private infant schools', and second that 'the Public Schools, in certain localities of the city, are so crowded with pupils that many of our citizens, among whom may be found numerous taxpayers, are thereby obliged to seek in private schools the means of instruction for their children. This unfortunate state of things exists more particularly in the southern portion of the city.'[30] There may have been some truth in these remarks, for whereas in 1861 only 3,884 children were attending public schools, against 2,777 in private ones, by June 1870 and after the expansion of the public school system in the mid-1860s there were 18,300 children at the public schools and only 4,582 in the private.[31] At this point it was the turn of the Catholic authorities to be anxious. *The Monitor* maintained in June 1869 that only 2,000 of the 8,000–10,000 Catholic children in the city were in Catholic day schools.[32] Consequently in the late 'sixties and 'seventies 'the educational activities of the Catholics were very marked' and new institutions permitted numbers to expand.[33] But there was some distance to go. According to the *Catholic Guardian* in February 1872 whereas 7,121 children on average attended Catholic Sunday schools, only 3,950 attended Catholic day schools.[34] If these figures are reliable, only 55 per cent of Catholic children attended Catholic day schools. In June 1875 the city reported that 6,155 children between the ages of five and seventeen were in private and Church schools when there were 5,350 children, presumably almost all Catholics, attending Church-run schools in San Francisco.[35] These figures suggest that by the mid-1870s over 85 per cent of the privately educated pupils in the city were in Church schools, slightly more females than males: 2,850 as against 2,500.[36]

Table 22

Numbers and percentages of Irish children attending school by ward, San Francisco, 1880

Ward	No. of Irish children aged 5–16	No. attended school	% attended school
1	911	641	70.4
2	841	614	73.0
3	27	20	74.1
4	695	517	74.4
5	15	10	66.7
6	265	196	74.0
7	1,064	738	69.4
8	837	626	74.8
9	2,172	1,365	62.8
10	2,841	2,028	71.4
11	7,341	5,342	74.0
12	3,314	2,312	69.8
N	20,323	14,499	71.3

By 1880 the Irish had either voluntarily or perforce accepted the necessity of sending their children to some school. Table 22 is based upon the reply given to the census marshal when he asked whether children had attended school during the last year. It will be seen that there was some little variation by wards. It is not clear, however, that even in a ward like the Ninth low attendance meant that families were rejecting schooling and, for instance, preferring to send children out to work. Only 177 of the 807 children not attending school there had been employed during the year. The figures include all children who were five, six, fifteen or sixteen years of age on 1 June 1880. Some of them may have been too young to go to school, others old enough to feel it was time they left. Fully 66.7 per cent of those who had not attended school in Ward Nine were of these four ages. By contrast only five ten-year-olds and five eleven-year-olds in the entire ward had not attended school, some through illness. The Irish attitude to education thus appears to have been all that a nativist could have demanded, particularly as the 1874 compulsory attendance law was probably of little use.

The way in which the Catholic authorities responded to their educational duties had much to do with this high school attendance. By 1875 the list of Church schools and colleges had become a long one. It included St Mary's College, founded in 1855 and incorporated as a college in 1872; St Ignatius' College, founded as an academy in 1855, becoming a college in 1859; Sacred Heart College, founded in 1874; St Joseph's School for Boys, St Mary's Cathedral School for Boys; St Francis' School for Boys and St Patrick's School, all for boys; together with two convents run by the Sisters of the Presentation, one on Taylor, the other on Eddy, founded in 1869 and 1855 respectively; one run by the Sisters of Notre Dame, founded as a school in 1851, and becoming an academy in 1858 and a college in 1868; another by the Sisters of Mercy, St Joseph's School; a fifth by the Sisters of St Dominic, St Rose's School, founded in 1862; and a sixth by the Sisters of the Holy Name, all for girls.[37] The total numbers attending private and Church schools did not rise very far in the late 'seventies, standing at 6,652 in 1880, no doubt limited in part by the buildings and staff available, whereas 38,320 children between six and seventeen years of age were enrolled at the public schools.[38] The cost of private schooling may, as Montgomery said, have helped to steady numbers. In 1880 the Preparatory Department of the Sacred Heart College cost $5 and $6 per quarter; the Intermediate Department, $8 and $10; the Commercial, $10 and $15; the Collegiate, $15 and $20. Music, drawing, the 'Banking Department', 'Telegraphy and Phonography' all cost extra, though there was 'No extra charge for study of French, German and Spanish languages'. There was, however, one for lunch, 'at an additional charge $10 per quarter'.[39] But if the Catholic community was willing to use the lower rungs of the educational ladder provided by the Church, it did not want, or could not afford, the higher. Between 1863, when St Ignatius' College gave its first degree, and 1880 only fifty-seven students received awards; thirty-one

B.A.s; eleven B.Sc.s; one M.Sc., and fourteen M.A.s.[40]

In as much as San Francisco society was created by men and women who had grown up in the eastern states it was very unlikely that the city would be able to deviate very far from the norms of eastern settlements, and, particularly, to have supported an educational system that shared funds equitably between Protestants and Catholics. New England influence was strong in the educational system, but what is surprising is that it was not exclusive. San Francisco's population was too mixed and too lately arrived for the ancestral habits of New England to be adopted completely, and it was therefore able to modify New England customs to some degree. But the city was in the nation, and the nation was under the constitution, and its freedom was therefore limited in that degree. Irish San Franciscans could not expect a successful crusade to restore the aberrant days of 1853–55 and did not attempt to wage one. This failure kept tension down. The Catholic community was, however, wealthy, and able to set up an alternative system without public money; this too helped to calm the atmosphere. The city authorities went as far as they could towards quietening Catholic fears without breaking the law of the constitution, and this too helped. Some Catholics accepted the public school system and they helped as well. Consequently education never approached the stage of serious controversy as in some cities of other parts of the Union, in which the parochial school became a burning question. Sometimes a zealous priest would comment on what he called the unfairness of taxing people to provide benefits for people who would not accept them, but the protest never took communal form, as it did in New York, demanding that the parochial schools be accorded a share of the state's moneys.[41] Moderation ruled at most levels in the period. In 1867 San Francisco voted by 7,428 to 6,361 in favour of the Reverend O. P. Fitzgerald for State Superintendent of Public Instruction, who was believed in some quarters to be in favour of dividing the public school money between Catholics and Protestants, but when the state-wide victor John P. Swett reported to the legislature after his term no fair-minded Catholic could have objected.[42] 'Occasionally,' said Swett, 'we hear something of sectarian difficulties in our public schools,' but 'common sense, concession, compromise, will bring us to a good understanding and harmonious action with regard to the education of our people. Catholics and Protestants and all others have a common interest in this matter, and mutual interest should lead to a final adjustment of all differences on a basis of justice, wisdom and charity.'[43] Swett reflected at the state level the tendency towards toleration by the end of the 1860s among many of the city's secular elite groups.

This is not to say that religious leaders were as happy with the situation as other men. It was impossible that they should be while they believed in the exclusive righteousness of their own cause. It was partly for this reason, and because Catholic parents continued to use the public schools, that the Catholic School Union was founded to give religious instruction on Sundays to children, some of whom might otherwise have failed to receive any. The Union went from seven Sunday schools in February 1872, with eighty-two teachers, to nine with eighty-six in April 1872; and to nine schools with 265 teachers by February 1873. At this later date the schools contained 7,425 pupils, of whom 2,870 came from the convent schools.[44] On 30 June 1873 the private schools had 5,285 pupils enrolled, suggesting that perhaps as many as 40 per cent of Catholic children attended the public schools.[45] Had there been strong lay discontent with this situation it should be manifest in contemporary sources, but the absence of complaint suggests that hostility to enrolment in the public schools came almost exclusively from the Church and was not shared by a large minority of the laymen.[46]

In a sense, the area of controversy over education was triangular, with one side being formed by the Catholic clergy, the second by the largely indifferent laity, Catholic and Protestant alike, and the third by some of the Protestant clergy, who were far from pleased by the level of toleration that had been reached in San Francisco schools. The third group were particularly displeased over what had happened to the reading of the King James Bible in the public schools, and in the late 1850s began an attack on the tendency to spare Catholic feelings by omitting Bible reading. In 1859 the Reverend William C. Anderson attacked 'the Romish element ... which never had the Bible in its own land, and which had kept the common people in darkness and ignornance', but which had demanded its exclusion from the Common Schools of the United States. He therefore called for an 'effort of the American people to maintain a religious privilege which they have enjoyed for two hundred years, and which intense sectarian bigotry is attempting to snatch from them.'[47] Despite this stern, uncompromising call for a religious crusade, nothing happened; indeed, the use of the Bible dwindled further, bringing into question the representativeness of his views. In 1873, however, Pastor Calvin A. Poage, of the Larkin Street Presbyterian Church, returned to the attack, but broadening it considerably by arguing that the assault on Bible-reading was a 'mere subterfuge' and that 'the real design' was to 'subvert the whole system' of the public schools. This 'glorious institution ... has enemies and opposers—enemies, fierce and bitter—enemies, bigoted and unscrupulous—who would rob it of its beauties; who would paralize its strength; who would trample it in the dust. These, I need not say, are the priests, and bishops, and adherents of the Roman Catholic Church.'[48]

In the same year the Reverend John Hemphill, a man of fixed ideas, also saw the exclusion of the Bible from the public schools as the first and near-fatal submission to the 'clamours of the Romish priests' that must lead to an attack on the schools themselves. Addressing such priests, he proclaimed,

> You ask us to pay you as educators, while history proves that you are no educators at all. Our public schools are maintained by the State for the purpose of training American citizens. You ask us to endorse your schools to train Jesuits.[49]

Two years later Hemphill was reported as saying with customary immoderation:

> The Republic is in danger. We have conciliated the Pope. We have lost the favour of the God of heaven. His heart sinks within him. He is cast down. He is in despair. All, all is lost.[50]

This was offensive enough, but more offensive was the highly dubious account of Zachariah Montgomery's speech to the

Roman Catholic Sunday school teachers on 6 July 1873, published with Hemphill's former remarks. According to the account, Montgomery began by pointing out that

> Roman Catholics are persecuted on all sides, in hotels, restaurants, and other places of common resort, by sneers, jeers and contemptible expressions about the leading Catholics, and eating meat on Friday.

Then he was supposed to have continued:

> In this country we have Catholic teachers in the public schools; they should teach the doctrines of our holy faith. (Applause.) But they are prevented by the laws. Now, for the present, they can whisper in the ear of the scholar at times, and tell them how, when and where they can obtain absolution from their sins. (Applause.) The institutions of this country must be made the institutions of the Church, and then our Sunday Schools and the so-called public schools will be one. The common schools of this country are nothing more nor less than so many schools for teaching the young scandal and wrong-doing. I am told by good authority it is almost impossible to make Christians of the children who attend the public schools. It is high time something was done to correct this evil, and I here venture to say that if the Roman Catholics do not stand up for their rights, they fail to do their duty.'

The veracity of the report was somewhat disingenuously betrayed by an editorial addition:

> The question will be asked why the above was not published in some of the daily papers. We understand that it was presented to the managers of the various dailies for publication, but all had reasons for not using it. The *Call* was more frank than the rest, stating the Bishop had requested them not to publish it.[51]

The purpose of this excited, implausible libel was to inflame passions, but it failed substantively. Public interest remained low; the distance between the temperature of clerical rhetoric and that of general feeling remained large. It was always difficult for the committed to avoid exaggeration, but the more voluble they became the less representative they were. Debates fuelled themselves, as when in 1883 Father Gleeson and Frank Pixley debated the 'Common School Question' in a series of accusations, replies and counter-replies that took both men over well trodden ground. Pixley's position was weak, as he was on record as opposing the public school system for its 'practical communism,' in educating children of persons able to provide that education; in providing too high salaries for teachers; and in educating the poor child 'beyond the rudiments of an English education'.[52] Even so, he was willing to defend them now against the Catholics. Father Gleeson began moderately by admitting that the wrong done Catholics through the schools might have been unconscious, but before long his pen carried him to statements that the system was 'irreligious and sectarian ... pagan and infidel'. Secularism, he felt, could not be distinguished from paganism and ended in infidelity, turning the Catholic victims of the school system into nothing better than 'disciples of such men as Buckner, Spencer, or Augustus Comte'.[53] Just as nativists could not divorce the idea of American Catholicism from the Roman Curia, so the Father had trouble distinguishing Protestantism from infidelity, a difficulty that was bound to ruin any attempt at impartiality. Pixley appeared to believe on his side that to give public money to Catholic schools was tantamount to handing over control of the public schools, arguing, 'whenever the American school-house shall be turned over to the Roman Catholic Church, American youth will be taught the civil supremacy of a spiritual power as the first and fundamental axiom of government'. Later changing his approach entirely, he was to argue that the system as it stood might have its faults:

but if it is accomplishing so grand a work as the destruction of the political power and influence of the Romish Church in America, and is undermining the authority of the Papal Church ... then we hail it as the last and grandest achievement of our American Commonwealth.[54]

One critic of Pixley called him 'a remarkable example of arrested development', which seems accurate enough, but the same hand less defensibly wrote that Gleeson was 'entirely free from the narrowness of bigotry or prejudice'.[55] As this particular debate showed, little but prejudice was excercised when the subject of the public schools in any aspect was discussed by the committed. The same immoderate sentiments were to inform the debates of the 'nineties surrounding the

Reverend J. Q. A. Henry's famous diatribe *Rome's Hand in Our Public Schools. A Protest*.⁵⁶ But the important point is to see such pieces in perspective. They may have articulated the muddled prejudices held by Catholics and Protestants alike but they had no effect on the course of events, since such prejudices were but historical and sterile appendices, incapable of moving anywhere near a majority to action. Indifferentism was not to the liking of clerical leaders on either side but it proved paramount. Further, there were even San Franciscans who struck down the middle and valued secularism for its own sake, not as Protestantism in disguise. J. R. Brandon, for instance, argued that the prohibition of the Lord's Prayer in school meant that he could rejoice that

> free thought, free education, free religion has gained a victory over the churchmen of all denominations; that the great principle has at last been enunciated, that the State, which should be the common parent and protector of all its children—majority or minority—few or many—will not lend its aid to dispense the particoloured light of any particular sect.⁵⁷

Such a positive approach may not have been directly representative of San Francisco opinion, but in the lack of an intellectual alternative it could stand for what effectually the community chose for itself, the path of non-sectarianism.

A good example of this feeling in action came in 1877 on the occasion of the hundredth anniversary of the founding of the Mission. The Hon. John W. Dwinelle was chosen to give the oration, which included the following remarkable passage:

> Protestant as I am, I am not afraid to say that I rejoice in the strength and prosperity of the Holy Apostolic Roman Catholic Church; and that when I predict that a hundred years from now she will be stronger than ever, and that her greatest strength will be in the United States, it is because my heart goes with the prediction; and when I consider that she has been the mother of all modern civilization, and the foster-mother of all free political institutions, I devoutly invoke Almighty God that this great empire of freemen may empty into her lap the Horn of Plenty in its widest abundance.⁵⁸

These sentiments, not those trotted out in by now redundant controversies over the role of the Inquisition, should be taken as exemplifying mainstream San Francisco thought. In such a libertarian context there need be little religious anxiety. Necessarily Catholics who hoped to see the results of the Reformation buried deeply by the end of the nineteenth century, who believed their Church to be the exclusive 'palladium of truth and of public and private morality... the root and bond of charity and faith,' and who believed that the appearance of the Stigmata on the body of Miss Collins was not produced by the lady herself, would be dissatisfied by religious pluralism.[59] Yet these were the conditions that obtained in San Francisco. There is no evidence that the rank and file of Irish Catholics felt they needed to be changed.

The level of loyalty to parochial schools was part and parcel of the larger relationship to the city. Every immigrant had to make up his or her mind what parts of the ancestral culture should be retained, what elements of that of the new society adopted. It is unlikely that the immigrant welcomed controversy and confrontation for its own sake, either at the behest of his own leaders or as the result of attacks by nativists. There was a need to retain the psychologically useful and to jettison what was irrelevant to life in a new home. Individuals would disagree on the precise amount of cutural divestment that was necessary, but only those who intended to return to their native land within a short time would insist on hanging on to all of their past. Whereas the attitudes to parochial schools show that they were regarded by a majority as necessary to group identity and security, feelings about two other matters, by contrast, illustrate what was readily given up in adjusting to life by the Pacific.

It proved very difficult to establish an exclusively Irish Catholic newspaper in San Francisco, despite what might have been thought to have been a large and obvious market. The *Catholic Standard Weekly* quickly went to an early grave in 1854; *Mooney's Express* lasted from possibly 1858 to 1863, when it merged with *The Irish News* founded in 1860, and together they rose and then fell with the Fenians.[60] On 6 March 1858 the first issue of the most successful newspaper, *The Monitor,* appeared, as a 'Catholic journal, free from the rancour of polemics and devoted to the cultivation of Catholic literature'.[61] *The Monitor* was the exception that proved the rule, because it asserted from the beginning that it had no aggressive Catholic intent. It did not want its founding to be interpreted as a sign that the Catholic community was dissatisfied with the rest of the press, for it was, it said, 'in no appreciable measure anti-Catholic, rather 'The Most Liberal in the Whole World'.[62] The refusal to indulge in either defensive or aggressive communal politics coincided with the mood of its readers, who supported it. Other attempts at a more committed line, on the contrary, failed. The *Irish Nationalist*, 'with a capital of thirty thousand dollars, belonging to the Irish men and women of this State ... flaunted to the view of its beguiled stock-holders for the space of six months, when it exploded—burst, like an empty bubble blown out of a pipe-stem'. The *Irish People* was intended to be a universal Fenian organ, but it 'perished, Unwept'.[63] In 1864 Zachariah Montgomery started *The Occident* for Catholic readers and in 1865 Thomas Brady began *The Universe,* but neither succeeded in firmly establishing his paper, Brady coming to grief within a year, Montgomery within five. Then in January 1872 Francis Dillon Eagan, a convert from Episcopalianism, started *The Catholic Guardian,* aimed directly at Irish Catholics, arguing that 'The great majority of Catholics have not, as yet, duly considered the nature and power of the instrumentality that is being employed against them'—that is, the Protestant press—'attacking the Church on every side, and seeking to corrupt the faith of her children', but if the disappearance of the paper in the middle of 1873 is anything to go by they continued to disbelieve.[64] The same year saw the short-lived *The United Irishman* come and go, showing that it too could not find the formula for success. *The Irish World*, founded by J. J. Donelly in 1879, and *The Review*, founded by Messrs Brady and Robinson in 1880, had no better fortune. They too were dead in a year.[65]

According to the *Irish News* in 1867 the leading organs for the Irish on the Pacific coast to that date had been the *Examiner,* the *Call* and the *Alta.*[66] There are reasons for disagreeing with this in part; for instance, the *Alta* was generally the paper of the employers, the People's Party and the Protestants, and the list omits *The Herald*, which was read by the Irish until its unfortunate demise in the wake of the 1856 Committee of Vigilance. Nevertheless the observation in general is important. The Irish read newspapers that were not permeated with the view that it was more important to know what was happening in Limerick or Dublin than in their new home. Likewise Irishmen in the city wishing to enter journalism did not restrict themselves to ethnic organs. When Philip Roach wanted to help float a newspaper after the Civil War he chose the new *Examiner,* not a new Catholic paper, as John Nugent had done before him with *The Herald.*[67] When Henry George went into journalism he joined the evening *Post.*[68] Such attitudes reflected one level of communal integration.

The fate of purely Irish theatre in the city also shows the limits of what would be retained. In the 'fifties and 'sixties Irish melodrama had a great vogue in San Francisco, particularly when acted by Mr and Mrs Barney Williams, who played the Irish boy and Yankee girl so successfully that they made a profit of $40,000 in one six-month season.[69] Even at this point the dramatic theme was Irish-American rather than Irish alone. Irish patrons were then solicited with similar programmes year after year, but slowly tastes changed.[70] In the 'seventies the 'Connie Soogah' and 'Arrah na Pogue' lost favour and were replaced by sketches that symbolised the transference of interest from Ireland to the New World by their settings in the tenements of New York. When Edward Harrigan came to San Francisco in 1878 for the first time since the late 'sixties with his sketches of New York life 'he was welcomed with open arms'.[71] For many in the city, life in New York was much more relevant in a number of senses than life in Ireland. The fact that there was a diminished need to proclaim a defensive Irishness against nativist attacks made it easier for the Irish theatregoer to turn to new dramatic interests, particularly since so many might have lived in New York before coming to San Francisco.

The maintenance of some aspects of Irish culture in the city in this period could be viewed in two ways. It might be seen as evidence of clannishness, or of tribalism, the refusal to adopt the values of the new society. It might also, and more properly would, be seen as inevitable in the nature of culture, which cannot be totally voluntarily surrendered. All immigrant groups faced the problem of cultural adjustment, while every American community had to find some level of assimilation for the newcomers. The result in the long run was what has been termed 'cultural pluralism', a cultural system made up of a mixture of sub-cultures with both shared and exclusive values. The development of the Irish immigrant into the Irish-American meant cutural pluralism for the individual as well, with some values from Ireland retained, others from the United States adopted. As the matter of education in particular showed, new developments did not take place at a uniform speed in all cases, and some values that were not of the new society were thought too valuable ever to be rejected. Other values were accepted, to give, at least, what has been called 'behavioural assimilation'. Full-scale, or 'structural', assimilation did not occur, not merely because of nativist hostility but also because the immigrants, even if they had the choice, did not want it to occur.[72] In matters like child-rearing or the selection of spouses, for instance, there was in any case little cutural free will.

It is important when looking at the level of satisfaction among the Irish of San Francisco to remember that some of its limits were, broadly, inevitable. It is possible to postulate a model or ideal society in which Irish immigrants would have experienced no form of dislocation, produced no sick, no criminal, no insane or no orphans; adopted the values and behaviour of their new society as easily as they put on their first new coats bought with their first wages; but it would not be very useful to do so. Definition implies distance, and the term 'Irish' means cultural standpoints distinct from those of Protestant British Americans. Thus, though there may be evidence of some limits to Irish life and progress in the city, it should not lead to a feeling of gloom or despondency. Despite the numbers in city institutions, despite the controversies over schooling, it is still possible to feel that the process of accommodation was well under way, that any agonies such evidence of dislocation might show were probably temporary and peripheral. The central core of Irish experience in the city was whole and satisfactory.

Chapter IX
Cosmopolitanism v. sectarianism

When Thomas Mooney was chosen to deliver the St Patrick's Day oration for 1868 at the Metropolitan Theatre, the editor of the *Irish News* felt it necessary to explain why he supported the decision not to ask a clergyman. 'There is no doubt,' he said,

> that our clergymen are fully equal to the task of delivering a sound oration or discourse upon almost any given subject. In education and ministerial ability, the Catholic clergy are not a whit behind, but in many cases in advance of the clergymen of other denominations. It is, however, difficult for a clergyman of any denomination, to make an oration for an hour or two without spicing it pretty freely with his own peculiar orthodoxy, both religious and moral, or political, which may be distasteful to many of his hearers. San Francisco is a cosmopolitan city; the American people are cosmopolitan. It is natural to think, therefore, that an audience composed of such, may be partial to cosmopolitan views, if such views do not conflict with sound morality and virtue'.[1]

The editor was correct. Sectarianism, here defined as the aggressive, extravagant pursuit of one religious philosophy deliberately at the expense of another, was impossible in the city of San Francisco in the period. It is difficult to argue that the cosmopolitanism that ruled instead was the attitude of open-minded freedom from ethnic or cultural prejudice, which stressed the value of free trade in ideas between groups, for a free choice between them, but in the end the cosmopolitanism of stalemate was as effective in producing an environment in which the Irish could pursue and express their own values without external interference or constraint. Sectarianism depended upon the possibility of religious monopoly, but as Hubert Howe Bancroft pointed out, 'Religious bigotry cannot flourish in a city or state where no church monopolises the wealth or the intelligence of either, and where in all public affairs the coin—the true test—of one is as good as that of another'.[2] What Bancroft, or, for that matter, Samuel Bowles, saw as 'the dominating materialism ... of all life' was another expression of the same lack of sectarianism, the failure of one set of religious ideas to feel secure enough to try to dominate others, so that men's minds were released to pursue other ends.[3] As Charles Loring Brace observed, coming from a different climate of opinion, the result was that 'The general tone of society' was 'far less sectarian and narrow' than in the east.[4]

The prevailing cosmopolitanism was important for the lack of support it gave to nativism. Robert Louis Stevenson went too far, however, when he explored the notion of San Francisco's cosmopolitanism at the end of the period:

The town is esssentially not Anglo-Saxon; still more essentially not American. The Yankee and Englishman find themselves alike in a strange country... Here, on the contrary, are airs of Marseilles and of Pekin... The passers-by vary in feature like the slides of a magic-lantern... You hear French, German, Italian, Spanish, and English indifferently. You taste the food of all nations in the various restaurants; passing from a French *prix-fixe* where everyone is French, to a roaring German ordinary where everyone is German; ending, perhaps, in a cool and silent Chinese tea-house. For every man, for every race and nation, that city is a foreign city; humming with foreign tongues and customs; and yet each and all have made themselves at home. The Germans have a German theatre and innumerable beer-gardens. The French Fall of the Bastille is celebrated with squibs and banners, and marching patriots, as noisily as the American Fourth of July. The Italians have their dear domestic quarter, with Italian caricatures in the windows, Chianti and polenta in the taverns. The Chinese are settled as in China.[5]

Stevenson's view was particularly faulty because, though the native stock were in a numerical minority, they had most firmly set their imprint on the form of San Francisco and settled, once and for all, what the major lines of development would be. Politics and the economy, not to mention the language of officialdom and the level of civic aspiration, were all guided by Anglo-American norms. All creeds and values were not equal, because cosmopolitanism did not mean relativism. When W. F. Rae wrote in 1871 that at one moment he was 'in Kearny-street or Montgomery-street, surrounded by tokens of Western Civilisation, and a few minutes afterwards... in what is a small section of an actual Chinese city', he was not describing a society which had somhow managed to overcome the prevalent beliefs in racial superiority and inferiority and had admitted the Chinese to an equality with the whites.⁶ Many, many visitors to San Francisco in the period tended to view the city as a cosmopolitian centre particularly because of the Chinese presence, to be enthralled by the mixture of East and West which they found in San Francisco's Chinatown.⁷ What they did not see, however, was any willingness to accept the Chinese as valuable, progressive members within society, rather, at best, a tendency to regard them as external curiosities and, if necessary because of their willingness to work for low wages, still quite unassimilable.

The Chinese presence was nevertheless of great importance to the Irish. The cultural gulf between Chinese and white society, which was ever being measured by contemporary references to appearance, clothing, hairstyles, accommodation, plays, operas, drugs, family life, language and religion, was so great as to diminish, by comparison, almost to vanishing point the differences between the natives of Cork and Boston, of Limerick and New York City. It is almost true to say that, if the Irish had required the degree of success they achieved in the city, they would have needed to invent the Chinese outsider. Be that as it may, what the Chinese inhabitants did was describe the limits to the city's cosmopolitanism, which could include some groups but definitely not others.⁸ As a philosophy permitting the culture of groups to express themselves within society as a whole, it had its narrowness, but, at the same time, by comparison with the tightly knit, historic communities in the east, it displayed a marked inclusive flexibility. One early example of this was given in *The Annals of San Francisco*, written in 1854, and dedicated to the 'Society of California Pioneers', a prestigious body contining no fewer than 153 Irish members. This work, which was, and still remains, a very effective summary of developments in the early American period, was co-authored by Frank Soule, a prominent Whig politician, but, as far as the Irish are concernèd, the tone is far from exclusive and nativist. In describing the population of the city in 1853 the authors make the very significant remark that in their calculations:

Under the term 'Americans' are included the natives of Great Britain and Ireland, who are less easily distinguishable from native Americans than are other foreigners. Many, however, of the British-born, are American by adoption and naturalisation. Since the common language of the Americans and British is English, and their customs and habits of thought are generally the same, there seems no impropriety in calling them all in California simply Americans.[9]

Thus what may be called the legitimisation of Irish culture, its acceptance into the ring for a fair fight with the native American one, occurred, it would seem, early on in the history of the city. This is not to say that much progress, if any at all, was made towards structural assimilation, or the production of a single amalgamated culture, comprising Irish and native American elements in a new and better conjunction. What is true is that, as far as the Irish were concerned, San Francisco, as a whole, exhibited an early example of cultural pluralism.

Cultural pluralism has never meant cultural disarmament. Consequently it is not surprising to see cultural tensions between the Irish and native stock, even in San Francisco. Since one of the determinants of cultural difference was religion, it is also unsurprising to find that cosmopolitanism as a major theme was accompanied by sectarianism as a minor one. There was bound to be controversy over the reading of the Bible in public schools, over the control of education and the distribution of taxation, because of the religious gulf. Since control over the distribution of taxes was political, there was bound to be political tension too. Since the native stock were by no means tolerant, in general, of cultural difference, there was bound to be dislike of any attempt to perpetuate those differences, whether it be by residential clustering or by ethnic associationalism. The crucial question to be answered is the extent and importance of the tension, whether it was created by the majority or only by the commitment of a minority of the population. The answer appears to be the latter, that only a minority on either side felt the dangers of accommodation and demanded the extreme of cultural purity. Thus Irish families sent Irish children to the public schools; thus the city saw pamphlet warfare and not physical violence on any large scale; debate, not demonstration, over cultural difference.

A relatively friendly environment thus gave the Irish the chances that they took. The cosmopolitanism of the city was a reflection of its youth, the lack of what an English upper-class visitor described as 'settled "society" ' with the unchallenged, pre-eminent right to dictate the tone and style of the city, order its affairs and exclude those who were, in its view, undesirable.[10] The massive growth of the city gave opportunity for the Irish to build into its central structure, which took form and character from their efforts. The San Francisco environment permitted the Irish family to flourish. This gave a psychological foundation stone on which much else could be built. The large numbers of Irish gave the opportunity for widespread development of societies, which further increased the psychological area on which more could be built. The school system was developed without sectarianism, to enable the second generation to learn more than its parents had known about how society worked, and to acquire the skills for upward mobility.

This is not to say there were no victims. There were those who felt that the pace of development was so fast as to be inevitably more than usually destructive. Walter Fisher, after three years' experience, wrote, 'San Francisco is full of social wrecks—wrecks more complete and miserable than any possible in calmer seas.'[11] In the winter of 1885–86 an English immigrant, who, perhaps, should have found fewer problems in adjusting to San Francisco than an Irishman or woman, unhappily discovered that 'For three months San Francisco was a city of sorrow and despair to me, of laborious occupation, or worse, of none at all, of poverty, of starvation, of discomfort'.[12] Irish immigrants found themselves in the hospital, in the asylums, in the prison, in the mortuary as a result of forces beyond their control. Nevertheless, it is impossible to agree with E. L. Godkin's general statement of 1859: 'The great mass of [Irish] have not, so far as I can see, very materially improved their condition, socially at least by emigration. Physically, they are perhaps better off though even in this respect their life in the large cities is pretty much what it is in London and Dublin...'. Godkin was partly correct that 'The prodigious influx of Irish during the last twenty years has created a large Irish class, apart from the rest of the people, poor, ignorant, helpless, and degraded, contemned by the Americans, used as tools by politicians of all parties, doing all the hard work and menial duties of the country, and filling the jails and almshouses, almost to the exclusion of everybody else', but he underestimated the amount of change that had already occurred, and was already under way, in areas like San Francisco.[13]

By the time Godkin wrote, San Francisco and its Irish had passed through the first period of their common experience, one that had been characterised by a series of false starts, themselves reactions to the ending of the Gold Rush and the sense of unease about the future of the city By the end of the 1850s it was clear that San Francisco would survive and would flourish. The second period, from the 1860s to the mid-1870s, saw widespread investment of capital, time and energy, by city and Irish community alike, in permanent forms and institutions of urban life. This period revealed that much of the work of the previous one survived and was of use, and was in many ways the Irish golden age. The mid-'seventies were plagued by economic depression, but this should not be seen as a blight as destructive to the Irish community in the city as another blight had been in Ireland; rather as a change in temperature that slowed down the growth rate, and which, if its variations could occasion a storm, never fell low enough to kill the roots, or discourage continuing growth. Overall, developments in San Francisco and its Irish community between 1848 and 1880 ensured that they were a generation ahead of much of the remainder of the United States, where only by 1900 were the Irish 'beginning to emerge from the immigrant community which the first and second generations had created'.[14]

A final word of caution needs to be added. It is not argued that the Irish performed as well as the native stock in San Francisco. The point is that, given the time, the mid- to later nineteenth century; the place, the United States; and the group, the Irish, their history in San Francisco was, by contrast with that elsewhere, comparatively successful and fortunate. Some may wish to see the story in terms of frontier opportunity, others in the light of urban history, some in terms of the urban frontier. Whatever the frame, perhaps the last word may be given to the loquacious champion of the Irish on the Pacific coast, Father Quigley. In his mind the Irish were almost boundlessly abreast of opportunity in San Francisco. It was, he said, no wonder that the Irish should be envied for the conspicuous position they occupy as statesmen, merchants, capitalists, legislators, miners, bankers, farmers and owners of real estate, and this in the face of very great opposition. Our countrymen [he continued] had the press, the sectarian pulpit and the nativist movement — legitimate offspring of Anglo-Saxon hate — against them. Yet, without secret societies or aid associations, and with nothing but their stout arms and simple but confiding faith, they own not far from one-half the real estate of the city, control, in a mooted degree, the legislation of the State, are most successful in business, and last, though not least, fill the churches.

Here were laid out the major and the minor themes, success and hostility, power and prejudice. For Quigley there was reason to rejoice in this, the result of the city's cosmopolitan outlook, which he recognised. There were 'ideas ... inspired by sectarian rancour; but among the commercial and educated portion of the community distinctions of creed and country become every day more obsolete and discreditable', he said.[15] Clearly the Father could be carried into hyperbole, but he did have some substantive truths to back him up against the doubters, particularly those who knew nothing of the Irish experience west of the Sierra Nevada.

Appendix
The Irish United States Senators from California in the middle nineteenth century

It may be argued that, since the Presidency was closed to immigrants, membership of the United States Senate was, in many ways, the highest position they could win in what was not far from being a plutocracy. Whatever voting patterns took Irishmen into the Senate in the middle of the nineteenth century, their arrival announced their full participation, if not their predominance, in the communities they represented. It is worth-while recalling that the Irish community of San Francisco and California sent four members to the United States Senate in this period, three from California and one from Nevada, the latter case showing that the Irish position in California was strong enough to extend to the colony east of the sierras. Though the accounts given in the *Biographical Dictionary of Congress* are vestigial, they may be of some interest in displaying the careers of four very different men who in their various ways found that California and San Francisco offered the Irish unrivalled opportunity for their day and age.

1. *Broderick, David Colbreth*: 'born in Washington, D.C., 4 February 1820, his father having emigrated from Ireland to work as a stonecutter in the Capitol; moved with his parents to New York, in 1823; attended the common schools; apprenticed to a stonecutter in early youth; unsuccessful candidate for election in 1846 to the Thirtieth Congress; moved to California in 1849 and engaged in smelting and assaying gold; delegate to the constitutional convention of California in 1849; member of the State senate in 1850 and 1851, serving as president of that body in the latter year; elected as a Democrat to the United States Senate and served from 4 March, 1857, until mortally wounded in a duel with David S. Terry, chief justice of the supreme court of California; died near San Francisco, California, 16 September, 1859; interment under a monument erected by the people of the State in Lone Mountain Cemetery, San Francisco'.

2. *Casserly, Eugene*: 'born in Mullingar, County Westmeath, Ireland, 13 November, 1820; immigrated to the United States in 1822 with his parents, who settled in New York, prepared for college by his father, who was a student of the classics; was graduated from Georgetown College, Washington, D.C.; studied law; was admitted to the bar in 1844 and commenced practice in New York City; editor of the *Freeman's Journal* and contributor to newspapers in other cities; corporation counsel of New York City in 1846 and 1847; moved to San Francisco, California, in 1850 and published the *Public Balance,* the *True Balance,* and the *Standard;* elected State printer 1 May, 1851; retired from journalism and resumed the practice of law; elected as a Democrat to the United States Senate and served from 4

March, 1869, until 29 November, 1873, when he resigned; again engaged in the practice of law in San Francisco, California, member of the constitutional convention of California in 1878 and 1879; died in San Francisco 14 June, 1883; interment in Calvary Cemetery'.

3. *Conness, John*: 'born in Abbey, County Galway, Ireland, 22 September, 1821; immigrated to the United States in 1833; learned the art of pianoforte making in New York; moved to California in 1849 and engaged in mining and mercantile pursuits; member of the State assembly in 1853 and 1854 and again in 1860 and 1861; unsuccessful candidate for Governor of California in 1861; elected as a Douglas Democrat (afterwards changed to a Union Republican) to the United States Senate and served from 4 March, 1863, to 3 March, 1869; moved to Boston, Mass., in 1869; retired from active business pursuits; died in Jamaica Plain, Mass., 10 January, 1909; interment in Cedar Grove Cemetery, Dorchester, Mass.'.

4. *Fair, James Graham*: 'born near Belfast, County Tyrone, Ireland, 3 December, 1831; immigrated to the United States in 1843 with his parents, who settled in Illinois; received a thorough business training; moved to California in 1849 and engaged in mining until 1860, when he moved to Virginia City, Nevada; again engaged extensively in mining and eventually formed a partnership with John W. Mackay, J. C. Flood, and William S. O'Brien in 1867; this firm purchased control of the Bonanza properties and various other well-known mines, from which the yield of gold and silver, while under the superintendency of Mr Fair, was estimated at about $200,000,000; also engaged in the real-estate business in San Francisco and was largely interested in various manufactures of the Pacific coast; elected as a Democrat to the United States Senate and served from 4 March, 1881, to 3 March, 1887; unsuccessful candidate for re-election in 1886; died in San Francisco, California, 28 December, 1894; interment in Laurel Hill Cemetery'.

Source: *Biographical Dictionary of Congress, 1774–1949* (Washington, D.C., 1950), pp. 892, 958, 1011, 1143. Reproduced by courtesy of the U.S. Government Printing Office.

A note on sources

Coming to the study of the Irish in America through Oscar Handlin's *Boston's Immigrants: a Study in Acculturation* (rev. and enl. edn. Cambridge, Mass., 1959) and Robert Ernst's *Immigrant Life in New York City, 1825–63* (New York, 1949), with Handlin only allowing, at best, that at the end of the period he studied there was 'An Appearance of Stability' (pp. 207–29), and Ernst, in his summing up (pp. 172–84), providing a grim view of the interaction of host and immigrant societies, it was something of a shock to discover the content and self-congratulatory tone of contemporary Irish and Irish-American writers in their discussions of Irish life on the Pacific coast and in San Francisco in particular. John Francis Maguire's *The Irish in America* (4th edn., New York, 1873), pp. 262–80, stated categorically that no Irish immigrant could do better than settle in California. The flood of Irish names that fills Father Hugh Quigley's *The Irish Race in California and on the Pacific Coast* (San Francisco, 1878), all apparently of immigrants or their descendants, impressively successful in a very favourable environment that led the Father to give the 'candid advice...to our countrymen to settle *anywhere* [original italics] in California' (pp. 283–4), had to suggest that there was a distinct difference between experiences in east and west, and that Irish life in San Francisco in the nineteenth century would have its own unusual contours, as well as the familiar ones. It could have been that Maguire, Quigley and others had special axes to grind—land to sell, for instance, since Maguire's brother was a Californian landowner — but as other evidence was uncovered their view did not seem to be far from the truth. Consequently, too, the tenor of three isolated articles, optimistic rather than pessimistic, laudatory rather than gloom-laden, also rang true, though these pieces are far from satisfactory to the modern reader, being mainly biographical, somewhat filio-pietistic and certainly analytically shallow. Nevertheless Maurice T. Moloney, 'The Irish pioneers of the west and their descendants', *American Irish Historical Society Journal*, viii (1909), 139–51; R. C. O'Connor, 'The Irish in California', *ibid.*, i (1916), 201–11; and George T. Crowley, 'The Irish in California', *Studies*, xxv (1936), 451–62, provide one starting-point; the biographies, drawn from secondary sources, contained in Thomas F. Prendergast, *Forgotten Pioneers: Irish Leaders in Early California* (San Francisco, 1942), provide a second.

Secondary literature is, however, less than full in its coverage of Irish San Franciscans and cannot take the story very much further. The Irish of San Francisco are conspicuous by their absence in Lawrence McCaffrey, *The Irish Diaspora in America* (Bloomington, Ind., 1976); are represented by a single

A note on sources 189

mention of Denis Kearney in John B. Duff, *The Irish in the United States* (Belmont, Cal., 1971); by Broderick and Buckley in Carl Wittke, *The Irish in America* (Baton Rouge, 1956); go nigh unnoticed in Joseph P. O'Grady, *How the Irish became Americans* (New York, 1973), beyond a general comment on the Irish bankers of the city and a remark that Irish politicians captured it in the 1890s; interestingly appear at one point in Arnold Schrier, *Ireland and the American Emigration, 1850–1900* (repr. New York, 1970), pp. 38–9, in the form of the only two Irish-American success stories quoted; do not receive mention in Andrew M. Greeley, *That Most Distressful Nation: the Taming of the American Irish* (Chicago, 1972), though the San Francisco experience would, in many ways, bring early evidence to support his general theory. No San Francisco detail appears in Edward M. Levine, *The Irish and Irish Politicians: a Study in Cultural and Social Alienation* (Notre Dame, 1966), though, again, it would have strengthened his case. William V. Shannon, *The American Irish* (New York, 1963), has a chapter on 'The gold coast Irish', which, depending as it does on Julia Cooley Altrocchi, *The Spectacular San Franciscans* (New York, 1949), has something of the air of the society column. It does, however, give an impression of extraordinary social achievement for San Franciscan Irish in pointing out that Peter Donahue left $4 million and married his daughter to a German baron, at the same time omitting general remarks on the whole Irish community in the city. Oscar Lewis, *Silver Kings: the Lives and Times of Mackay, Fair, Flood, and O'Brien, Lords of the Nevada Comstock Lode* (New York, 1947), deals narrowly, too, with one section of what became the Irish upper class in the city, but without connecting it to the generality. George Potter, *To the Golden Door: the Story of the Irish in Ireland and America* (Boston, 1960), quotes Maguire, mentions the 1856 Committee of Vigilance and Broderick, but scarce gives a dozen pages to California in a massive work. The main reason why so little on the San Francisco Irish appears in these general works is clear: there is little in print, based on research among primary materials, available for use.

This work therefore rests on primary sources. One major item was the manuscript schedules of the United States census for 1860, 1870 and 1880, and of the California census for 1852, this in the edition prepared by the Genealogical Records Committee of the Daughters of the American Revolution in 1934. Frequent reference to Stephan Thernstrom's *The Other Bostonians: Poverty and Progress in the American Metropolis, 1880–1970* (Cambridge, Mass., 1973), and to other publications in the series 'Harvard Studies in Urban History', greatly helped analysis of data. A second major source was the San Francisco newspapers of the period, principally the *Daily Alta California*, the *Daily Morning Call*, the *Examiner*, and, importantly, the three Irish newspapers, the *Irish News*, the *Monitor* and the *Catholic Guardian*. Other newspapers were consulted where necessary. The San Francisco *Municipal Reports*, particularly those from 1860 to 1880, were very useful, as were, to a lesser extent, the *Legislative Journals*, published, after 1854, at Sacramento. Henry G. Langley, the compiler of the principal *Directories* of the city, amassed a wealth of detail that could be supplemented by the *Great Registers of Voters*, which gave more than the names of the electorate. Pamphlet literature was also extremly valuable.

The best history, overall, of San Francisco in the period remains John P. Young, *San Francisco: a History of the Pacific Coast Metropolis* (2 vols., Chicago, 1912), but this has been superseded for the earliest period by Roger W. Lotchin, *San Francisco, 1846–56: from Hamlet to City* (New York, 1974). F. Soule et al., *The Annals of San Francisco* (New York, 1855), remains a good read and a major source for much of these same years. Gunther Barth, *Instant Cities: Urbanization and the Rise of San Francisco and Denver* (New York, 1975), pursues an idea, not altogether successfully, but contains much insight into the period. Lawrence Kinnaird, *History of the Greater San Francisco Bay Region* (3 vols., New York and West Palm Beach, 1966); Mel Scott, *The San Francisco Bay Area: a Metropolis in Perspective* (Berkeley and Los Angeles, 1959); and James E. Vance Jr., *Geography and Urban Evolution in the San Francisco Bay Area* (Berkeley, 1964), were all useful. Further detail of the San Francisco background was drawn from the rich source of travellers' reports.

The Catholic dimension has been created over the years principally by John B. McGloin, S.J., and the Reverend Francis J. Weber, whose *Select Guide to California Catholic History* (Los Angeles, 1966) is especially important. John B. McGloin's *California's First Archbishop* (New York, 1966) and his *Eloquent Indian: the Life of James Bouchard, California Jesuit* (Stanford, 1949), are particularly outstanding. These works differ from the present one in emphasis, being less favourable to communal and religious attitudes in San Francisco in the period, but the secular and religious minds have differed before now, and may have to again. Moses Rischin, 'Beyond the Great Divide: Immigration and the Last Frontier', *Journal of American History*, lv (1968), especially pp. 46–7, has emphasised western nativism. No one would wish to deny that it existed, since no one presumably would wish to argue that easterners shed their prejudices at the Mississippi or the Isthmus of Panama. There is, however, an important distinction to be made between an area where nativism, for historical reasons, is crucial to social activity and an area where, for the same reasons, it is more peripheral, more verbal, less realistic and less effective. It is necessary to separate rhetoric and reality on many occasions in the study of history. The sources seem to say that, in San Francisco in the later nineteenth century, nativist rhetoric did not have much real effect on Irish life, though this is not the same as saying that native-born and Irish shared a life style, or lived entirely without friction.

Notes

Chapter 1

1. *Historical Statistics of the United States Colonial Times to 1957* (Washington, D.C., 1960), p. 57; M. A. Jones, *American Immigration* (Chicago, 1960), pp. 109–10; Lawrence J. McCaffrey, *The Irish Diaspora in America* (Bloomington, 1976), p. 61.
2. Francis A. Walker, *A Compendium of the Ninth Census* (Washington, D.C., 1872), pp. 396, 448–9; McCaffrey, *op. cit.*, p. 63.
3. Donald B. Cole, *Immigrant City: Lawrence, Massachusetts, 1845–1921* (Chapel Hill, 1963), pp. 27–41; Oscar Handlin, *Boston's Immigrants: a Study in Acculturation* (rev. and enl. edn., Cambridge, Mass., 1959), pp. 54–150; 178–229; Robert Ernst, *Immigrant life in New York City, 1825–63* (New York, 1949), pp 48–72; Dennis Clark, *The Irish in Philadelphia: Ten Generations of Urban Experience* (Philadelphia, 1973), pp. 38–87; Earl F. Niehaus, *The Irish in New Orleans 1800–60* (Baton Rouge, 1965), pp. 23–58.
4. Ray Allen Billington, *The Protestant Crusade 1800–60: a Study of the Origins of American Nativism* (repr. Chicago, 1964), pp. 1–31, 68, 70, 71–6.
5. Michael Feldberg, *The Philadelphia Riots of 1844: a Study of Ethnic Conflict* (Westport, Conn., 1975), *passim*; Billington, *op. cit.*, pp. 220–37.
6. Adrian Cook, *The Armies of the Streets: the New York City Draft Riots of 1863* (Lexington, Ky., 1974), *passim*.
7. John Higham, *Strangers in the Land: Patterns of American Nativism 1860–1925* (New Brunswick, N.J., 1955), pp. 12–34
8. Barbara M. Solomon, *Ancestors and Immigrants: a Changing New England Tradition* (repr. New York, 1965), pp. 3, 22, 29, 43–58; Edward Pessen, 'The marital theory and practice of the Antebellum urban elite', *New York History*, 53 (1972), 389–410; E. Digby Batzell, *Philadelphia Gentlemen: the Making of a National Upper Class* (New York, 1958), especially chapter VI.
9. The Irish in the Middle West have been studied in Dean R. Esslinger, *Immigrants and the City: Ethnicity and Mobility in a Nineteenth-century Midwestern Community* (Port Washington, N.Y., 1975); in Merle Curti, *The Making of an American Community: a Case Study of Democracy in a Frontier County* (Stanford, 1959); Mary J. McDonald, *History of the Irish in Wisconsin in the Nineteenth Century* (Washington, D.C., 1954); Kathleen Neils Conzen, *Immigrant Milwaukee, 1836–60: Accommodation and Community in a Frontier City* (Cambridge, Mass., 1976).
10. The change has been studied in Leonard Pitt, *The Decline of the Californios: a Social History of the Spanish Speaking Californians 1846–90* (Berkeley

and Los Angeles, 1966).

11. Roger W. Lotchin, *San Francisco 1846–56: from Hamlet to City* (New York, 1974), pp. 3–30.

12. The official figures given by the United States Bureau of the Census were disputed by local observers, partly through local pride. In 1879 one city directory claimed a population of 'about 330,000', See D. M. Bishop, comp., *Bishop's Directory of the City and County of San Francisco, 1879* (San Francisco, 1879), p. 30. The U.S. census officials were willing to agree that their figures were suspect. See U.S. Bureau of the Census, *Compendium of the Tenth Census* (2 parts, Washington, D.C., 1883), I, xxvii; and Carroll D. Wright, *The History and Growth of the United States Census* (Washington, D.C., 1900), p. 69.

13. Walker, *Compendium Ninth Census,* pp. 444, 448.

14. The figures for second and later generations of Irish were personally compiled from the microfilm schedules of the United States censuses of San Francisco, 1860, 1870 and 1880, and the state census of 1852. See also U.S. Bureau of the Census, *Statistics of the Population of the United States at the Tenth Census* (Washington, D.C., 1883), p. 51. The figures compiled from the manuscript schedules of the 1880 census are not quite complete, as some of them, covering about five hundred first-generation Irish, and a proportionate number of later generations, are now missing. This study concerns itself almost exclusively with the first and second generations. A study of the second generation opens the question of whether those with only one Irish parent should be included. Purists might correctly argue that only those second-generation with two Irish parents should properly be thought to belong to the Irish community and certainly that no third generation with only one Irish-born grandparent should be. The study of marriage patterns reveals, however, that parents on the surface not Irish very often had Irish blood, in more cases than not. At the same time, it is arguable that the true definition of whether an individual was Irish, in the sense of what community gave him or her the basic values, would depend, in an ethnically mixed marriage, on which partner was dominant. Since this cannot be known, and since it seems unacceptable to leave the products of ethnically mixed marriages in some form of limbo, the Irish community is defined here as all those who had one Irish grandparent. If a large percentage of the Irish so defined had only one Irish grandparent, such a definition would be absurd. It is the case, however, that about ninety per cent of those now defined as Irish had three or more Irish-born grandparents.

15. [Henry G. Langley], *Langley's San Francisco Directory for the Year commencing April 1880* (San Francisco, 1880), p. 1118; *The Scotch-Irish in America: Proceedings and Addresses of the Third Congress* (Nashville, Tenn., 1891), pp. 1, 139–59, 301–6.

16. San Francisco *Monitor,* 17 April 1869.

17. John F. Maguire, *The Irish in America* (New York, 1868), pp. 261, 273–80. At least one Irishman left a record of the impact of Maguire's work, even if in the end the reader did not follow the advice to go west. The Attorney General of Illinois, Maurice T. Moloney, described how 'as a boy in Ireland, reading his lectures on the subject, and subsequently, after graduating at the University of Virginia, I determined to go to California'. See Maurice T.

Moloney, 'The Irish pioneers of the west and their descendants', *American Irish Historical Society Journal*, viii (1909), 141.

18. [J. Alemany], *Pastoral Letter, 17 July 1862, to the Clergy of the Diocese of San Francisco assembled in Diocesan Synod* (San Francisco, ?1862).

19. Rev. Hubert Vaughan, 'California and the Church', *The Catholic World*, ii (1866), 800, 807, 811.

20. Rev. William Gleeson, *History of the Catholic Church in California* (2 vols., San Francisco, 1872), ii, 280.

21. Walker, *Statistical Atlas of the United States, based on the Results of the Ninth Census, 1870* (Washington, D.C., 1874), plate XXXI; U.S. Bureau of the Census, *Statistics of the United States (including Mortality, Property, etc.) in 1860* (Washington, D.C., 1866) p. 359; id., *The Statistics of the Population of the United States, Ninth Census-Volume I* (Washington, D.C., 1872), p. 531.

22. P. J. Thomas, comp., *Our Centennial Memoir. Founding of the Missions. San Francisco de Assis and its Hundredth Year* (San Francisco, 1877), p. 163.

23. Rev. Hugh Quigley, *The Irish Race in California, and on the Pacific Coast* (San Francisco, 1878), pp. 418–19.

24. San Francisco *Alta California*, 4 January 1849.

25. P.R.O. Foreign Office Papers, Series 5, vol. 536, 14 June 1851; vol. 571, 30 June, 16 October 1853.

26. William V. Shannon, *The American Irish* (New York, 1963), pp. 73, 182.

27. *Biographical Dictionary of the American Congress, 1774–1961* (Washington, D.C., 1961), pp. 672, 730. Conness did not receive much support from the San Francisco delegation at Sacramento, partly because he was an ex-Democrat and the delegation consisted largely of ex-Republicans, both now in the Union party. Only two members of the city's legislative delegation were supporting him on the sixty-first ballot; only six of a possible seventeen voted for him in the final sixty-ninth ballot of the Union Senatorial Caucus. By contrast, eleven members of the city's delegation voted for Casserly in his victorious fifth ballot of the Democratic Senatorial Caucus. Sixteen members of the delegation were Democrats. See *Sacramento Daily Union*, 9, 10 February 1863; 20 December 1867.

28. David A. Williams, *David C. Broderick: a Political Portrait* (San Marino, 1969), esp. pp. 12, 84, 118–19, 137, 166; Hubert Howe Bancroft, *History of California* (7 vols., San Francisco, 1884–90), vi, 678–739.

29. San Francisco, *Irish News*, 11 July 1868.

30. Thomas F. Prendergast, *Forgotten Pioneers; Irish Leaders in Early California* (San Francisco, 1942), chapter XXIV, *passim*.

31. *Ibid.*, chapter XI, *passim*.

32. *Alta California*, 17 May 1861; 26 May 1863.

33. Quigley, *Irish Race*, pp. 397–9; R. C. O'Connor, 'The Irish in California', *Journal of the American Irish Historical Society*, xv (1916), 208; Bancroft, *California*, vii, 754 n.

34. *Irish News*, 11 July 1868.

35. Prendergast, *op. cit.*, p. 177; Quigley, *op. cit.*, pp. 326–31. The detail on real estate drawn from the manuscript schedules of the Eighth U.S. Census.

36. *Irish News*, 11 July, 8 August 1868.

37. *Irish News*, 2 May 1868.

38. Bancroft, *op. cit.*, vii, 177.
39. Alonzo Phelps, *Contemporary Biography of California's Representative Men* (2 vols., San Francisco, 1881), i, 330.
40. Prendergast, *op. cit.*, chapters V, IX, *passim*.
41. Bancroft, *op. cit.*, vii, 315; Prendergast, *op. cit.*, chapter XIX, *passim; Report of the Trustees of the R.C. Orphan Asylum and Free School Association, of the City of San Francisco, August 6th, 1854* (San Francisco, 1854); *Report of the Trustees of the R.C. Orphan Asylum of San Francisco, January 1st, 1857* (San Francisco, 1857).
42. *Appendix to Journals of Senate and Assembly, 1867–68, 17th Session*, (Sacramento, 1868), III, *Report of the Joint Hospital Committee in Relation to Charitable Institutions Aided by the State of California*, *passim*.
43. Frances Cahn and Valeska Bary, *Welfare Activities of Federal, State and Local Governments in California, 1850–1934* (Berkeley, 1936), pp. 9–11.
44. *Ibid.*, p. 66.
45. Table 1 is taken from Peter R. Decker, 'Social mobility on the urban frontier: the San Francisco merchants, 1850–80' (Ph.D. thesis, Columbia University, 1974), p. 452.
46. The heritage of the Reformation has been stressed in Colman J. Berry, 'Some roots of American nativism', *Catholic Historical Review*, xliv (1958), 139, 141–3, and by Gordon A. Cahill in his 'Comments' on Berry in *ibid.*, 159–64.
47. San Francisco, *Catholic Guardian*, January 1872.

Chapter II

1. *Statistics of the Population . . . Tenth Census*, p. 855.
2. Lotchin, *San Francisco*, p. 48; Decker, *Fortunes and Failures: White-collar Mobility in Nineteenth-century San Francisco* (Cambridge, Mass., 1978), p. 34; Bancroft, *History of California*, vii, 110–12, 113, 173–80, 182–3.
3. Figures personally compiled from the manuscript schedules of the Tenth Census.
4. Lotchin, *op. cit.*, pp. 45–6; Bancroft, *op. cit.*, vii, 116–19.
5. Lotchin, *op. cit.*, p. 54; Bancroft, *op. cit.*, vii, 121–3.
6. Decker, 'Social mobility', p. 345.
7. Bancroft, *op. cit.*, vii, 73; Neil L. Shumsky, 'Tar Flat and Nob Hill: a social history of industrial San Francisco during the 1870s' (Ph.D. thesis, University of California, Berkeley, 1972), 22–3, 58–9; Decker, *Fortunes and Failures*, pp. 70, 76, 163–64, 167, 168.
8. Lotchin, *op. cit.*, pp. 65–7; Bancroft, *op. cit.*, vii, 67–71.
9. U.S. Bureau of the Census, *Manufactures of the United States in 1860* (Washington, D.C., 1865), pp. 28–9.
10. Bancroft, *op. cit.*, vii, 115, 687.
11. U.S. Bureau of the Census, *The Statistics of Wealth and Industry of the United States . . . Ninth Census* (Washington, D.C., 1872), pp. 496, 640.
12. W. F. Rae, *Westward by Rail: a Journey to San Francisco and Back and a Visit to the Mormons* (2nd edn., London, 1871), pp. 269–71.
13. Samuel Bowles, *Our New West* (Hartford, 1869), pp. 358–9; see also John Erastus Lester, *The Atlantic to the Pacific: What to See and How to See it*

(London, 1873), pp. 85–6; J. G. Player-Frowd, *Six Months in California* (London, 1872), pp. 33–4.

14. Francis A. Walker and Charles W. Seaton, eds., *Compendium of the Tenth Census* (2 parts, Washington, D.C., 1883), II, 1092–5; U.S. Bureau of the Census, *Report on the Manufactures of the United States... Tenth Census* (Washington, D.C., 1883), pp. 26, 435–7. See also Gunther Barth, *Instant Cities: Urbanisation and the Rise of San Francisco and Denver* (New York, 1975), pp. 208–28.

15. U.S. Bureau of the Census, *Agriculture of the United States in 1860* (Washington, D.C., 1864), pp. 10–12, 194.

16. *Wealth and Industry, Ninth Census*, pp. 104–7, 346.

17. U.S. Bureau of the Census, *Report on the Productions of Agriculture... Tenth Census* (Washington, D.C., 1883), pp. 34, 144, 256, 257.

18. Bancroft, *History of California*, vi, 768; Lotchin, *San Francisco*, p. 140.

19. Lotchin, *op. cit.*, pp. 137–8.

20. John P. Young, *San Francisco: a History of the Pacific Coast Metropolis* (2 vols., San Francisco, 1912), i, 192.

21. Bancroft, *op. cit.*, vi, 772.

22. Young, *op. cit.*, ii, 517.

23. Bancroft, *op. cit.*, vi, 774 n. 42; vii, 690 n. 31; Young, *op. cit.*, ii, 556. Considering that wages were high in San Francisco, local taxation was comparatively low. In Baltimore the rate peaked at $1·18¼ in the decade 1855–64, generally remaining at $1·15 and below, but the troubles of Reconstruction sent it up to between $1·50 and $1·90 in the decade 1869–78. In Cleveland the rate stayed below $1 before 1860, but reached $2·01½ in 1865, peaked at $2·07½ in 1870 and fluctuated between $1·25 and $1·88 during the remainder of the decade, with the median rate being $1·78¼ per $100 of assessed property. See J. M. Hollander, *The Financial History of Baltimore* (Baltimore, 1899), pp. 382–3; Charles C. Williamson, 'The finances of Cleveland' (Ph.D. thesis, Columbia University, 1907), p. 228.

24. Anthony Trollope, *North America* (repr. Harmondsworth, Middx, 1968), p. 79. An urban philosophy, that is, a view that the community should act positively to improve material and moral conditions, is visible in the American colonies of the mid-eighteenth century. See Carl Bridenbaugh, *Cities in Revolt: Urban Life in America, 1743–1776* (repr. New York, 1971). It informed some urban activity in the early nineteenth century. See Richard D. Brown, 'The emergence of urban society in rural Massachusetts, 1760–1820', *Journal of American History*, lxi (1974), 37–42, 46–7; John Higham, *From Boundlessness to Consolidation: the Transformation of American Culture, 1848–60* (Ann Arbor, 1969), pp. 26–7; Richard C. Wade, *The Urban Frontier: the Rise of Western Cities, 1790–1830* (Cambridge, Mass., 1959), pp. 316–21. That it did not develop confidently or uninterruptedly, as it did not in San Francisco, as will be seen, is the theme of Michael H. Frisch, *Town into City: Springfield, Massachusetts, and the Meaning of Community, 1840–80* (Cambridge, Mass., 1972).

25. U.S. Bureau of the Census, *Report on the Social Statistics of Cities* (2 parts, Washington, D.C., 1887), II, p. 805.

26. Young, *San Francisco*, ii, 518; *Valedictory of the Hon. Geo. Hewston, M.D.*,

and Inaugural Address of the Hon. A. J. Bryant (San Francisco, 1875), p. 12.

27. Lotchin, *op. cit.*, p. 171; Dwight L. Clarke, *William Tecumseh Sherman: Gold Rush Banker* (San Francisco, 1969), p. 23.

28. *Valedictory of the Hon. Thos. Selby and Inaugural Address of the Hon. Wm. Alvord* (San Francisco, 1871), p. 14.

29. *Valedictory of the Hon. Wm. Alvord and Inaugural Address of the Hon. James Otis* (San Francisco, 1873), p. 20; Lotchin, *op. cit.*, p. 172, Hewston, *Valedictory*, p. 6.

30. *Social Statistics of Cities*, II, p. 811.

31. Young, *op. cit.*, i, 182; Bancroft, *California*, vi, 214, n. 68; Lotchin, *op. cit.*, pp. 201–3.

32. Young, *op. cit.*, i, 447.

33. *Ibid*, ii, 451; Lotchin, *San Francisco*, p. 204

34. Alvord, *Valedictory*, p. 10; Board of Supervisors, *San Francisco Municipal Reports for the Fiscal Year 1879–80* (San Francisco, 1880), p. 284.

35. Alvord, *Valedictory*, pp. 10–11.

36. Hewston, *Valedictory*, p. 22

37. *Municipal Reports, 1879–80*, p. 284.

38. Young, *op. cit.*, ii, 541; *Municipal Reports, 1879–80*, p. 284.

39. *Municipal Reports, 1879–80*, p. 295.

40. Frederick Whymper, *California and its Prospects*, in H. W. Bates, ed., *Illustrated Travels: a Record of Discovery, Geography and Adventure* (London, n.d.), p. 103, Isabelle Saxon, *Five Years within the Golden Gate* (London, 1868), pp. 27–52; Sir Charles Wentworth Dilke, Bt., *Greater Britain: a record of Travel in English-speaking Countries* (8th edn., London, 1885), pp. 159–70; Charles Loring Brace, *The New West: or, California in 1867–68* (New York, 1869), p. 41; Rae, *Westward by Rail*, pp. 265–6; Player-Frowd, *Six Months*, p. 1.

41. *Municipal Reports, 1879–80*, p. 284.

42. *Ibid.*, pp. 281–3.

43. Young, *San Francisco*, i, 255–6.

44. See, for instance, *Constitution, By-Laws, and Rules of Order of Young America Engine Co. No. 13* (San Francisco, 1856), Article IV; *Constitution and By-laws of St. Francis (Hook and Ladder No. 1)* (San Francisco, 1857), Article 8, sec. 1; *Constitution and By-laws of Volunteer Engine Co. No. 7* (San Francisco, 1860), Article 3.

45. Lotchin, *San Francisco*, pp. 177–80.

46. A London Parson, *To San Francisco and Back* (London, ?1870), p. 76. See also Saxon, *Five Years*, pp. 69–70.

47. Young, *San Francisco*, i, 442; Saxon, *op. cit.*, p. 69.

48. Young, *op. cit.*, ii, 569–70.

49. *Langley's Directory, 1880*, p. 1090.

50. J. W. Boddam-Whetham, *Western Wanderings: a Record of Travel in the Evening Land* (London, 1874), p. 155.

51. Brace, *op. cit.*, p. 41; Saxon, *op. cit.*, p. 70. See also Emily Faithfull, *Three Visits to America* (Edinburgh, 1884), p. 214.

52. *Social Statistics of Cities, 1880*, II, p. 812.

53. Lotchin, *San Francisco*, pp. 181–3.

54. *The Charter of the San Francisco City Water Works together with Copies of the*

Acts of the Legislature and Ordinances of the City of San Francisco (San Francisco, 1863), p. 6.

55. Young, *San Francisco*, i, 407–8; *Laws, Ordinances, and Acts of Incorporation affecting the Property and Franchises of the Spring Valley Water Works* (San Francisco, 1879), p. 2.
56. Young, *op. cit.*, ii, 586.
57. *The State*, 7 June 1879.
58. Mel Scott, *The San Francisco Bay Area: a Metropolis in Perspective* (Berkeley and Los Angeles, 1959), p. 203.
59. Young, *op. cit.*, i, 326
60. *Ibid.*, ii, 582–3.
61. *Social Statistics of Cities, 1880*, II, p. 806.
62. Young, *op. cit.*, ii, 531.
63. Scott, *op. cit.*, p. 68. Young says the service opened in 1880. See *San Francisco*, ii, 583.
64. *Ibid.*, ii, 583.
65. I. H. Stallard, *The Problem of the Sewerage of San Francisco: a Polyclinic Lecture* (San Francisco, 1892), pp. 18–19.
66. *Municipal Reports, 1879–80*, p. 829.
67. See *An Act to Establish a Quarantine and Sanitary Laws for the City and County of San Francisco, and Orders and Regulations Adopted by the Board of Health* (San Francisco, 1870), *passim*.
68. Lotchin, *San Francisco*, p. 312; J. C. Pelton, *Origin of the Free Public Schools of San Francisco* (San Francisco, 1865), pp. 12–13: Pelton, *Life's Sunbeams and Shadows* (San Francisco, 1893), p. 224.
69. *Langley's Directory, 1880*, pp. 32–4.
70. *Municipal Reports, 1879–80*, pp. 660–2, 685; *Department of Public Schools, . . . Twenty-fifth Annual Report . . . 1878* (San Francisco, 1878), p. 38.
71. William Warren Ferrier, *Ninety Years of Education in California, 1846–1936: a Presentation of Educational Movements and their Outcome in Education Today* (Berkeley, 1937), p. 79. Boston's first High School was established in 1821.
72. *Ibid.*, pp. 81, 86–7, 89–90.
73. Lotchin, *op. cit.*, p. 312; John Swett, *Public Education in California: its Origin and Development, with Personal Reminiscences of Half a Century* (New York, 1911), p. 202.
74. *Ibid.*, pp. 202, 204.
75. Swett, *Public Education in California*, pp. 207, 221, 224, 235. See also David B. Tyack, *The One Best System: a History of American Urban Education* (Cambridge, Mass., 1974), p. 100.
76. Ferrier, *op. cit.*, pp. 163, 168, 169; *Municipal Reports, 1879–80*, p. 733; Faithfull, *op. cit.*, p. 221.
77. Cahn and Bary, *Welfare Activities*, pp. 33, 153.
78. *Langley's Directory, 1880*, pp. 17, 18; Bancroft, *op. cit.*, vi, 722; Cahn and Bary, *op. cit.*, pp. 46–8.
79. *Langley's Directory, 1880*, p. 18.
80. Cahn and Bary, *op. cit.*, pp. 138–44, 156–7, 170–1 and 132, 199.
81. *Langley's Directory, 1880*, p. 18.

82. Brace, *New West*, p. 74. See also Rev. John Todd, *The Sunset Land; or, The Great Pacific Slope* (London, 1869), p. 266; Bowles, *Our New West*, pp. 353–4.

83. Lester, *Atlantic to the Pacific*, p. 85.

84. Faithfull, *Three Visits*, p. 222.

85. *The School Scandal of San Francisco* (San Francisco, 1878), *passim*; Young, *San Francisco*, ii, 645; Walter M. Fisher, *The Californians* (London, 1876), p. 147; E. R. Highton, *Some General Observations on Matters of Public Interest with Special Reference to the Municipal Government of San Francisco* (San Francisco, 1866), p. 17. Pelton, *Life's Sunbeams and Shadows*, p. 234. When Henry George went to investigate the Industrial School a gun was pulled on him. See Charles A. Barker, *Henry George* (New York, 1955), p. 218. Joseph C. Merrill, *The Industrial School Investigation. With a Glance at the Great Reformation and its Results* (San Francisco, 1872), *passim*. Player-Frowd, *Six Months*, pp. 213–14.

86. Guy and Helen Griffen, *The Story of Golden Gate Park* (San Francisco, 1949), pp. 10–12.

87. Alvord, *Inaugural*, p. 19.

88. *Municipal Reports, 1879–80*, p. 619.

89. *The State*, 12 April 1879; Young, *San Francisco*, ii, 637; *Municipal Reports 1879–80*, p. 830.

90. George August Sala, *America Revisited: from the Bay of New York to the Gulf of Mexico, and from Lake Michigan to the Pacific* (2 vols., 3rd edn., London, 1883), p.445.

91. *Langley's Directory, 1880*, pp. 36–38. The number marked a slight falling off from earlier days. By 1856 there were at least fifteen libraries in San Francisco, five of which could, in some sense, be described as public. See Hugh S. Baker,'"Rational Amusement in our Midst": public libraries in California, 1849–59', *California Historical Society Quarterly* (hereafter cited as *C.H.S.Q.*), xxxviii (1959), 303.

92. Brace, *The New West*, p. 41; Lester, *Atlantic to the Pacific*, p. 96; R.P. Spice, *The Wanderings of the Hermit of Westminster between New York and San Francisco in the Autumn of 1881* (London, ?1882), p. 31; Young, *op. cit.*, ii, 606, 638; *Sacramento Union*, 12 September 1855; Rae, *Westward by Rail*, p. 318.

93. Lester, *op. cit.*, p. 96.

94. *Ibid*, p. 95.

95. Lotchin, *San Francisco*, p. 333; Young, *San Francisco*, i, 262; Saxon, *Five Years*, p. 100; Bancroft, *History of California*, vi, 780 n. 58.

96. Player-Frowd, *Six Months*, p. 203.

97. Young, *op. cit.*, i, 262; Saxon, *op. cit.*, p. 100; Boddam-Whetham, *Western Wanderings*, pp. 150–1; Lady Dufus Hardy, *Through Cities and Prairie Lands: Sketches of an American Tour* (London, 1881), pp. 148–50.

98. Young, *San Francisco*, ii, 410; William L. MacGregor, *San Francisco, California, in 1876* (Edinburgh, 1876), pp. 49–50; M. Davenport, *Under the Gridiron: a Summer in the United States and the Far West, including a Run through Canada* (London, 1876), pp. 82–3.

99. Boddam-Whetham, *Western Wanderings*, pp. 170–3. Another good description can be found in William Minturn, *Travels West* (London, 1877), pp. 242–4.

100. Saxon, *Five Years*, p. 101; Player-Frowd, *Six Months*, p. 201; Minturn, *op. cit.*, p. 246; Wallis Nash, *Oregon: There and Back in 1877* (London, 1878), pp. 47–49; W. H. Russell, *Hesperothen; Notes from the West* (2 vols. in one, London, 1882), ii, 62–6.

101. Minturn, *Travels West*, p. 342. See also Bowles, *Our New West*, p. 345; Lester, *Atlantic to the Pacific*, p. 95; [P. W. Hamer], *From Ocean to Ocean, Being a Diary of a Three Months' Expedition from Liverpool to California and Back, from the Atlantic to the Pacific by the Overland Route* (n.p., 1871), p. 42; G. A. Lawrence, *Silverland*, (London, 1873), p. 108; Nash, *Oregon*, p. 53.

102. Bowles, *op. cit.*, p. 346.

103. *Social Statistics of Cities, 1880*, II, p. 806; *Langley's Directory, 1880*, p. 19.

104. Player-Frowd, *Six Months*, pp 30–1; Minturn, *Travels West*, pp. 241–2, 304; William M. Bell, *Other Countries* (2 vols., London, 1872), ii, 179, 180.

105. *Social Statistics of Cities, 1880*, II, p. 807.

106. Russell, *Hesperothen*, ii, 45; Lawrence, *Silverland*, p. 143; Boddam-Whetham, *Western Wanderings*, p. 147; MacGregor, *San Francisco*, pp. 14–16; Davenport, *Under the Gridiron*, p. 80; Lester, *Atlantic to Pacific*, p. 72; Willard Glazier, *Peculiarities of American Cities* (Philadelphia, 1885), p. 459; Player-Frowd, *Six Months*, pp. 18–19, 22–3.

107. S. B. Sutton, ed; *Civilising American Cities: a Selection of Frederick Law Olmsted's Writings on City Landscapes* (Cambridge, Mass.; 1971), p. 128.

108. Sir Rose Lambart Price, Bt., *The Two Americas; an Account of Sport and Travel with Notes on Men and Manners in North and South America* (London, 1877), pp. 202–3. See also Saxon, *Five Years*, p. 10.

109. *Municipal Reports, 1879–80*, pp. 421, 468.

110. Young, *San Francisco*, i, 327.

Chapter III

1. R.A. Burchell, 'The gathering of a community: the British-born of San Francisco in 1852 and 1872', *Journal of American Studies*, 10 (1976), 279–312.

2. Figures personally compiled from the manuscript schedules of the census. Where no source is given for figures used in this chapter, it should be assumed that they have been compiled from these manuscript schedules.

3. Burchell, 'Gathering', 303–4; *Annual Reports of the Commissioners of Emigration of the State of New York from May 5, 1847, to 1860, inclusive* (New York, 1861); *Annual Reports of the Commissioners of Emigration for the State of New York for the years ending December 31, 1861–70* (New York, 1862–71), 10 vols.

4. Bancroft, *California*, vii, 696–8; F. Soule, H. Gihon and James Nisbet, *The Annals of San Francisco* (New York, 1855), pp. 411, 413. A survey in 1859 of one overland route suggested that it was being used by migrants from states west of Ohio, and not from the eastern states that provided the bulk of San Francisco's Irish. See W. Turrentine Jackson, *Wagon Roads West* (repr. New Haven, 1965), pp. 213–14.

5. John H. Kemble, *The Panama Route 1848–69* (Berkeley and Los Angeles, 1943), pp. 54–57, 65, 69, 77, 82, 92, 94, 148.

6. *Irish News*, 4 April 1868.

7. San Francisco *Daily Morning Call*, 12 August 1870; San Francisco, *The*

Monitor, 15 May, 31 July 1869.

8. California Immigrant Union, *All about California and the Inducements to Settle There* (3rd 10,000, San Francisco, 1871), pp. 36, 74.

9. M. Phillips Price, *America after Sixty Years: the Travel Diaries of Two Generations of Englishmen* (London, 1936), p. 36.

10. Robert Louis Stevenson, *Across the Plains* (London, 1913), p. 36. Interestingly, Stevenson noted that on his emigrant train 'There were no emigrants direct from Europe'. See p. 39.

11. California, *Appendix to Journals of Senate and Assembly, 19th Session* (Sacramento, 1872), III: *Memorial and Report of the California Immigrant Union*, p. 20; Bancroft, *California*, vii, 697 n. 2.

12. R. Byron Johnson, *Very Far West Indeed: a Few Rough Experiences on the North West Pacific Coast* (London, 1872), pp. 12–13.

13. *History of Merced County* (San Francisco, 1881), pp. 151–2.

14. California, *Appendix to Journal of Assembly, 12th Session* (Sacramento, 1861), *Report of Committee on Commerce and Navigation*, pp. 1–9.

15. *Ibid.*, p. 3

16. California, *Appendix, Journal of Assembly, 12th Session, Annual Report of Controller of State for the Year 1860*.

17. Frances Cahn and Valeska Bary, *Welfare Activities of Federal, State and Local Governments in California, 1850–1934* (Berkeley, 1936), pp. 336–8.

18. Caspar T. Hopkins, *Common Sense applied to the Immigration Question: Showing why the 'California Immigrant Union' was Founded, and What it Expects to Do* (San Francisco, 1869), *passim*.

19. See *Articles of Incorporation and By-laws of the Immigration Association of California Incorporated November 18 1881* (San Francisco, 1882).

20. It has been suggested, in general, that migrants within the United States are not 'average' people. Sece George W. Pierson, *The Moving Americans* (New York, 1973), pp. 167–8, 176–8. It is tempting to see the Irish story in San Francisco as in part a result of this basic 'law' of migration, but in the absence of firm corroborative evidence the temptation must be resisted. See also Everett S. Lee, 'A theory of migration', *Demography*, 3 (1966), 47–57.

21. Scott, *San Francisco Bay Area*, p. 19.

22. Samuel Smiles, ed., *A Boy's Voyage round the World; including a Residence in Victoria, and a Journey by Rail across North America* (London, 1871), p. 245.

23. Young, *San Francisco*, i, 414, 415.

24. Scott, *op. cit.*, p. 79.

25. Lotchin, *San Francisco*, pp. 17, 22–3.

26. Scott, *op. cit.*, p. 63; Young, *op. cit.*, i, 275.

27. *Langley's Directory, 1880*, p. 13.

28. Lotchin, *op. cit.*, pp. 25, 70.

29. Young, *op. cit.*, i, 412–13. Steam traction was forbidden in the city in 1868.

30. Bancroft, *California*, vii, 684 n. 8; *Langley's Directory, 1880*, pp. 20–3; *Social Statistics of Cities*, II, p. 805; Scott, *op. cit.*, pp. 41–42.

31. Scott, *op. cit.*, p. 35; Lester, *Atlantic to the Pacific*, p. 87.

32. Young, *San Francisco*, i, 413; J. E. Ollivant, *A Breeze from the Great Salt Lake; or, New Zealand to New York by the New Mail Route* (London, 1871),

pp. 24–25.
33. Young, *op. cit.*, ii, 531.
34. MacGregor, *San Francisco*, p. 24; T. S. Hudson, *A Scamper through America, or, Fifteen Thousand Miles on Ocean and Continent in Sixty Days* (2nd thousand, London, 1882), p. 139; W. G. Marshall, *Through America; or, Nine Months in the United States* (London, 1881), p. 264.
35. Lotchin, *San Francisco*, p. 24; Young, *op. cit.*, i, 417.
36. Sala, *America Revisited*, pp. 446–7, 452.
37. Lawrence Kinnaird, *History of the Greater San Francisco Bay Region* (3 vols., New York and West Palm Beach, 1966), i, 436–41. See also *Irish News*, 12 October 1867; Bancroft, *California*, vi, 755–60.
38. Kinnaird, *op. cit.*, i, 445.
39. Young, *San Francisco*, i, 347.
40. *Ibid.*, i, 327.
41. Henry G. Langley, comp., *The San Francisco Directory . . . 1869* (San Francisco, 1869), p. 47.
42. *Langley's Directory, 1880*, pp. 13–14.
43. *Irish News*, 25 January 1868; Ira B. Cross, *Financing an Empire: History of Banking in California* (4 vols., Chicago, 1927), i, 243, 372, 375.
44. *Langley's Directory, 1869*, p. 46. The *Irish News*, 18 April 1868, said, 'There are 104 Homestead Associations in San Francisco, as recorded in the Hall of Records,' presumably an item of news to interest the Irish reader.
45. *Articles of Association, Certificate of Incorporation, Rules of Order, Map, Officers, Remarks, etc., of the Abbey Homestead Association. Incorporated February 20th, 1869* (San Francisco, 1869), p. 7.
46. *Articles of Association and By-laws of the Sunny Vale Homestead Association* (San Francisco, 1869), *passim*.
47. Brace, *New West*, pp. 49, 50.
48. Sala, *America Revisited*, p. 457.
49. Boddam-Whetham, *Western Wanderings*, p. 178.
50. *Daily Morning Call*, 26 November 1863.
51. *Alta California*, 4 June 1861; Lotchin, *San Francisco*, pp. 11–14.
52. See *An Act to Establish a Quarantine and Sanitary Laws for the City and County of San Francisco, and Orders and Regulations Adopted by the Board of Health* (San Francisco, 1870).
53. Johnson, *Very Far West*, pp. 17–18; See also Saxon, *Five Years*, pp. 10–12; Smiles, *Boy's Voyage*, p. 245.
54. Highton, *Some General Observations*, pp. 25, 61.
55. *Chinatown Declared a Nuisance!* (San Francisco, 1880), pp. 15, 16.
56. William Hepworth Dixon, *White Conquest* (2 vols., London, 1876), ii, 250–1.
57. Lawrence, *Silverland*, p. 143, quoting Mark Twain.
58. Young, *San Francisco*, i, 413–14.
59. Alvin Averbach, 'San Francisco's South of Market District, 1858–1958: the emergence of a Skid Row', *California Historical Society Quarterly* (hereafter cited as *C.H.S.Q.*), lii (1973), 200–3.
60. Nash, *Oregon*, p. 46. See also Boddam-Whetham, *Western Wanderings*, pp. 155–6.

61. Robert P. Porter et al., *The West from the Census of 1880* (Chicago, 1882), p. 510: Richard A. Van Orman, 'San Francisco: hotel city of the west', in John A. Carroll, ed., *Reflections of Western Historians* (Tucson, 1969), pp. 10–18.
62. Saxon, *Five Years*, p. 191.
63. Lotchin, *San Francisco*, p. 120; Bradford Luckingham, 'Immigrant life in emergent San Francisco', *Journal of the West*, 12 (1973), 602.
64. Cross, *A History of the Labor Movement in California* (Berkeley, 1935), pp. 69, 313 n. 30.
65. Soule, *Annals*, pp. 300, 358, 484.

Chapter IV

1. Peter M. Blau and Otis Dudley Duncan, using mid-twentieth-century evidence, have discussed class barriers to free mobility. See their *The American Occupational Structure* (New York, 1967), especially pp. 76–79; also Duncan and Robert W. Hodge, 'Education and occupational mobility: a regression analysis', *American Journal of Sociology*, lxviii (1963), 629–44. Some of the evidence presented in Decker, 'Social mobility on the urban frontier', especially pp. 120–34, suggests the same factors at work in mid-nineteenth-century San Francisco.
2. A point made strongly by Stephan Thernstrom in *Poverty and Progress: Social Mobility in a Nineteenth Century City* (Cambridge, Mass., 1964), chapter V.
3. Figures here and throughout the chapter compiled from the manuscript schedules of the censuses.
4. The German-born white-collar group is discussed further in Decker, *op. cit.*, pp. 137–45.
5. There were always concentrations or clusterings of Irish, but these were always relative, that is, importantly, they did not mean a marked or significant absence of Irish in other areas. See Lotchin, *San Francisco*, p. 120; Luckingham, 'Immigrant life', 602. The broad dispersal of Irish in San Francisco was similar to that in other parts of the United States, suggesting that Irish ghettoes were never a reality, even in the mid-nineteenth century. See Sam Bass Warner Jr. and Colin Burke, 'Cultural change and the ghetto', *Journal of Contemporary History*, 4 (1969), 178–80; David Ward, 'The emergence of central immigrant ghettoes in American cities, 1840–1920', *Annals of the Association of American Geographers*, 58 (1968), 347, 352–3; Howard P. Chudacoff, 'A new look at ethnic neighborhoods: residential dispersion and the concept of visibility in a medium-sized city', *Journal of American History*, lx (1973–74), 77–9, 86.
6. Bancroft, *California*, vi, 190–1.
7. Saxon, *Five Years*, p. 191.
8. Bancroft, *op. cit.*, vii, 104, 110 n. 17; MacGregor, *San Francisco*, p. 63.
9. P.R.O. Foreign Office Papers, Series 5, vol. 785, 20 February 1862; vol. 911, 3 March 1863; MacGregor, *op. cit.*, p. 63.
10. Clarence D. Long, *Wages and Earnings in the United States, 1860–90* (Princeton, 1960), p. 84.
11. Shumsky, 'Tar Flat and Nob Hill', pp. 47–8. The figures given there,

the basis for Table 13, were derived from U.S. Department of Labor, *Wages in the United States and Europe, 1870 to 1898* (Washington, D.C., 1898), Bulletin 18. Massachusetts wage rates can be compared by looking at the figures given by MacGregor, *San Francisco*, p. 63, and at Carroll D. Wright, *A Compendium of the Census of Massachusetts, 1875* (Boston, 1877), pp. 270–6. In Massachusetts a labourer reportedly earned $1.63 per day.

12. Quoted in J. Ross Browne, *Resources of the Pacific Slope* (San Francisco, 1869), pp. 610–11.

13. John S. Hittell, *A History of the City of San Francisco and Inadvertently of the State of California* (San Francisco, 1878), pp. 457–8.

14. Browne, *Resources*, p. 269. In fact during 1868 the average New York wholesale price of flour was $7.912 per 100 lb, while the San Francisco wholesale price, in March, was between $6.25 and $6.50. See U.S. Bureau of the Census, *Historical Statistics of the United States to 1957* (Washington, D.C., 1960), p. 107; *Irish News*, 21 March 1868.

15. Quoted in Oscar Lewis, *This was San Francisco* (New York, 1962), pp. 180–1.

16. MacGregor, *op. cit.*, p. 69; Lester, *Atlantic to the Pacific*, p. 95.

17. Henry Lucy, *East by West* (2 vols., London, 1885), i, 143.

18. *Catholic Guardian*, 22 March 1873.

19. [California Labour Exchange], *Facts about California* (San Francisco, 1869), p. 10.

20. Shumsky, 'Tar Flat and Nob Hill', pp. 128–30.

21. *Ibid.*, pp. 130–1.

22. Long, *Wages and Earnings*, p. 84.

23. In 1868 a teamster in a flour mill in New York could have been paid between sixty-nine and seventy-six cents a day; one in California, three dollars. If it is assumed that the length of the working day was equal at ten hours, for which, strictly, there is little evidence beyond the fact that in 1880 61·0 per cent of a sample of 123 New York firms worked a day of ten to eleven hours, as did 58·0 per cent of a sample of Californian firms, then it would have taken the New York teamster 1·04 to 1·14 working days to earn enough to buy a pound of flour at wholesale prices (see note 14); the Californian, between 0·208 and 0·216. Even if the New York wage seems very low, the difference is remarkable. The length of the working day was taken from Joseph D. Weeks, *Report on the Statistics of Wages in Manufacturing Industries, Vol. XX, Tenth Census of the United States, 1880* (Washington, D.C., 1886), p. xxxi.

24. Cross, *Labour Movement*, pp. 34–6.

25. Lucile Eaves, *A History of California Labour Legislation with an Introductory Sketch of the San Francisco Labour Movement* (Berkeley, 1910), pp. 198–209, 229–57.

26. *Alta California*, 2 July 1869, 8 July 1870, 7 July 1871. See also *California, Appendix to Journals of Senate and Assembly, 18th Session* (Sacramento, 1870), III, *Report of the Trustees of the California Labour and Employment Exchange from April 27, 1868, to November 30, 1869*.

27. *The State*, 12 April 1879.

28. Fisher, *Californians*, p. 72.

29. The picture presented in this chapter of the occupational history of the Irish in San Francisco in the period has been in the form of a series of 'snap-shots' taken at ten-year ar intervals. There is no doubt that it would be more precise to approach the subject by following the particular careers of a number of Irish through these years. It can, however, be questioned whether the end result would be much different unless it was the case that the total Irish community in the city was largely uniformly mobile, with departing groups being continuously replaced by others of a slightly higher socio-economic status. Though this is theoretically possible it would demand a virtually open society in which other groups, less transient, more powerful, more entrenched, would allow free entry into the more prized higher-status occupations, as well as a society that did not disproportionately reward commitment, persistence and the insider. The unlikelihood of this provides a defence for the method of analysis used here.

Chapter V

1. J. D. B. De Bow, *A Compendium of the Seventh Census* (Washington, D.C., 1854), pp. 56, 204–5, 394. Irish statistics personally compiled. In this chapter, as in previous ones, it should be assumed, where no source is given for statistics, that they have been personally compiled from the manuscript schedules of the appropriate census.

2. Burchell, 'Gathering of a community', 282–3.

3. The figures in Tables 14 and 15 do not include either women or men who seemingly had no occupation. This is because, first, male and female occupational statistics are not comparable; second, for the obvious reason that the tables break down boarders and lodgers by occupational status. The omission of males without occupations is not serious: there were only six first-generation and four second-generation in the ward.

4. The area contained in the Seventh ward is well described in Alvin Averbach, 'San Francisco's South of Market District', 196–223.

5. Margaret Lear, 'Irish Californians: some aspects of occupational and family patterns among the Irish of the Eleventh ward of San Francisco in 1880' (M.A. thesis, University of Manchester, 1977), pp. 33–42.

6. Marshall, *Through America*, pp. 269–70; Bryant, *Inaugural* (1875), p. 29. See also Fisher, *Californians*, p. 79.

7. *Catholic Guardian*, 12 October, 23 November 1872; 8 February, 19 April, 10 May 1873.

8. Lear, *op. cit.*, pp. 22–3.

9. There is a slight discrepancy between the figures used in Table 16 and those used in Table 18. Analysis was done personally and therefore suffered from human error.

10. The British-born group was defined as natives of England, Scotland, Wales, British North America (though the inclusion of French Canadians here needs remembering), Australasia, including New Zealand, but not other parts of the Empire such as the West Indies or Malta because of their population mixture.

11. The factor of increasing or decreasing Irishness proved difficult to

analyse conclusively. For instance, the German and French connections did not move in a uniform way, either increasing or decreasing according to the number of Irish parents to a couple. Where three parents were born outside Ireland, 33·3 per cent of the remainder were born in Germany, 6·5 per cent in France. Where two parents were born outside Ireland, 48·1 per cent of the rest were born in Germany, 14·1 per cent in France. The percentages for the category where three parents were born in Ireland were, respectively, 32·8 and 32·8, equal, but in the end uninforming.

12. The 'Chinese' who appear in Tables 16 and 18 were white, presumably Europeans living in China.

13. U.S. Bureau of the Census, *Population at the Tenth Census* (Washington, D.C., 1883), pp. 538–41, 649.

14. Rev. Zephyrin Engelhardt, O.F.M., 'The First Ecclesiastical Synod of California (March 19–23, 1852)', *Catholic Historical Review*, i (1915–16), 35–6.

15. Rt. Revd. Doctor Amat, *A Treatise on Matrimony, According to the Doctrine and Discipline of the Catholic Church* (San Franscisco, 1864), pp. 8, 21–2, 40–1, 42, 44–5, 46, 53–4, 61.

16. *Catholic Guardian*, 30 November 1872.

17. Engelhardt, *op. cit.*, 36.

18. John B. McGloin, S.J., *California's First Archbishop* (New York, 1966), pp. 181–2 n. 62; Amat, *op. cit.*, p. 42.

19. Figures for 1852 and 1870 personally compiled; for 1880 taken from Lear, *op. cit.*, p. 27.

20. Excluding St Boniface, established for the German community in 1870; Notre Dame des Victoires, for the French in 1856; and Yglesia de Neustra Senora de Guadalupe, set up for Spanish, Portuguese and Italian Catholics in 1875.

21. Lotchin, *San Francisco*, p. 120; Luckingham, 'Associational life on the urban frontier: San Francisco, 1848–56' (Ph.D. thesis, University of California, Davis, 1968), pp. 53–4.

22. *Catholic Guardian*, 28 December 1872.

23. Thomas D. McSweeny, *Cathedral on California Street: the Story of St. Mary's Cathedral, San Francisco, 1854–91, and of old St. Mary's, a Paulist Church, 1894–1951* (Fresno, Cal., 1952), p. 46.

24. Young, *San Francisco*, i, 454; *Langley's Directory, 1880*, pp. 1106–8; McGloin, *Eloquent Indian: the Life of James Bouchard, California Jesuit* (Stanford, 1949), p. 99.

25. Player-Frowd, *Six Months*, p. 32.

26. Rev. Francis J. Weber, *California's Reluctant Prelate: the Life and Times of Right Reverend Thaddeus Amat, C.M. (1811–78)* (Los Angeles, 1964), pp. 81–3, 85; also 'The Pious Fund of the Californias', *Hispanic American Historical Review*, 43 (1963), 88, 93. Payments were only made for thirteen years following 1877 and during 1903–14.

27. Quoted in McGloin, *Eloquent Indian*, p. 7. Cf. Young, *op. cit.*, i, 238: 'The Catholic faithful of San Francisco were [then] as poor as the founders of the Christian religion.'

28. Young, *op. cit.*, i, 238, 239; McSweeny, *op. cit.*, pp. 12, 23.

29. McSweeny, *op. cit.*, pp. 12, 23.

30. Rev. Dennis J. Kavanagh, S.J., *The Holy Family Sisters of San Francisco: a Sketch of their First Fifty Years, 1872–1922* (San Francisco, 1922), p. 27.
31. *Ibid.*, p. 85.
32. *Ibid.*, pp. 85–6, 93.
33. *Irish News*, 2 May 1868; cf. *The Monitor*, 18 April 1868.
34. *Catholic Guardian*, 18 May 1872.
35. San Francisco, *Fair Messenger*, 1–10 December 1870.
36. *Catholic Guardian*, 21 December 1872.
37. *Irish News*, 22 February, 13 June 1868.
38. Quoted in McGloin, *Eloquent Indian*, pp. 141–2.
39. Quoted in *ibid.*, p. 145.
40. *Langley's Directory, 1880*, p. 1110.
41. *Ibid.*, p. 1118; Luckingham, 'Associational life', p. 89.
42. *Langley's Directory, 1880*, p. 1118; *Catholic Guardian*, 1 February 1873.
43. *Langley's Directory, 1880*, p. 1121.
44. *Appendix to Journals of Senate and Assembly*, 17th Session (Sacramento, 1868), II, *Report and Petition of the Managers of the Magdalen Asylum of San Francisco From Jan. 1864 to Feb. 1 1868*, pp. 4–7; *Appendix to Journals of Senate and Assembly*, 18th Session Sacramento, (1870), III, *Report on the Magdalen Asylum to the Legislature of California at its 18th Session*, p. 7; *Langley's Directory, 1880*, p. 1117.
45. *Langley's Directory, 1880*, p. 1117.
46. *Ibid.*, p. 1117.
47. *Ibid.*, p. 1120.
48. Luckingham, 'Associational life', *passim*, describes the variety of roles played by such societies. The positive side of associationalism has been stressed by Oscar Handlin, both in *Boston's Immigrants* and in *The Uprooted* (Boston, 1951). See also Eric L. McKitrick and Stanley Elkins, 'Institutions in motion', *American Quarterly*, xii (1960), 193–4. Just as the variety of Irish associations in San Francisco shows the vitality and positive commitment of the Irish community, so, by contrast, the weakness of such institutions in contemporary Milwaukee has been seen as evidence of a stunted Irish community there. See Conzen, *Immigrant Milwaukee*, pp. 162–3, 170–2.

Chapter VI

1. *Alta California*, 18 March 1851.
2. *The San Francisco Directory, 1852–53* (San Francisco; 1852), p. 18; Henry G. Langley, *The San Francisco Directory for the Year commencing June 1859* (San Francisco, 1859), p. 388.
3. *Alta California*, 18 March 1852; Charles P. Kimball, *San Francisco City Directory, Sept. 1, 1850* (San Francisco, 1850), p. 122.
4. *Langley's Directory, 1859*, p. 388.
5. *Langley's Directory, 1859*, p. 388; *Directory, 1880*, p. 1120; *The Monitor*, 25 July 1868.
6. *Langley's Directory, 1880*, p. 1121.
7. Ira B. Cross, *Financing an Empire*, i, 233–4.
8. Langley, *The San Francisco Directory for the Year commencing December 1869*

(San Francisco, 1869), p. 47.

9. *The Monitor,* 18 January 1868, 13 February 1869; *Langley's Directory, 1869,* p. 841.

10. Langley, *The San Francisco Directory for the Year commencing April 1871* (San Francisco, 1871), p. 903; *Langley's Directory, 1880,* pp. 1139–40.

11. *Langley's Directory, 1871,* p. 902; *Directory, 1869,* pp. 840–51; San Francisco, *The United Irishman,* 28 July 1873; *Irish News,* 8 August 1868; William L. Cole, *California: its Scenery, Climate, Productions and Inhabitants. Notes of an Overland Trip to the Pacific Coast* (New York, 1872), pp. 24, 32.

12. *Langley's Directory, 1869,* p. 850.

13. *Articles of Incorporation, Constitution, Rules, By-laws and Rules of Order of the Irish-American Benevolent Society* (San Francisco, 1871), pp. 28–9; Langley, *The San Francisco Directory for the Year commencing July 1860* (San Francisco, 1860), p. 442.

14. *The Monitor,* 13 March, 13 November 1869; San Francisco, *The Call,* 30 December 1890; *Irish News,* 8 May 1869.

15. *Langley's Directory, 1869,* p. 833; *Directory, 1880,* p. 1121; *The Catholic Guardian,* 18 January 1873.

16. *Irish Fine Arts Aid Society: the First Annual Report* (San Francisco, 1861), *passim.*

17. Hibernicus (pseud.), *Humbuggery and its Victims* (San Francisco, 1863), *passim.*

18. W. A. D'Arcy, *The Fenian Movement in the United States, 1858–86* (Washington, D.C., 1947), pp. 18–19, 20.

19. *Langley's Directory, 1871,* p. 878.

20. Langley, *The San Francisco Directory for the Year commencing October 1864* (San Francisco, 1864), p. 557; *Proceedings of the First National Convention of the Fenian Brotherhood, held in Chicago, Illinois, November, 1863* (Philadelphia, 1863), p. 5.

21. D'Arcy, *op. cit.,* pp. 18–19, 20.

22. *Proceedings of the First General Convention of the Fenian Brotherhood of the Pacific Coast, held in San Francisco, California* (San Francisco, 1864), *passim.*

23. *Irish News,* 14 October 1865; *Langley's Directory, 1869,* p. 828.

24. Hibernicus, *op. cit.,* pp. 1–2.

25. *Anniversary Celebration of the St. Patrick's Brotherhood* (San Francisco, 1862), p. 1.

26. *The Monitor,* 19 September 1868, 16 January 1869.

27. *Alta California,* 21 May 1866.

28. *Ibid.,* 7 September 1867.

29. See, for instance, *The Monitor,* 6 July 1867, 16 May, 6 June, 6 July, 11 July 1868, 15 May 1869, 14 May 1870; *Irish News,* 2 May 1868.

30. *Irish News,* 16 May 1868.

31. *The Monitor,* 14 May 1870.

32. *Ibid.,* 11 July 1868.

33. *Irish News,* 14 October 1865.

34. *Ibid.,* 13 July 1867.

35. *Ibid.,* 19 September 1868.

36. *The Monitor,* 27 November 1869; *Daily Morning Call,* 29 December

1870; Quigley, *Irish Race in California*, p. 291.
37. *The Monitor*, 5 December 1868.
38. *Irish News*, 27 February 1869; *The Monitor*, 20 February 1869.
39. *Langley's Directory, 1871*, pp. 875–6; *Directory, 1880*, p. 1111; *The United Irishman*, 28 July 1873.
40. *The Monitor*, 27 November 1869; 27 April 1872.
41. San Francisco *Daily Examiner*, 1 June 1878.
42. *Daily Morning Call*, 7 July 1870.
43. Cross, *Financing an Empire*, i, 243; *Irish News*, 18 January 1868; *Langley's Directory, 1869*, pp. 839, 841.
44. *Alta California*, 14 September 1870; quoted in Cross, *op. cit.*, i, 372.
45. *Irish News*, 21 March 1868.
46. *Alta California*, 14 September 1870.
47. *The Monitor*, 24 April, 15 May 1869, 7 May 1870; *Irish News*, 22 August 1868; 'The California recollections of Caspar T. Hopkins', *C.H.S.Q.*, xxvii (1948), 165.
48. *Langley's Directory, 1871*, p. 893; *The Monitor*, 9 January 1869.
49. *The Monitor*, 27 June 1868.
50. *Langley's Directory, 1880*, pp. 1113, 1121.
51. *Ibid.*, p. 1121.
52. Gilman M. Ostrander, *The Prohibition Movement in California, 1848–1933*, University of California Publications in History, volume 57 (Berkeley and Los Angeles, 1957), p. 38.
53. *Langley's Directory, 1869*, p. 834; Ostrander, *op. cit.*, p. 31. It had eighty converts in January 1868: *The Monitor*, 18 January 1868.
54. *Daily Morning Call*, 25 May 1869; *The Monitor*, 22 January 1870; *Langley's Directory, 1880*, pp. 1125–6.
55. Ostrander, *op. cit.*, pp. 30–1.
56. *Langley's Directory, 1880*, p. 1126.
57. *Ibid*, p. 1126.
58. *Ibid.*, p. 1127.
59. Luckingham, 'Associational life', pp. 28–30; Lotchin, *op. cit.*, pp. 90, 92–3.
60. Fifteen per cent of the total labour force, or 20 per cent of the non-Chinese labour force, was Irish in 1870. See Alexander Saxton, *The Indispensable Enemy: Labour and the Anti-Chinese Movement in California* (Berkeley, 1971), p. 11. These percentages do not include second-generation Irish.
61. *Anniversary Celebration . . . 1862*, p. 1.
62. *Irish News*, 8 February 1868.
63. Young, *op. cit.*, i, 372–5.
64. *Langley's Directory, 1871*, pp. 893–5.
65. *Langley's Directory, 1880*, pp. 1127–30.
66. *Ibid.*, p. 1131.
67. *The Monitor*, 6 March 1869.
68. *Langley's Directory, 1880*, p. 1132.
69. *Alta California*, 4 May 1853; Young, *op. cit.*, i, 445; *Daily Morning Call*, 1 January 1867.

70. *The Monitor*, 25 January, 29 August 1868.
71. *Ibid.*, 2 January 1869.
72. *Langley's Directory, 1871*, p. 900.
73. Cole, *op. cit.*, pp. 34–5.
74. *Irish News*, March 1872.
75. *The Monitor*, 20 April 1872.
76. *Ibid.*, 27 April 1872.
77. *Langley's Directory, 1880*, p.1116.
78. *Report of the Fifth Annual Banquet of the Knights of St. Patrick, held in San Francisco, March 17, 1879* (San Francisco, 1879), p. 3.
79. *Langley's Directory, 1880*, p. 1116; *Fifth Annual Banquet*, p. 3.
80. *Fifth Annual Banquet*, p. 3.
81. Quigley, *Irish Race*, p. 291.
82. Barker, *Henry George*, pp. 244-5.
83. *Langley's Directory, 1880*, p. 1118.
84. *Daily Morning Call*, 24 May 1867, 24 May 1868, 23 May 1869, 27 May 1870; *The Monitor*, 23, 30 May, 25 July 1868; *Irish News*, 2 May, 13, 27 June 1868; *Celebration of St. Patrick's Day, 1863, by the Sons of the Emerald Isle at Hayes Park* (San Francisco, 1863), *passim*.
85. *The Monitor*, 18 January, 29 February, 4 April, 9 May 1868; *Daily Morning Call*, 22 May 1870.
86. *Daily Morning Call*, 9 March, 19 November 1858; *The Monitor*, 27 November 1869, 23 April 1870.
87. *Irish News*, 8 February 1868; *The Monitor*, 1 February 1868, 9 January 1869.
88. *The Monitor*, 20 April 1872.
89. *Alta California*, 18 March 1851; F. Soule *et al.*, *The Annals of San Francisco* (New York, 1855), p. 523; *The Monitor*, 20 March 1858.
90. *Irish News*, 27 March 1869.
91. *Ibid.*, March 1872.
92. MacGregor, *op. cit.*, p. 41. There was trouble at the 1872 procession. A German objected to being held up while it passed and attempted to break through, 'using profane language'; see *The Monitor*, 20 April 1872.
93. *The Monitor*, 20 March 1858.
94. Rev. Fr. Rooney, *Oration on St. Patrick's Day ... Together with his Crushing Reply to the Strictures of the Commercial Advocate, the Organ of the American Protestant Association and of Chinese Labour* (San Francisco, 1878), esp. pp. 12–14; *The Monitor*, 20 March 1858; *Irish News*, 21 March 1868, March 1872.
95. Rooney, *op. cit.*, p. 9.
96. *The Monitor*, 20 March 1858.
97. *Irish News*, 27 February 1869.
98. *Catholic Guardian*, 8 February 1873. Cf. *The Monitor*, 27 February, 7 March 1868; 13 March 1869, 19 March 1870.
99. *The Monitor*, 23 January 1869.
100. *Ibid.*, 29 January 1870.
101. *Ibid.*, 14 March 1868.
102. *Irish News*, 13 July 1867.
103. *The Monitor*, 11 July 1868.

104. *Daily Morning Call,* 7 July 1870.
105. Fisher, *Californians,* p. 171; Lambert Price, *Two Americas,* pp. 206–7.
106. *The Monitor,* 13 June 1868.
107. Thomas N. Brown, *Irish-American Nationalism* (Philadelphia, 1966), *passim.*
108. *Daily Morning Call,* 19 April 1865.
109. Cole, *op. cit.,* p. 24.
110. P. J. Thomas, comp., *Our Centennial Memoir: Founding of the Mission. San Francisco de Assis in its Hundredth Year* (San Francisco, 1877), pp. 69–70, 71–4, 124.

Chapter VII

1. Report of Louis Kaplan, *Registrar of Voters . . . 1879* (San Francisco, 1879), p. 14.
2. *Social Statistics of Cities,* II, p. 902.
3. Large numbers of Irish voters on the register could also mean corrupt entries. The precise figures are unlikely to be recovered.
4. *County Clerk's Report* in *Municipal Reports . . . 1866–67,* p. 147.
5. Figures taken from the annual *Reports of the County Clerk* contained in the annual *Municipal Reports* published in San Francisco at the end of each fiscal year, ending 30 June. For 1867–68 see pp. 145–7; for 1868–69 see pp. 245–6; for 1869–70 see pp. 119–120; for 1870–71 see pp. 347–9; for 1871–72 see pp. 8–9; for 1872–73 see pp. 7–9; for 1873–74 see pp. 89–91; for 1874–75 see pp. 85–6; for 1875–76 see pp. 7–8; for 1876–77 see pp. 87–8; for 1877–78 see pp. 8–9; for 1878–79 see pp. 412–13; for 1879–80 see pp. 582–3.
6. Saxon, *Five Years,* p. 195.
7. *Alta California,* 7 September 1865.
8. See, for instance, *Irish News,* 17, 31 August 1867, 17 October 1868; *Alta California,* 30 October, 2 November 1868, 3 September 1871; *The United Irishman,* 28 July 1873.
9. San Francisco *Daily Examiner,* 29, 30, 31 August, 2 September 1867. Because the registers of voters are unreliable it is not possible to correlate Irish presence with Democratic strength. For fraudulent registration see Kaplan, *op. cit.,* pp. 4–5. Henry George's view of the register of 1872 was that it contained 10,000 voters who had left the city and 15,000 in the wrong wards. See Charles A. Barker, *Henry George* (New York, 1955), p. 218. It is instructive in June 1871 40,715 were reported enrolled on the register of voters, whereas in June 1879, despite years of great population growth, only 37,915 were. For the 1871 figure see *Municipal Reports, 1871,* p. 527.
10. *Alta California,* 14 November 1856.
11. The even-numbered wards voted in 1865; the odd-numbered in 1866; *Alta California,* 10 May 1865, 7 September 1866. Before 1856 the city had a bi-cameral legislature of aldermen and assistant aldermen, elected from eight wards. The charter of 1856 set up a unicameral body with twelve members, at first elected by ward, and then, from 1873, at large. Ward boundaries were changed once after 1856, in 1864.
12. *Alta California,* 9 November 1864. There was very probably a class

dimension to abstentionism. The People's Party, despite its name, was believed by many to be the vehicle of the business classes. Since many Irish were of the working class, their interests clashed. For unconvincing denials of class bias in the People's Party see *Alta California*, 28 August 1858, 16 May 1861, 16 May 1863. The demoralisation of the Irish vote is interesting. It suggests that the Irish were not attracted to politics under all conditions.

13. *Alta California*, 7, 9 September 1867.

14. The *Alta California* argued that when the state legislature reunited the dates of local elections with those of the state and federal it sounded the party's knell. In fact the party had won a number of elections before those dates had been separated in 1861. See *Alta California*, 15 May 1861, 3, 4 September 1866.

15. *Alta California*, 1 September 1867.

16. *The United Irishman*, 28 July 1873; *Alta California*, 3 September 1871, 25 August 1879; *Irish News*, 31 August 1867.

17. *Alta California*, 1 September 1879; San Francisco, *The Argonaut*, 12 July, 23, 30 August 1879.

18. *Argonaut*, 18 May 1878.

19. Figures personally compiled from the manuscript schedules of the 1870 census.

20. *San Francisco Ward Register* (San Francisco, 1880), *passim*; *Social Statistics of Cities*, II, p. 902.

21. *Ward Register, 1880, passim*.

22. It lost the area between Bush and Market in 1864.

23. *Ward Register, 1880, passim*.

24. Williams, *Broderick*, p. 15, *contra* Jeremiah Lynch, *A Senator of the Fifties: David C. Broderick of California* (San Francisco, 1911), p. 31.

25. James O'Meara, *Broderick and Gwin* (San Francisco, 1881), pp. 22–3; Lotchin, *San Francisco*, p. 219; Mary F. Williams, *The History of the San Francisco Vigilance Committee of 1851: a Study of Social Control on the California Frontier in the Days of the Gold Rush* (Berkeley, 1921), pp. 130–1; Bancroft, *California*. vi, 659–62.

26. Andrew J. Newman, 'The formation of the first political parties in California, 1849–51 (M.A. thesis, University of California, Berkeley, 1918), p. 30.

27. *Ibid.*, p. 33.

28. Lotchin, *op. cit.*, p. 219.

29. Bancroft, *op. cit.*, vi, 694.

30. Franklin Tuthill, *The History of California* (San Francisco, 1866), p. 305. Cf. *Alta California*, 8 December 1856.

31. O'Meara, *Broderick and Gwin*, p. 111.

32. John M. Myers, *San Francisco's Reign of Terror* (New York, 1966), p. 73.

33. *Ibid.*, p. 75.

34. *Alta California*, 11 April 1851.

35. San Francisco, *Public Balance*, 20 December 1850. Associate Justice Edward McGowan of the Court of Sessions had a reputation for putting politics before the law. See Williams, *op. cit.*, p. 177. This should be recalled in the light of future events. Duane continued to be a menace: he attacked

two men, attempting to shoot one. See Williams, *op. cit.*, p. 321; also George R. Stewart, *Committee of Vigilance: Revolution in San Francisco, 1851* (Boston, 1964), pp. 223 ff.

36. *Alta California*, 13 June 1851; Williams, *op. cit.*, pp. 23, 130–1, 211, 218–20. It is an interesting comment on the links between politics and disorder that the 'Hounds', the group that plagued San Francisco in the summer of 1849 and who were put down extra-legally, had their headquarters in a tent known as Tammany Hall. See Williams, *op. cit.*, p. 105; also Stewart, *Committee of Vigilance*, pp. 107, 112, 119, 122, 204.

37. *Alta California*, 14 June 1851. See also the same, 13 June 1851.

38. Williams, *op. cit.*, p. 220; San Francisco, *Herald*, 2 June 1856; James O'Meara, *The Vigilance Committee of 1856* (San Francisco, 1890), pp. 46, 47, makes the interesting observations that though Duane had Irish blood, he was at this time a Whig, 'yet felt kindly to Broderick'. Such confused relationships should lead to hesitant generalisation.

39. Williams, *op. cit.*, pp. 233–51; S. L. Ricards and G. M. Blackburn, 'The Sydney Ducks: a demographic analysis', *Pacific Historical Review*, 42 (1973), 20–31.

40. Williams, *op. cit.*, pp. 274–75; Burchell, 'The gathering of a Community', 281–85.

41. Williams, *op. cit.*, pp. 324–7.

42. *Ibid.*, p. 327.

43. *Alta California*, 17, 30 October, 19 November, 2, 9 December 1851; 4 January, 3 February, 6 October 1852; 12 April, 1 October 1853; 13 June 1854.

44. Clarke, *Sherman*, p. 134.

45. *Alta California*, 16 March 1852; 20 June, 16, 28 August 1854.

46. *Ibid*, 16 March, 5 Ocotber 1852; 19 August 1854.

47. *Ibid.*, 16 March 1852. See also the same 4, 6 October 1852.

48. Interestingly, when in January 1853 the *Alta* reviewed the position of the foreign born in the city it did so in terms of German-and French-born, omitting the Irish. See *Alta California*, 21 January 1853.

49. *Ibid.*, 14, 25 October 1852.

50. *Ibid.*, 11 November 1852.

51. *Ibid.*, 26 July 1853.

52. *Ibid.*, 26 May 1854.

53. *Ibid.*, 27 May 1854.

54. *Ibid.*, 11, 13 September 1854; Clarke, *op. cit.*, p. 57; Lotchin, *op. cit.*, p. 232; Tuthill, *op. cit.*, p. 430; Peyton Hurt, 'The rise and fall of the "Know Nothings" in California', *C.H.S.Q.*, ix (1930), 27, 118–19. In its early days Know Nothingism in San Francisco was somewhat muddled in its philosophy. Its original candidate for the mayorship in 1854 was Lucien Hermann, a Roman Catholic. His supersession was a sign of nativism, as his original nomination had been an attempt to bypass established politics. See Hurt, *op. cit.*, 27–8.

55. The American Party platform can be found in Winfield J. Davis, *History of Political Conventions in California, 1849–92* (Sacramento, 1893), p. 42.

56. *Alta California*, 24 May, 1 June 1855; Hurt, *op. cit.*, 108.

57. *Alta California*, 30 May 1855.
58. [William R. Rhodes], *The Political Letters of 'Caxton'* (San Francisco, 1855). Reflecting the comparatively low level of ethnic acrimony in the city, the Irish community in 1869 paid Rhodes to write the poem 'The Emerald Isle' for the 1869 St Patrick's Day celebrations.
59. [Rhodes], *op. cit.*, p. 14.
60. *Ibid.*, p. 15.
61. *Ibid.*, pp. 15–16.
62. *Alta California*, 30 September 1854.
63. *Ibid.*, 22 August 1855.
64. *Ibid.*, 30 May, 12 September 1855.
65. William T. Coleman, 'San Francisco Vigilance Committees', *Century*, November 1891, 144.
66. *Ibid.*, 138.
67. Thomas G. Cary, 'The San Francisco Committee of Vigilance', *Atlantic Monthly*, xl (December, 1877), 702; Tuthill, *op. cit.*, pp. 426–7; *Proclamation of the Vigilance Committee of San Francisco, June 9th, 1856* (San Francisco, 1856), *passim*.
68. *Alta California*, 26 August 1856. There is disagreement over the ethnic dimension to the episode of the 1856 committee. Lotchin, *op. cit.*, pp. 384–5 n. 23, discounts ethnic tensions in general. He would not distinguish the Irish on the one hand from the Germans and French on the other, who certainly seem to have supported the committee: see *The Herald*, 29 May, 4, 19, 24 June, 3, 12 July 1856. The distinction should be made. There were no French and perhaps two German victims of the committee, whereas the Irishness of the committee's targets cannot be disputed. This is not to say that the view of Richard Maxwell Brown, given, for instance, in his *Strain of Violence: Historical Studies of American Violence and Vigilantism* (New York, 1975), pp. 134–43, is altogether correct in over-stressing the ethnic dimension. As has been shown, some of the victims of the committee had gone too far. Even opponents of the committee could accept that there had been violence at the polls: see O'Meara, *Vigilance Committee of 1856*, pp. 10, 25–6, and *The Herald*, 18 May 1856. The impulses producing the committee came generally from the state of San Francisco society. The Irish, however, were given the role of scapegoat. That is the true meaning of their role in the episode.
69. San Francisco, *Pacific*, 12 June 1856. Cf. Tuthill, *op. cit.*, p. 439.
70. John S. Hittell, *A History of the City of San Francisco and Incidentally of the State of California* (San Francisco, 1878), p. 295.
71. Quoted from the German *San Francisco Journal* in *Alta California*, 29 June 1856.
72. *Herald*, 28 May, 24 June, 5 July 1856.
73. *Ibid.*, 27 June 1856.
74. San Francisco *Evening Bulletin*, 17 October 1856. The paper's crusade against Broderick continued for at least eight months, suggesting that it was not so confident that the committee had won a permanent triumph and that Broderick was a major target. See *Bulletin*, 29 October, 16, 18 December 1856; 10, 12 January, 24, 25, 26 June 1857.
75. *Alta California*, 10, 13, 24 October, 14 November 1856.

76. Eugene Casserly to Isaac V. Fowler, 19 May 1857. Original in the Bancroft Library, University of California, Berkeley.

77. Ernest Seyd, *California and its Resources: a Work for the Merchant, the Capitalist, and the Emigrant* (London, 1858), pp. 22–3. Italics in the original.

78. *Alta California*, 12 September 1858, 22 October, 9 November 1860, 8 April 1867. Both Young and Gaven made their money from dealing in real estate. The People's Party would have served their economic interests better than the Democratic, so that in their case class might have weighed more heavily than ethnicity in politics. It is also possible, however, that Young was a Protestant. He was born in Northern Ireland.

79. *Alta California*, 17 May 1861, 26 May 1863. Sweeny was, however, a prominent Catholic.

80. *Ibid.*, 2 July 1863; 9 February 1864.

81. *Ibid.*, 12 September 1858, 10 September 1859.

82. *Ibid.*, 11 September 1859, 17 May 1861.

83. *Ibid.*, 24 November 1860.

84. *Ibid.*, 26 May 1863.

85. O'Meara, *Broderick and Gwin*, pp. 48, 98; William C. Cullinan, 'History of party politics in California, 1849–54' (M.A. thesis, University of California, 1928), pp. 29, 157.

86. *Alta California*, 22 May, 11 September 1859.

87. *Sacramento Daily Union*, 9 July 1861.

88. *Alta California*, 2 September 1861.

89. *Ibid.*, 1 September 1861.

90. *Ibid.*, 8 November 1860, 7 September 1861.

91. *Sacramento Daily Union*, 10 February 1863.

92. Hittell, *History of San Francisco*, p. 343.

93. Conness was always a controversial character, partly because he managed to use the open political conditions of the state to his advantage and not to limit himself to obvious Irish allies. See *Sacramento Daily Union*, 11 July 1861.

94. *Evening Bulletin*, 11 February 1863.

95. *Alta California*, 11 February 1863. Cf. *ibid.*, 10 February 1863.

96. San Francisco *Daily Examiner*, 31 July 1867.

97. *Alta California*, 5 September 1863. John G. Downey, born in Castle Sampson, Roscommon, in 1827, came to the United States in 1842, to California in the Gold Rush and settled in Los Angeles. He became Governor of California in 1860 from the Lieutenant-governorship, to which he had been elected on the Lecompton Democratic ticket, when the Governor resigned to take up a United States Senate seat. Such success in Sacramento might compensate for the depressed state of Irish politics in San Francisco. See Prendergast, *op. cit.*, chapter XXI, *passim*, for Downey.

98. Davis, *Political Conventions*, pp. 213–15; *Alta California*, 22 March 1864.

99. *Ibid.*, 19 October 1864.

100. *Ibid.*, 22 October 1864.

101. *Ibid.*, 24 October 1864.

102. *Ibid.*, 9 November 1864.

103. Saxon, *Five Years*, pp. 193–4, 195.

104. *Alta California,* 9, 10 November 1864.
105. Davis, *op. cit.,* pp. 224, 226.
106. *Alta California,* 5 September 1865.
107. Saxton, *Indispensable Enemy,* pp. 69–7.'
108. *Alta California,* 5, 6 June 1867.
109. Quoted in Saxton, *op. cit.,* pp. 90–1.
110. *Alta California,* 7 September 1867.
111. *California Blue Book or State Roster, 1907* (Sacramento, 1907), p. 536.
112. *Sacramento Daily Union,* 20 December 1867.
113. *Alta California,* 22 December 1867.
114. Langley, *Directory, 1867,* p. 643; *Directory, 1868,* p. 725.
115. *Alta California,* 22 May 1861.
116. Farquhar, ed., *Up and Down California,* p. 453. Other anti-Irish jokes can be found in the San Francisco *Daily California Chronicle,* 19 February 1858; San Francisco *Puck,* 21 January 1865.
117. *A Goose Pie and How it was Cooked* (?San Francisco, ?1867), *passim.*
118. *A Political Stew* (?San Francisco, n.d.) pp. 1–2. The original was published in the San Francisco *Newsletter,* apparently.
119. *Bribery; or, The California Senatorial Election. A Comedy. In III Acts* (San Francisco, 1868), p. 4.
120. *Ibid.,* addendum.
121. To be more precise, with one Jesuit in particular, James Bouchard. See McGloin, *Eloquent Indian,* pp. 112–21, where the archbishop attacks Bouchard's beard, and p. 127.
122. *Anniversary Celebration, 1862,* p. 2.
123. *Alta California,* 17 February 1862, 17 May 1864.
124. *Daily Morning Call,* 16 April 1865.
125. McGloin, *California's First Archbishop,* p. 14.
126. *The Monitor,* 30 May 1868.
127. Quoted in *Alta California,* 7 November 1864.
128. *Monitor,* 23 April 1870; *Alta California,* 4 November 1868; 3, 4 September 1869.
129. *Ibid.,* 26 June, 27, 28, 30 August 1869.
130. *Ibid.,* 3 September 1869.
131. *Ibid.,* 7 September 1867; 4 September 1869.
132. *Ibid.,* 1, 8 September 1873.
133. *Ibid.,* 9, 15 September 1870, 8 September 1873.
134. *Ibid.,* 11 September 1875, 10 September 1877.
135. Quigley, *Irish Race,* pp. 264–70. Father Quigley had rather a broad definition of an Irishman. He included J. P. Shine, born in Massachusetts, and George W. Hayes, born in New York; J. Henley Smith, born in Washington, D.C., and J. O. Rountree, born in Mississippi, all of whom might have been second-generation Irish, as well as M. Mangels, who was born in Hanover, and was very likely not. He also conflated two elections, those of 1875 and 1877. Nevertheless, what is remarkable is the boundless enthusiasm for the Irish position in the city which made him so cavalier with facts.
136. Birthplaces of state legislators were drawn from a variety of sources,

including Richard Lambert, *Legislature of California* (Sacramento, 1852); Lambert, *Statistical Chart, Fourth Session,* (San Francisco, 1853); William Fassender, *Statistical Chart, Fifth Session* (Sacramento, 1854); Lambert, *Statistical Chart, Sixth Session* (Sacramento, 1855); Lambert, *Homographic Chart, Seventh Session* (Sacramento, 1856); Lambert, *Homographic Chart, Eleventh Session* (Sacramento, 1860); Lambert, *Homographic Chart, Twelfth Session* (Sacramento, 1861); *A Homographic Chart, 1862* (Sacramento, 1862); C. D. Bonestal, *Homographic Chart, 1863* (Sacramento, 1863); *Anthropographic Chart, Fifteenth Session* (Sacramento, 1863); H. T. Burr, *Chart, Sixteenth Session* (Sacramento, 1866); *Anthropographic Chart, Seventeenth Session* (Sacramento, 1867); W. A. Ransom, *Anthropographic Chart, Eighteenth Session* (Sacramento, 1869); Kean and Dudley, comps., *Legislative Guide* (Sacramento, 1871); William Halley, *Directory, Twenty-first Session* (Sacramento, 1875); *Halley's Handbook, Twenty-second Session* (Sacramento, 1878); Hugh J. Mohan et al., *Pen Pictures of our Representative Men* (Sacramento, 1880): all short titles. The San Francisco district sent three state senators and seven assemblymen to the first legislature, of total delegations of sixteen and thirty-six respectively. The city and county sent two state senators and six assemblymen to the second legislature, in which the total number of seats remained unchanged. The third legislature was expanded to twenty-seven senators and sixty-three assemblymen. San Francisco sent three senators and seven assemblymen to it and to the fourth. The fifth legislature consisted of thirty-four senators and eighty assemblymen. San Francisco was given four senatorships and nine Assembly seats, which the city retained until the ninth legislature, when the number of Assembly seats was lowered to eight. In 1862 the thirteenth legislature met with forty senators and eighty assemblymen. San Francisco was given five senatorships and twelve Assembly seats. The total number of seats in both houses now remained fixed, but in the twenty-first legislature, of 1875–76, the San Francisco delegation was increased and given one quarter of the seats in both houses, namely ten in the Senate and twenty in the Assembly. See *California Blue Book or State Roster, 1907* (Sacramento, 1907).

137. San Francisco *Flag*, quoted in Bancroft, *op. cit.*, vii, 326 n. 12.

138. *Alta California*, 17 December 1867.

139. *Ibid.*, 25 August, 3 September 1869. The Irish saw McCoppin, at least at the outset of his mayoralty, as a reformer. See *Irish News*, 31 August 1867.

140. *Alta California*, 1 September 1870.

141. Young, *San Francisco*, ii, 519.

142. *Alta California*, 26 June 1869; Selby, *Valedictory*, p. 4.

143. *Alta California*, 26 July 1870. Henry George charged that there was bribery in the 1871 elections. See Barker, *op. cit.*, p. 157. R. J. Canfield, Clerk of Election in the Fourth ward, was arrested for fraudulent enrolment of voters: see *Alta California*, 4 September 1871.

144. Bancroft, *op. cit.*, vii, 319; Young, *op. cit.*, ii, 519, 560–3.

145. *Ibid.*, i, 405; Richard Reinhardt, 'Tape worms and shoulder strikers', *American West* (November 1966), 85–6.

146. *Alta California*, 5 September 1871.

147. Philip A. Roach, *The Presidential Contest. The Candidate and the Issues. Speech at the Tenth Ward Wigwam, San Francisco, September 19th, 1872* (San

Francisco, 1872), p. 2.
   148. Roach, *Address . . . on the Three Hundred and Eighty-Fifth Anniversary of the Discovery of America by Columbus. Delivered Oct. 14, 1877, at South San Francisco Park, by Invitation of the Italian Population of San Francisco* (San Francisco, 1877), p. 2.
   149. *The Monitor*, 1 July 1871.
   150. *Ibid.*, 20 April 1872.
   151. *Ibid.*, 4 May 1872.
   152. *Ibid.*, 4 May 1873.
   153. *Ibid.*, 19 June 1869.
   154. *Ibid.*, 26 June 1869.
   155. *Catholic Guardian*, 8 February 1873.
   156. *Newsletter*, 11, 18 August 1877.
   157. Minturn, *Travels West*, pp. 354–5.
   158. San Francisco *Argonaut*, 1 April 1877.
   159. *Ibid.*, 16 June 1877.
   160. *Ibid.*, 12 July 1879.
   161. *Examiner*, 18 June 1878.
   162. *Ibid.*, 22 June 1878. Cf. *ibid.*, 23 June 1878.
   163. *Ibid.*, 29 August 1879.
   164. *Ibid.*, 29 August 1879; *Argonaut*, 18 May 1878.
   165. *The Labor Agitators; or, the Battle for Bread. The Party of the Future: The Workingmen's Party of California, its Birth and Organization – its Leaders and its Purposes* (San Francisco, n.d.), p. 7; J. C. Stedman and R. A. Leonard, *The Workingmen's Party of California: an Epitome of its Rise and Progress* (San Francisco, 1878), pp. 23, 26, 74.
   166. Marshall, *Through America*, p. 289.
   167. See illustration to Neil L. Shumsky, 'San Francisco's Workingmen respond to the Modern City', *C.H.Q.*, lv (1976), 45–58, at p. 73.
   168. *Argonaut*, 23 August 1879.
   169. *Ibid.*, 30 August 1879. White came to the United States at one year old, had been in the country approximately fifty-six years in 1879 and in California thirty years. He had been educated at the Academy of Oxford, Shenango County, New York. See T. J. Vivian and D. G. Waldron, eds.; *Biographical Sketches of the Delegates to the Convention to Frame a New Constitution for the State of California, 1878* (San Francisco, 1878).
   170. Stedman and Leonard, *op. cit.*, pp. 95–109; Ira B. Cross, ed., *Frank Roney, Irish Rebel and California Labor Leader: an Autobiography* (Berkeley, 1931), pp. 1–164.
   171. Davis, *Political Conventions*, p. 391; Vivian and Waldron, *op. cit., passim*.
   172. Mohan *et al.*, *op. cit., passim.*
   173. *Alta California*, 19 May 1878.
   174. *Ibid.*, 1 September 1879.
   175. *Loc. cit.*
   176. (Kaplan), *Report of Registrar of Voters . . . 1879*, pp. 88–91.
   177. *Alta California*, 1 September 1879.
   178. Quoted in *ibid.*, 1 September 1879.
   179. See *State Platform of the W.P.C.* (San Francisco, 1879).

180. Quoted in Stedman and Leonard, *op. cit.*, pp. 68–9, 70.
181. *Labor Agitators*, p. 9.
182. Charles E. Pickett, *Philosopher Pickett's Anti-Plundercrat Pamphlet* (San Francisco, 1879), p. 11; *Labor Agitators*, pp. 9–10.
183. Stedman and Leonard, *op. cit.*, pp. 9–10.
184. David Kennedy, Jr., *Kennedy's Colonial Travels: a Narrative of a Four Years Tour Through Australia, New Zealand, Canada, etc.* (Edinburgh, 1876), p. 333.
185. Jeremiah Lynch, *Buckleyism: the Government of a State* (San Francisco, 1889), pp. 6–8; Young, *op cit.*, ii, 562–4.
186. Lynch, *op. cit.*, pp. 5, 14–16, 21, 26; Alexander Callow, Jr., 'San Francisco's blind boss', *Pacific Historical Review*, 25 (1956), 261–79.
187. See Edward P. Levine, *The Irish and Irish Politicians* (Notre Dame, 1966).

Chapter VIII

1. *San Francisco Municipal Reports . . . 1879–80* (San Francisco, 1880), pp. 303–4, 457–8, 498, 535, 588.
2. Bureau of the Census, *Statistics of the Population, 1880*, p. 855.
3. Figures in Table 21 drawn from *San Francisco Municipal Reports . . ., 1859–80* (20 vols., San Francisco, 1860–80). For 1859–60 see pp. 122, 125; for 1861–62, pp. 182–4; for 1862–63, pp. 198–9; for 1863–64, pp. 223, 224; for 1864–65, pp. 248, 249; for 1865–66, pp. 217, 237; for 1866–1867, pp. 262, 276–7, 286–7; for 1867–68, pp. 149, 302, 306, 326, 332–3, 341; for 1868–69, pp. 192–3, 224–5, 235–49 (*a*this includes smallpox statistics March 1868– June 1869 as follows:
    Cases   Total 968   Irish 61   % Irish 6·3
    Deaths   Total 303   Irish 22   % Irish 7·3).
For 1869–70 see pp. 124-5, 167, 206-7, 226-7; for 1870–71, pp. 307, 321–2, 334–5, 352; for 1871–72, pp. 11–12, 232–3, 245–6, 258; for 1872–73, pp. 12, 359–60, 364, 375–6, 390–1 (*b* includes Smallpox Hospital report: cases 50, Irish 2, % Irish 4·0); for 1873–74, see pp. 93–4, 401–2, 407, 421–2, 438 (*c* includes Smallpox Hospital report:
    Cases 78   Irish 4   % Irish 5·1
    Deaths 20   Irish 2   % Irish 10·0).
For 1874–75 see pp. 103, 240, 335–6, 356, 386–7; for 1875–76, pp. 13–14, 28, 417–18, 423, 430–1, 451 (*d* includes Smallpox Hospital report:
    Cases 88   Irish 7   % Irish 8·0
    Deaths 13   Irish 1   % Irish 7·7).
For 1876–77 see pp. 91–2, 341, 427–8, 438, 459, 530 (*e* includes Smallpox Hospital report:
    Cases 875   Irish 62   % Irish 7·1
    Deaths 245 Irish 23   % Irish 9·4).
For 1877–78 see pp. 13, 95, 118–9, 251–2, 276, 306 (*f* includes suicides: total 103, Irish 17, % Irish 16·5). For 1878–79 see pp. 129, 133–4, 221–2, 252, 260,

294, 416, 734 (*includes suicides: total 86, Irish 5, % Irish 5·8; includes autopsies made by police surgeons: total 169, Irish 46, % Irish 27·2). For 1879–80 see pp. 303–4, 358–9, 457–8, 535, 588. (^h includes suicides: total 90, Irish 13, % Irish 14·4). In the cases of both suicide and smallpox the Irish provided comparatively few victims.

4. Figures here and otherwise unacknowledged personally compiled from the manuscript schedules of the census.

5. California, *Appendix to Assembly Journal, Sixth Session, 1855* (Sacramento, 1855), *Appendix to Annual Report of the Inspector of State Prisons to the Legislature ... February 15, 1855, passim; Appendix to Legislative Journals* (Sacramento, 1862), *Report of Committee Relative to the Condition of the State Prison of San Quentin, 1862, Roll of State Prison, March 3, 1862, passim.*

6. U.S. Bureau of the Census, *Report on the Mortality and Vital Statistics of the United States, Part II* (Washington, D.C., 1886), p. 788.

7. Handlin, *Boston's Immigrants*, pp. 245, 257; Ernst, *Immigrant Life*, pp. 193, 202–3.

8. The general background to the educational issue is given in Paul Goda, S.J., 'The historical background of California's constitutional provisions prohibiting aid to sectarian schools', *C.H.S.Q.*, xlvi (1967), 149–71.

9. David F. Ferris, *Judge Marvin and the Founding of the California Public School System* (Berkeley and Los Angeles, 1962), University of California Publications in Education, vol. XIV, p. 73.

10. Swett, *History of the Public School System*, p. 15. The precise meaning of this section is debatable.

11. Luckingham, 'Associational life', pp. 61–2; Swett, *op. cit.*, p. 18; Ferrier, *Ninety Years of Education in California*, p. 46, says that the total number of children in Catholic schools at the end of 1852 was 230.

12. Quoted in Ferris, *Judge Marvin*, p. 81; see also Swett, *op. cit.*, p. 20.

13. Ferris, *op. cit.*, pp. 91–2; Luckingham, 'Associational life', p. 68.

14. Swett, *op. cit.*, p. 21; Ferrier, *op. cit.*, p. 7.

15. Swett, *Public Education in California*, p. 115.

16. Ferrier, *op. cit.*, pp. 93–4.

17. *Ibid.*, p. 95.

18. Quoted in Lotchin, *San Francisco*, p. 317.

19. Luckingham, *op. cit.*, p. 71.

20. Quoted in Swett, *Public School System*, p. 71.

21. Lotchin, *op. cit.*, p. 318; Swett, *Public Education in California*, p. 116. The Rev. F. C. Ewers was rector of Grace Church and, as an Episcopalian, was perhaps doctrinally suited for the delicate job of mediating between New England and Rome. His view can be found in Pelton, *Origin of the Free Schools of San Francisco*, p. 44.

22. *Journal of the Proceedings of the Senate, Twelfth Session, 1861* (Sacramento, 1861), pp. 534, 652–3; Swett, *Public School System*, p. 31.

23. Rev. Francis J. Weber, *Catholic Footprints in California* (Newhall, Cal., 1970), pp. 70–1.

24. *Journal of the Proceedings of the Assembly, Fifth Session, 1854* (Sacramento, 1854), pp. 430–1, reveals that Conness supported the proposal to allow public money for private schools in that year, but *Journal of the Proceedings of*

the Senate, Twelfth Session, 1861 (Sacramento, 1861), p. 680, shows the position he adoped in the long run, presumably having decided that the fight for public funds was futile. See also *Alta California*, 1 September 1861.

25. Quoted in Swett, *Public School System*, pp. 31–2.
26. *Catholic Guardian*, February 1872.
27. *Ibid.*, 31 August 1872.
28. See the speech of the Rev. P. Harrington, delivered while laying the corner stone of the Sacred Heart College: *Catholic Guardian*, 21 December 1872.
29. Zachariah Montgomery, *Speeches: Address in Stockton on St. Patrick's Day, for the Benefit of St. Mary's Catholic Free School, 1874* (n.p., 1874).
30. Board of Supervisors, *San Francisco Municipal Reports for . . . 1861–62* (San Francisco, 1862), pp. 202–3. In 1858 it was calculated that there were 1,000 children in the private schools of San Francisco, of whom 650 attended Catholic schools. See *Eighth Annual Report of the Superintendent of Public Schools of the City and County of San Francisco* (San Francisco, 1858), p. 15.
31. *San Francisco Municipal Reports, 1869–70* (San Francisco, 1870), p. 275.
32. *The Monitor*, 26 June 1869.
33. Young, *San Francisco*, ii, 645.
34. *Catholic Guardian*, February 1872.
35. *San Francisco Municipal Reports, 1874–75* (San Francisco, 1875), pp. 584–5.
36. Kavanagh, *Holy Family Sisters*, pp. 20–1.
37. Kavanagh, *op. cit.*, pp. 20–1; Ferrier, *Ninety Years*, pp. 139–43, 205–11; Young, *op. cit.*, i, 457; ii, 645; McGloin, *Jesuits*, pp. 12–14; *Catholic Guardian*, 21 December 1872; *The Monitor*, 1 July 1871; *Appendix to Journals of Senate and Assembly, Nineteenth Session* (Sacramento, 1872), I, 212–13.
38. *San Francisco Municipal Reports, 1879–80*, pp. 660–2; *Langley's Directory, 1880*, pp. 34–5, gives figures for four schools that show little growth since 1875.
39. *Municipal Reports, 1879–80*, p. xvii. There was free schooling, too, for instance at the two associated schools attached to the Roman Catholic orphan asylum. There 'To those who cannot afford to pay, tuition is free'. See *Report of the Trustees, 1854*, p. 8.
40. McGloin, *Jesuits*, pp. 38–9.
41. Young, *San Francisco*, i, 456–7.
42. *Alta California*, 17 October 1867.
43. *Appendix to Journals of Senate and Assembly, Eighteenth Session* (Sacramento, 1870), I, *Third Biennial Report of the Superintendent of Public Education*, p. 14.
44. *Catholic Guardian*, February, 27 April 1872, 1 February 1873.
45. *Municipal Reports, 1872–73*, p. 283. This very rough estimate was derived by assuming that 85 per cent of those at 'private schools' were Catholics at Catholic schools and that there were at least 7,500 Catholic children of school age in the city. Consequently 4,500 of the 7,500 would be at Catholic day schools, or 60 per cent.
46. The eighteenth legislature (1869–70) made a state grant to the Presentation Convent Schools, showing that even at this late date there was

the possibility of state grants to sectarian schools. Unfortunately the schools never received any money from the grant, possibly because it was always on the cards that the following legislature would rescind the grant as against general policy, which it did. See *Alta California*, 22, 26, 27 January 1872.

47. Rev. William C. Anderson, *The Substance of Four Discourses on the Bible in Common Schools, Delivered in the First Presbyterian Church, San Francisco, by the Pastor* (San Francisco, 1859), p. 7.

48. Calvin A. Poage, *Lecture on 'Our Public Schools'* (San Francisco, 1873), pp. 10–12.

49. Rev. Father Bouchard, S.J., *The Inquisition, and a Reply by Rev. John Hemphill, Pastor of Calvary Presbyterian Church. Our Public Schools by Rev. John Hemphill. Together with the Remarks of Honourable Zach. Montgomery, before the R.C. Sunday-school Teachers, and other Interesting Reading Matter* (2nd edn., San Francisco, 1873), pp. 39–40, 43.

50. Quoted in J.R. Brandon, *A Reply to the Rev. Mr. Hemphill's Discourse on 'Our Public Schools', 'Shall the Lord's Prayer be Recited in Them?'* (San Francisco, 1875), p. 15.

51. Bouchard et al., *The Inquisition, etc.*, pp. 10–12.

52. Rev. W. Gleeson and Frank M. Pixley, *The Common School Question: A Discussion* (San Francisco, 1883), p. 65.

53. *Ibid.*, pp. 8–10, 13–14.

54. *Ibid.*, pp. 29, 44.

55. *Ibid.*, pp. 63–4.

56. San Francisco, 1894.

57. Brandon, *op. cit.*, p. 20.

58. Thomas, *Our Centennial Memoir*, pp. 96–7.

59. *Catholic Guardian*, 14 September 1872, 19 April, 17 May 1873.

60. John P. Young, *Journalism in California: Pacific Coast and Exposition Biographies* (San Francisco, 1915), pp. 53–4; Rev. Francis A. Weber, *A Select Guide to California Catholic History* (Los Angeles, 1966), p. 149. It is stated in Weber that the *Irish News* lasted to 1865. The latest extant copy I have seen was dated March 1872.

61. Weber, *Select Guide*, p. 149.

62. *The Monitor*, 20 March 1858.

63. *Irish News*, 16 May 1868.

64. *Catholic Guardian*, January, February 1872; Weber, *Select Guide*, p. 149.

65. The *United Irishman* is not mentioned by Weber. By 1880 only *The Monitor* was listed as a Catholic organ out of 109 periodicals published in San Francisco. This is extremely revealing about the value of an ethnic newspaper to Irish San Franciscans. See S. N. D. North, *History and Present Conditions of the Newspaper and Periodical Press of the United States* (Washington, D.C., 1881), pp. 206–7.

66. *Irish News*, 14 September 1867.

67. Young, *Journalism in California*, p. 63; Barker, *Henry George*, p. 111.

68. Barker, *op. cit.*, p. 172.

69. Young, *San Francisco*, i, 439; Edmund M. Gagey, *The San Francisco Stage: a History* (New York 1950), pp. 57, 118–9; Carl Wittke, 'The immigrant theme on the American stage', *Mississippi Valley Historical Review*, xxxix (1952),

211–32, especially 216, 220.

70. *Alta California,* 16 April 1866, 6 September 1870, 25 August 1877; *The Monitor,* 13 April 1872.

71. Young, *San Francisco,* ii, 613.

72. See Milton M. Gordon, *Assimilation in American Life* (New York, 1964), *passim.*

Chapter IX

1. *Irish News,* 7 March 1868.
2. Bancroft, *California,* vii, 731.
3. Bowles, *Our New West,* p. 341
4. Brace, *New West,* p. 72
5. James D. Hart, ed., *From Scotland to Silverado* (Cambridge, Mass., 1966), pp. 182–3.
6. Rae, *Westward by Rail,* p. 303.
7. See, for instance, Dilke, *Greater Britain,* pp. 182–8; Lester, *Atlantic to the Pacific,* pp. 88–94; Alfred Gurney, *A Ramble through the United States. a Lecture Delivered (in part) in S. Barnabas' School, February 3, 1886* (n.p., n.d.), pp. 23–5; Sala, *America Revisited,* pp. 220–73; Nash, *Oregon,* pp. 56–64; H. Hussey Vivian, *Notes of a Tour in America, from August 7th to November 17th, 1877* (London, 1878), pp. 135–46.
8. A similar pattern of relationships was seen in the contemporary society of San Antonio, with the Mexican playing the role of the Chinese. See Alwyn Barr, 'Occupational and geographical mobility in San Antonio, 1870–1900', *Social Science Quarterly,* 51 (1970–71), 400.
9. Soule, *Annals,* p. 485.
10. Lady Duffus Hardy, *Through Cities and Prairie Lands: Sketches of an American Tour* (London, 1881), p. 157.
11. Fisher, *Californians,* p. 73.
12. Morley Roberts, *The Western Avernus, or, Toil and Travel in Further North America* (London, 1887), p. 297; see also pp. 284–99.
13. Rollo Ogden, ed., *Life and Letters of Edwin Lawrence Godkin* (2 vols., New York, 1907), i, 182.
14. Shannon, *American Irish,* p. 131.
15. Quigley, *Irish Race,* p. 275.

Index

Abbey Homestead Association, 42–3
Adams, James F., 141
Alemany, Archbishop Joseph S., 5, 6, 9, 10, 86, 91, 139, 140, 152–3
Alvord, Mayor William, 23
Amat, Archbishop Thaddeus, 85–6
Ancient Order of Hibernians, 102, 114
Anderson, Rev. William C., 170–1
Anti-Irish feeling in the east, 1–2
Asbury, Monroe, 144

Bagley, J. W., 128, 129
Bartol, A., 96
Beck, Thomas, 109
Bowles, Samuel F. 180
Boyston, John, 143
Brace, Charles Loring, 30, 43, 180
Brady, Owen, 153
Brady, Thomas, 176
Brandon, J. R., 174
Brannan, Samuel, 124
Bribery; or, The California Senatorial Election, 138–9
Broderick, David C., 7, 121–2, 124, 125, 126, 127–8, 129, 130–1, 186
Broderick, William, 109, 143
Bryan, Thomas, 142
Bryant, Mayor Andrew Jackson, 28, 148
Buckley, Christopher A., 153
Builders' Insurance Company, 103
Burke, Martin, 23
Burns, John, 150

California Building and Loan Society, 41–2, 102
California Labour Exchange, 70–1
California Rifles, 97
Callaghan, James, 102
Canavan, Matthew, 142
Canavan, P. H., 108, 119, 136, 141
Canney, Pat, 122
Carr, Billy, 130
Carson, James G., 143
Cary, Thomas G., 129
Casey, James P., 122, 128, 129, 130
Casserly, Eugene, 7, 8, 108, 131–2, 133, 135–6, 148, 186–7
Catholic Labourers Union, 106
Catholic Total Abstinence Mutual Beneficial Association, 106
Catholic Total Abstinence Union of the Arch-Diocese of San Francisco, 105
'Caxton', *The Political Letters of*, 127–8
Cazneau, T. N., 108
Celtic and Teutonic Farm Association, 103
Celtic Insurance Company, 103
Celtic Protective and Benevolent Society, 104
Chinatown and Chinese, 45, 153, 180–1
Church Society of St Francis' Parish, 92
Cody, M., 133
Coleman, William T., 129
Commins, Edward, 119, 142
Committee of Vigilance, 1851, 124–5
Committee of Vigilance, 1856, 22, 118, 120, 128–132
Condon, John D., 150
Connelly, J. D., 151
Connelly, James E., 143

Conness, John, 7, 133–4, 135, 143–4, 164–5, 187
Conroy and O'Connor, 9
Cooney, Michael, 141
Corkery, Charles, 141
Crowley, Patrick, 23
Curtiss, James, 23
Cusick, James, 130

Daly, P. H., 136
Desmond, Thomas, 151
Dolan, Michael, 98
Donahue, James A., 8, 10, 21, 27
Donahue, Mary Ann, 8
Donahue, Michael, 8
Donahue, Mrs P., 90
Donahue, Peter, 8, 9, 10, 40, 126
Donnelly, J. J., 176
Donnelly, Thomas, 150
Donohue, Joseph A., 9, 108
Donohue, Kelly & Co., 9
Donovan, M. J., 143
Dowling, Patrick T., 150
Downey, John G., 133–5
Doyle, John T., 9
Doyle, Luke D., 150
Duane, Charles P., 123–4, 130
Dunn, John P., 150, 151
Dwinnelle, John W., 174
Dwyer, David, 142

Eagan, Francis Dillon, 176
Emmet Life Guard, 97
'Ewer Settlement', 163–4, 165

Fair, James G., 187
Faithfull, Emily, 30
Farren, J. W., 142
Father Mathew Total Abstinence and Benevolent Society, 105, 114
Female Catholic Orphan Asylum, 92
Fenians, 99–101, 110, 113
Fitzgerald, Rev. O. P., 169
Flaherty, Edward, 141
Foley, John, 109, 142
Forsyth, William K., 143
Fortune, H. W., 142

Gaffey, P. T., 150
Gallagher, Reverend J. A., 112
Gallagher, Martin, 128, 130
Gaven, Dominic, 132
George, Henry, 26, 177
Gildea, Charles, 143
Gleeson, Rev. William, 5, 172–3
Godkin, E. L., 183–4
Goodwin, Robert, 142
A Goose Pie, and How It Was Cooked, 137
Gorham, George C., 136
Gorman, Joseph C., 150
Gray, Thomas, 142

Haight, Henry H., 136
Hamill, John, 142
Harrison, Thomas, 150
Hayes, George R. B., 142
Hayes, Maria, 9
Hayes, Colonel Thomas, 8–9
Hemphill, Rev. John, 151–2, 171–2
Henry, Rev. J. Q. A., 173–4
Hibernia Green Baseball Club, 107
Hibernia Homestead Association, 43
Hibernia Provident Association, 103
Hibernia Savings and Land Association, 104
Hibernia Savings and Loan Society, 8, 9, 41, 97
Hibernian Rifles, 97, 114
Hibernian Society, 96
Hittell, John S., 131
Hossefross, George H., 24
Humphreys, William P., 28
Hynes, David J., 102

Ignation Literary Society, 107
Industrial School, 11, 29
Irish-American Benevolent Society, 71, 97–8, 113, 114
Irish-American Hall, 108
Irish American Mutual Association, 103
Irish Battalion, 113
Irish Confederation, 108
Irish Fine Arts Aid Society, 99

Index

Irish in the east, 1–2
Irish National Union, 108
Irish Republican Army, 97, 113–4

Jackson Dragoons or Guards, 97, 131
Jewell, Rev. F. E., 91
Joyce, Peter J., 150

Kane, Thomas, 150
Kavanagh, Jeremiah, 100
Kearney, Denis, 149, 150, 151, 153–4
Kearny, Wooley, 128
Kelley, John Jr., 9
Kelly, James R., 98
Kelly, Martin, 150
Kelly, M. J., 141
Kelly, Terence, 130
Kennedy, E. C., 133
Kennedy, J. F., 133
Kennedy, John O'B., 143
Kenny, Bernard R., 150
King, James (of William), 129
Knights of St Patrick, 109
Knights of the Red Branch, 101
Know Nothings, 125–8, 163

Labourers' Benevolent Society, 106
Labourers' Protective Association, 114
Labourers' Protective Benevolent Society, 106
Labourers' Protective Society, 106
Labourers' Protective Union, 113
Labourers Union Benevolent, 113
Ladies' Protection and Relief Society, 158
Lane, Michael, 150
Legion of St Patrick, 97, 114
Lester, John Erastus, 30
Lewis, William, 130
Little Sisters' Infant Shelter, 92, 93
Loyal Orange Institution of the United States, 109–10
Lynch, John, 133, 142

Magdalen Asylum, 10, 11, 92, 93, 160

Maginnis, Rev. John, 162
Maguire, John Francis, 5
Mahon, Frank, 142
Mahoney, David, 143
Mann, A. L., 109
Mann, Horace, 162
Mannix, Jack, 153
Marwedel, Emma, 29
Mater Misericordiae, 92, 93–4
Mayo, Charles, 141
McCallion, J. J., 150
McCarthy, Michael, 143
McCarthy, Timothy, 141, 143
McCloskey, John Henry, 36–7
McColliam, T. W., 142
McCoppin, Frank, 7, 9, 30, 118, 119, 136, 139, 141, 143, 144, 145, 146
McGlynn, D. C., 9
McGlynn, John A., 10
McGowan, Edward, 122, 128, 129
McHugh, John, 97
McInery, Thomas, 143
McKibben, William, 133
McMahon Grenadier Guard, 97, 113
McManus, Terence Bellew, 7, 100
McNally, Rev. J. B., 105
Meagher Guard, 97, 114
Meagher, John F., 141
Merrifield, Azro D., 26
Minturn, William, 146
Mitchell, John, 7
Mitchell, William, 109
Monitor, The, damage to building, 139–40
Montgomery Guard, 97
Montgomery, Zacariah, 164, 165, 168, 171–2, 176
Mooney, Thomas, 41–42, 102–3, 179
Mulligan, William, 130
Murphy, Daniel J., 8, 9
Murphy, John C., 143
Murphy, Timothy, 10
Murray, Martin, 104
Myrick, Judge M. L., 109

Nevins, Thomas J., 163
Nolan, James H., 104
Nunan, Edward, 136, 141, 143

Nunan, Matthew, 109
Nunan, Miss M., 90
Nuttall, Dr R. K., 96

O'Connell, Bishop, 86
O'Connell, W., 71, 142, 143
O'Connor, Mrs B., 90
O'Connor, Joseph, 29
O'Donohue, Patrick, 7
O'Farrell, Jasper, 10, 89
Oliver, D. J., 8, 9
Olmstead, Frederick L., 30, 32
O'Malley, J. J., 142
O'Meara, James, 122
O'Reilly, J. P., 141
O'Sullivan, C. D., 9, 108
O'Sullivan, Mrs C. D., 90
O'Sullivan, James, 150

Parochial (Ward) Schools, 161–174
People's Party, 19, 120, 131, 132, 136
Pickett, Garrett, 150
Pius IX, 114
Pixley, Frank, 127, 172–3
Poage, Pastor Calvin A., 171
A Political Stew, 138
Press, 175–77

Quigley, Father Hugh, 6, 184–5

Rae, William F., 180
Ralston, William C., 9
Ring, Richard, 141
Roach, Philip A., 10, 109, 143, 144–5, 177
Roman Catholic Orphan Asylum, 10, 92–3, 158, 160
Roney, Frank, 150
Rooney, Rev. Father, 112

San Francisco:
  Death rate, 33
  Economy, 16–19
  Education, 28–9
  Electricity, 27
  Entertainments, 31–2
  Fire service, 24–5
  Gas, 27
  Government, 19
  Homestead associations, 42–4
  Hospitals, 46
  Hotels, 46
  Industrial School, 29, 158
  Labour unions, 70
  Land titles, 40–1
  Law and order, 24
  Libraries, 31
  Mortgage rates, 41, 43
  Parks, 30–1
  Police, 22–4
  Politics, 19, 116–154
  Population, 3
  Prices, 68–70
  Prisons, 30
  Reception of immigrants, 37
  Rents, 46, 66, 69
  Residential patterns, 38–9
  Restaurants, 32
  Roads, 21
  Sewerage, 27–8
  Slums, 44–5
  Street cleaning, 22
  Street lighting, 21–2
  Taxation, 19–20
  Telephone, 27
  Theatres, 32
  Transport, 39–40
  Unemployed, 30
  Urban services, 20–46
  Villas, 45
  Wages, 66–8, 70, 71
  Water supply, 26
San Francisco Irish:
  Ages, 50–1
  Almshouse inmates, 155, 157, 158, 159, 160
  Associationalism, 94–5, 96–115
  Bible-reading in public schools, 163, 170–1
  Catholicism, 4–6, 9–11, 85–94
  Criminality, 155, 156–8, 159, 160–1
  Deaths, 155, 157, 159
  Dislocation, statistics of, 155–161
  Education, 161–174

Index

Electorate, 116–120
Family patterns, 73–6, 77–8, 87
Fenians, 99–101, 113
Hospital admissions, 155, 156, 157
Insanity, 155, 157
Juvenile delinquency, 76–7, 158
Labour organisations, 106–7
Length of residence, 11–12
Living patterns, 73–6
Marriage patterns, 78–87
Numbers, 3–4
Occupational mobility, 52–60
Politics, 7, 116–154
Press, 175–7
Previous residence, 34
Processions, 110, 113–115
Property ownership, 61–4
Protestants, 4, 109–10
Residential patterns, 38–9, 46–9, 63–6
Routes to San Francisco, 34–6
St Patrick's Day, 110–13
Self-organised migration, 37–8
Sex ratios, 49–50, 73
Summary of position, 12–14, 179–185
Sunday schools, 166, 170, 172
Temperance, 105–6
Theatre, 177
Workforce, 16

St Boniface Orphan Asylum, 92, 93, 158
St Francis Literary Society, 107
St Joseph's Benevolent Society, 98–9, 114
St Joseph's Benevolent Society of St Francis' Parish, 104
St Joseph's Infant Asylum, 158
St Joseph's Temperance and Benevolent Society, 114
St Mary's Ladies Society, 96
St Mary's (Temperance) Benevolent and Library Association, 105, 113
St Patrick's Day, 110–13
St Patrick's Mutual Alliance of California, 104

St Patrick's Society of San Francisco, 108
Sarsfield Rifle Guards, 97
Schools, 28–9, 161–170
Seyd, Ernest, 132
Shields Guard, 97
Smith, M. C., 141
Smith, Colonel M. D., 100
Smyth, Charles F., 108
Society of St Vincent de Paul, 92, 94
Sodality of the B.V.M., 91
Sons of the Emerald Isle, 96, 113, 114
Stallard, I. H., 27
Stanford, Leland, 139
Stevenson, Robert Louis, 180
Sullivan and Cashman, 9
Sullivan, Catherine, 89
Sullivan, D. C., 143
Sullivan, Eugene L., 108
Sullivan, John, 8, 9, 10, 71, 89, 97
Sunny Vale Homestead Association, 43
Sweeny, Mary, 44
Sweeny, Miles D., 8, 9, 92, 132
Sweeny, Mrs Miles D., 90
Swett, John, 29, 163, 169–70

Teschemacher, H. F., 132
Theatre, 177
Tilford, Frank, 123
Tobin, John J., 143
Tobin, Richard, 9, 127
Tobin, Mrs Richard, 90
Tobin, Robert J., 23, 89, 92
Tobin, Mrs Robert, 90
Tobin, Thomas, 9–10

Van Ness, James, 9
Vaughan, Father Hubert, 5

Wellin, Patrick M., 150
White, William F., 150
Wolfe Tone Guard, 97
Workingmen's Party, 119, 120, 148–53

Yale, Gregory, 9
Yale, Nellie, 9
Young, Thomas, 118, 132

www.ingramcontent.com/pod-product-compliance
Lightning Source LLC
Chambersburg PA
CBHW021704230426
43668CB00008B/722